DATE DUE

MAY 2 4 1993			
DEC 2 1998			
APR 1 9 1999			
GAYLORD			PRINTED IN U.S.A.

ANIMAL MARKING

Recognition Marking of Animals in Research

ANIMAL MARKING

Recognition Marking of Animals in Research

Edited by
BERNARD STONEHOUSE

School of Environmental Science
University of Bradford

UNIVERSITY PARK PRESS
Baltimore

© The Contributors, 1978

First published 1978 by
The Macmillan Press Ltd
London and Basingstoke

Published in North America by
UNIVERSITY PARK PRESS
233 East Redwood Street
Baltimore, Maryland 21202

Printed in Great Britain

Library of Congress Cataloging in Publication Data

Main entry under title:

Animal marking.

Bibliography: p.
Includes index.
1. Animal marking. I. Stonehouse, Bernard.
QL60.5.A54 $591'.07'2$ 78-3777
ISBN 0-8391-1274-2

Contributors

AMLANER, C. J.–Animal Behaviour Research Group, Department of Zoology, University of Oxford, South Parks Road, Oxford OX1 3PS

ASHTON, D. G.–Zoological Society of London, Whipsnade Park, Dunstable LU6 2LF

BROWN, S. G.–Sea Mammal Research Unit, c/o British Antarctic Survey, Madingley Road, Cambridge CB3 OET

DELANY, M. J.–School of Environmental Science, University of Bradford, Bradford BD7 1DP

ELTRINGHAM, S. K.–Department of Applied Biology, University of Cambridge, Pembroke Street, Cambridge CB2 3DX

INGRAM, J. C.–Department of Psychology, University of Bristol, 8–10 Berkeley Square, Bristol BS8 1HH

JORDAN, W. J.–Royal Society for the Prevention of Cruelty to Animals, Causeway, Horsham RH12 1HG

KEAR, J.–The Wildfowl Trust, Martin Mere, Bursclough, Nr. Ormskirk, Lancs.

LAIRD, L. M.–Department of Zoology, University of Aberdeen, Tillydrone Avenue, Aberdeen AB9 2TN

LANE-PETTER, W.–Animal House, School of Clinical Medicine, University of Cambridge, Hills Road, Cambridge CB2 2QL

LINN, I.–Department of Biology, University of Exeter, Exeter EX4 4PS

MACDONALD, D. W.–Animal Behaviour Research Group, Department of Zoology, University of Oxford, South Parks Road, Oxford OX1 3PS

MEDWAY, LORD–Great Glemham House, Great Glemham, Saxmundham, IP17 1LP

NEWTON, D.–Universal Livestock Services Ltd., Universal House, Riverside, Banbury, OX16 8TF

PATTERSON, I. J.–Culterty Field Station, University of Aberdeen, Newburgh, Aberdeenshire

PENNYCUICK, C. J.–Department of Zoology, University of Bristol, Woodland Road, Bristol BS8 1UG

PRESTT, I.–Royal Society for the Protection of Birds, The Lodge, Sandy SG19 2DL

RYDER, R. D.–Department of Psychology, The Warneford Hospital, Oxford

SCOTT, D. K.–Sub-department of Animal Behaviour, University of Cambridge, Madingley, Cambridge CB3 8AA

SOUTHWOOD, T. R. E.–Department of Zoology and Applied Entomology, Imperial College, Silwood Park, Ascot, Berks.

SPELLERBERG, I. F.–Department of Biology, University of Southampton, Southampton SO9 5NH

SPENCER, R.–British Trust for Ornithology, Beech Grove, Tring HP23 5NR

STEBBINGS, R. E.–Institute of Terrestrial Ecology, Monks Wood Experimental Station, Abbots Ripton, Huntingdon PE17 2LS

STONEHOUSE, B.–School of Environmental Science, University of Bradford, Bradford BD7 1DP

SUMMERS, C. F.–Sea Mammal Research Unit, c/o British Antarctic Survey, Madingley Road, Cambridge CB3 OET

SWINGLAND, I. R.–Animal Ecology Research Group, Department of Zoology, University of Oxford, South Parks Road, Oxford OX1 3PS

TWIGG, G. I.–Department of Zoology, Royal Holloway College, Englefield Green, Surrey TW20 9TY

WITTHAMES, S. R.–Sea Mammal Research Unit, c/o British Antarctic Survey, Madingley Road, Cambridge CB3 OET

Contents

1 Introduction: marking animals for research

M. J. Delany*

The Wild Animal Advisory Committee of the R.S.P.C.A. meets several times a year to consider comments received by the Society on a wide range of wildlife management practices in which cruelty may be, or is claimed to be, involved. In addition, the Committee looks into a number of topics at its own initiative. At these sessions expert advice and comment is frequently invited which, together with the expertise within the Committee, provides a basis for recommendation to the Council of the Society. Examples of topics that have been discussed are rabies, use of strychnine to poison moles, management of seals and the status of the otter. It was at a meeting in late 1976 that a discussion on recognition marking of animals for research was first proposed. As this possibility was explored in more detail it soon became apparent that the Committee would be embarking on a very wide subject which, in order to give it the full treatment it merited, necessitated reference to a far wider range of experience than existed within the Wild Animals Advisory Committee. In view of the clearly recognised need to include a comprehensive range of specialist interests it was considered desirable that the discussions should be held in an open meeting and that both contributors and audience should have the opportunity of discussion and seeking further information on the marking methods described. It was also felt that the proceedings would be of sufficient interest to many persons not able to attend the meeting to justify publication. It was intended that this should be a definitive reference work of value to non-professional as well as professional biologists, providing guidance on the most useful techniques in marking or other methods of recognition of individual animals. These, then, are the reasons why the conference on *Recognition Marking of Animals in Research* was held, in the meeting room of the Zoological Society of London, on July 12–14, 1977.

The meeting was sponsored by the R.S.P.C.A. and, while expressing gratitude for its support, it is pertinent to draw attention to the interest which the Society had in it. To some extent this can be obtained from the R.S.P.C.A. Statement

*Professor M. J. Delany is a graduate of the Universities of Manchester and Glasgow. His first research, between 1950 and 1953, was on the ecology of wingless insects (Thysanura) at the University of Exeter. From there he proceeded to a Fulbright Fellowship at the University of Florida, and thence to the Universities of Glasgow and Southampton. Research on the ecology of British mammals was initiated in 1956, and on tropical rodents in 1961. He was Professor of Zoology at Makerere College, Uganda, from 1965 to 1969, and is currently Professor of Environmental Science at the University of Bradford.

of Policies which was approved by the Council in 1976. This includes the following:

Animal Experimentation. (1) The R.S.P.C.A. is opposed to all experiments on animals which cause pain, suffering or stress. It realises that until practicable and reliable alternatives are available, experimental work on animals appears to be scientifically indispensable in some areas of genuine veterinary or medical research. (2) The R.S.P.C.A. is opposed to animal experiments which involve unnecessary repetitions or are for scientifically trivial ends, or which involve techniques to which satisfactory and humane alternatives have already been developed. (3) In cases where animals have to be used, suffering should be controlled as far as possible by the proper use of anaesthetics and/or analgesics.

Snares and Traps. The R.S.P.C.A. is opposed to the use of snares and any trap which causes suffering. It condones live traps when certain conditions are adhered to.

Conservation. The R.S.P.C.A. is concerned with the welfare of wildlife.

While some of these statements might, with justification, provoke discussion (what criteria are used for assessing the 'scientifically trivial' and who establishes these criteria? What is the 'welfare of wildlife'?) the very broad area of concern expressed by the Society is that stress, suffering and pain should be avoided in experiments on animals. These are very laudable objectives to which I am sure all who were involved in the symposium would subscribe.

No-one is more aware of the absolute necessity to minimise discomfort to an animal than the field biologist who wishes to obtain meaningful scientific information over a period of time on the animal he has marked. The prime requirements of a marking technique are that it should not modify the behaviour, mobility, dispersal, health or any other facet of the life history of the marked animal. In short, a marked animal should be able to live in the wild in precisely the same way as it would had it not been marked. If the animal as a result of marking were to suffer debilitation, severe and continued stress, prolonged pain or incapacitating mutilation it is very highly improbable that it would meet the experimental requirements of the biologist. These practical considerations are additional to the biologist's ethical concern for the welfare of the animal. Thus, on these issues the R.S.P.C.A. and the field biologist have much of common interest as well as considerable areas of agreement in the attainment of virtually identical objectives.

A further important aspect of the work of the Society is in the field of education in animal welfare. This is achieved through its publications, visual aids, field education officers, courses for teachers, the Society's education and field studies centre and in a variety of other ways. In the educational context, R.S.P.C.A. was particularly interested in supporting the conference as it plans to make considerable use of the guidelines on the most desirable methods of marking and recognition that have emerged through the experience of the contributors and their papers. Those of us working on wild populations of animals are very conscious of the need for readily accessible published information on marking techniques for students, amateur naturalists and our own research programmes. Furthermore, the R.S.P.C.A. is prepared to assist with the improvement of marking techniques by providing logistic and financial support to individual research workers, subject to the availability of funds and providing that the work falls within the Society's objectives.

The Development of Marking Techniques

Before outlining the uses and application of marking techniques it is appropriate to consider briefly the background knowledge on animals against which most methods have been developed. Not only does this place their scientific relevance and objectives in perspective but it also indicates how the development of new techniques has accompanied the expansion of biological research into new and previously unexplored fields.

The British interest in natural history was well established during the last century through the collections, observations, thinking and writings of naturalists. In addition to the formulation and testing of fundamental concepts, such as Darwin's theory of organic evolution, many workers were producing the intellectually less exciting but nevertheless extremely valuable contributions on the systematics and biology of the British fauna and flora. F. O. Morris's treatise on *The History of British Birds* which first appeared in 1857, and J. G. Millais's *Mammals of Great Britain and Ireland* published in 1904, are excellent examples of these types of works. They were comprehensive, detailed and rich in illustration. But of greater significance for our present discussion is the type of information these authors, and other contemporary naturalists, had obtained on the animals they described. Through careful field observation, much was known on the general habits and ecology of birds and mammals. For the former there were detailed accounts of the food, structural characters, nesting habits of particular pairs, and geographical distribution. By way of contrast, information was scant on territory, social structure, the size and configuration of areas occupied and exploited and the routes of migration. There was a similar imbalance of information on the mammals. Here data were given on the habits and longevity of readily identifiable deer stags, but there was scant information on individual female deer as well as the individuals of other mammal species. Millais's account, like Morris's almost fifty years earlier, represented a most useful accumulation of fragmentary information from a large number of sources. However, both lacked the depth of study which naturalists were beginning to recognise as essential to a better understanding of the life histories of animals.

From this phase of descriptive natural history there evolved a more critical, imaginative and quantitative approach to the study of animals in the field. This was accompanied by the emergence and expansion of the sciences of ecology and ethology which demanded the adoption of more refined analytical and field techniques than had generally been in use up to the turn of the century. A more rigorous approach to field studies was essential if the fundamental questions being posed by these new disciplines were to be answered. Clearly, diagnostic marking had a recognisable role and widespread application in providing basic information in ecology and behaviour.

Recognition marking had, in fact, been attempted with varying degrees of success on two groups of animals prior to the nineteenth century. The earliest and apparently most powerful motivation for recognition marking stemmed from ornithologists and ichthyologists, who wanted to establish ownership, transport messages, and ascertain the movement patterns of birds and fish.

Modern scientific bird banding was probably pioneered during the 1890s, although prior to this numerous successful attempts at marking birds had been

achieved since very early times. Fisher and Peterson (1964) cogently described
some of this earlier work:

> The earliest man known to have marked a bird . . . was one Quintus Fabius
> Pictor. Sometime between 218 and 201 BC, when the second Punic War was
> on, this Roman officer, was sent a swallow taken from her nestlings, by a
> besieged garrison. He tied a thread to its leg with knots to indicate the date
> of his relief attack, and let the bird fly back. In the later Roman days of Pliny
> (1st century AD), a certain knight fond of chariot racing in Rome used to take
> swallows with him from Volterra, 135 miles away, and released them with
> the winning colours painted on them, no doubt enabling his friends at home
> to confound the local bookmakers.

From the thirteenth to eighteenth centuries a variety of markings were used.
As early as the thirteenth century falconers marked their birds with name plates
or bands. Herons were similarly marked, while swans and ducks were marked
with metal collars by landowners in the seventeenth and eighteenth centuries.
During the nineteenth century there were numerous, haphazard and for the most
part unsuccessful attempts at marking a large number of bird species. However,
in 1890 a Dane called Mortensen marked starlings using zinc rings. These were
inscribed with the year and the name of his home town, Viburg. The experiments
were not entirely successful, but in 1899 he refined his technique by using
aluminium rings, each marked with a return address. Mortensen marked 164
starlings in this way. It was this work that provided the foundation for subsequent
bird-banding studies which have been adopted throughout the world.

One of the earliest references to fish marking appears in Izaak Walton's
The Compleat Angler which was first published in 1653. He alludes to experiments
where ribbons were tied to the tails of young salmon. These marked animals
demonstrated that salmon returned to the same part of the river after visiting
the sea. Marking of salmon and sea trout was being practised in a number of
Scottish rivers during the first half of the nineteenth century. The first of these
reported by Calderwood (1907) was in March 1823, when Mackenzie of Ardross
marked a grilse kelt with a brass wire and recaptured the fish a year later. In
1834, 524 sea trout from the River Nith were marked by removal of the adipose
fin. Sixty-eight were recaptured in 1835 when a third of the dorsal fin was
removed. Those recaptured in 1836 had half the anal fin removed and the one
fish caught in 1837 was killed. These and other early experiments were undertaken
by private individuals. However, between 1851 and 1865 and between 1870 and
1873, the Experimental Committee of the Tweed Commissioners undertook two
marking programmes. Various marks were used including fin cutting, pieces of
wire in various parts of the body such as the tail and jaws, and numbered labels
attached to the tail or the operculum. By the turn of the century techniques
had been refined and improved. The Fishery Board for Scotland was then using
a small numbered, silver plate attached to the base of the dorsal fin, and in
1905 the Tay Salmon Fisheries Company marked 6500 smolts with silver wire
loops passed through the skin of the back close to the adipose fin.

Seals appear to be the first group of wild mammals to have been subjected to

systematic marking programmes. The earliest records I have obtained go back
to the middle of the last century when attempts were being made, as with the
first marking experiments on fish, to obtain information on their movement
and dispersion patterns. Seal marking was probably first undertaken on the northern
fur seal on the then Russian-owned Pribilof Islands in the 1860s. Little information is available on these experiments, which were designed to establish whether
young males returned to the rookery of their birth. The animals were marked by
removal of their ears.

Following the purchase of Alaska by the United States, a Captain Charles
Bryant marked seal pups in 1870 and 1871 on two rookeries on St Paul Island
within the Pribilofs. He clipped the right ear of pups from Lukanin Rookery
and the left ear of those from Reef. Sufficient seals were killed in 1872 and 1873
to show that young animals did not invariably return to the rookery of their
birth (Scheffer, 1950). Several thousand fur seals were branded on the Pribilofs
between 1896 and 1903. This work was actually undertaken with a view to
protecting seal stocks, as the resulting scarring made the skins less attractive to
sealers. All these methods involved mutilation, and it was not until the 1920s
that extensive tagging programmes of the fur seal got under way. Between
1927 and 1950 just under 70 000 seals had been tagged. The first use of markers
in the United Kingdom was in 1951, when Mrs G. Hickling used tags for marking
grey seals on the Farne Islands (Hewer, 1974).

For the remaining groups of mammals, recognition marking has had much more
recent origins. The first sytematic marking of whales was in about 1920, when a
Norwegian called Hjorst fired copper lances into the blubber of whales off the
Faroes and South Georgia. The method was unsuccessful as either the marks
were lost or infection set in. It was not until 1934, after the Discovery Committee
had developed a new type of mark (a stainless steel tube about $10\frac{1}{2}$ inches long)
which could not be ejected, that extensive and successful whale marking could
be initiated (Slijper, 1962).

Among small mammals marking was frequently initiated in the 1930s. During
this decade Chitty (1937) described the use of rings on small mammals,
Krassovksii (1935) placed discs on the ears of arctic foxes, and Southern (1940)
used numbered ear discs on rabbits. Bat banding was undertaken by Reyberg
(1947) in 1932, and Eisentraut described in 1935 his marking of 600 noctules.

The marking of large terrestrial wild mammals has posed particular difficulties,
as there are the combined problems of applying a suitable mark and capturing and
immobilising the subject. These constraints have probably been responsible
for the relatively slow development of studies making use of markers on these
animals. Two references to the literature illustrate this. Describing in 1967
the use of an immobilising drug on waterbuck, Hanks stated, 'Before the start of
this decade the only method available to widlife research workers for capturing a
wild animal for marking was to chase it with a vehicle almost to the point of
exhaustion, and then rope it.' And in a second paper published in 1969 he
reviews the available techniques for marking large African mammals. Inevitably,
in this account, reference is made to sources of information from other parts
of the world, but it is significant to note that in a bibliography of forty references
only five appeared before 1960 and none prior to 1953.

Among the invertebrates, the marking of insects using paints and dyes was being practised during the 1920s (Dudley and Searles, 1923; Meder, 1926) and by the 1930s its use was widespread. By this time researches were well under way into the assessment of insect population densities.

From this brief and incomplete summary we can see that marking was used to a limited extent on a relatively small range of animals up to the turn of the century. Apart from on birds and fish, effective recognition marking techniques were being developed only between the wars when they were used in a quite small number of experimental situations. Their greatest application has been in the post second war period at the same time as there has been a considerable expansion in studies in animal ecology and behaviour.

The Information Obtained from Recognition Marking

It would be neither appropriate nor feasible to consider at this stage the results of the numerous experiments, using marked animals, that have produced valuable scientific information. Instead, and with scant reference to particular examples, it is possible to identify broadly those major areas where results have been obtained or can reasonably be anticipated. In putting forward these ideas I will be stressing the relevance of marking to studies of animals in the wild. It should also be mentioned here that recognition marking can be carried out in one of two major ways. It can either permit identification of a particular animal, or enable the experimenter to know that the marked animal is one of a group, each member of which bears an identical mark. The information derived from these two methods is not necessarily the same. For the most part I shall be referring to the former, although where appropriate the merits of uniform marking will be mentioned.

Migratory and Non-Migratory Movements

The use of markers has provided much information on migrations of birds, bats and fish. Many of their species traverse enormous distances—for example the arctic tern, which can travel 10 000 miles or more at each migration. Migratory movement can be over appreciably shorter distances, as is witnessed by the distances covered by many of our winter visitors from Europe. Not only is information provided on the origin and destination of the migrant; further data from marked animals can indicate the route of the migration. Records of dates of recoveries provide an insight into rate of movement and the time spent at intermediate points. All are parameters of considerable relevance to understanding how a species lives and makes use of its available resources.

The non-migratory movements include the localised movements witnessed in the day-to-day life of the animal. The places of feeding, resting, courtship, rearing of young and so forth are frequently accommodated within a common area which can be defined through continued observation of one or more identifiable animals. Such information also forms a basis for recognising territorial boundaries and home ranges. These spatial limits may be within two dimensions, as with exclusively ground-dwelling species, or in three as for most birds and scansorial mammals. Dispersal is another type of non-migratory movement involving the permanent vacating of one area in favour of another. It frequently involves a segment of a population rather than the whole. Data from marked animals can shed light on rates and times of dispersal, the types of habitat moved into, the distances traversed, and the proportions and members of the population involved in this type of movement.

Ethology

In animal behaviour the ability to recognise individual animals in the field and the laboratory is probably the prime requirement of a wide spectrum of research studies. Observations on the individual permit a detailed characterisation of its full panoply of diurnal and (with supporting techniques) nocturnal activities. The times spent in various behavioural events such as feeding, foraging, hunting, drinking, resting, scent marking, grooming, preening and vocalising can be recorded, as well as the way in which each of these activities is carried out. There is also the complex array of intraspecific and interspecific social activities that animals indulge in. The detailed and sustained investigation of hierarchical organisations and the determination of their biological significance, courtship, mating, rearing of young, group activities such as communal feeding, the maintenance of territories and interactions between species, almost invariably require identification of members of the groups concerned. This facility provides considerable strength to the quality and detail of the achievable ends.

Demography

Statistical data on populations can be obtained through marking. The length of time individuals are recorded within a population provides information on longevity, survivorship and mortality rates, while the reproductive habits of known animals can, in conjunction with other sources of information, provide back-up data on natality and recruitment rates. But perhaps the most widespread use of marking in population studies *per se* has been in the estimation of densities. The recognition of particular animals can, of course, provide a means of obtaining total numbers when the investigator is confident that he had identified every animal within a defined area. This method can be labour intensive; it has probably been applied to a relatively small number of species, although some (for example primates and buffalo) have proved amenable to this type of assessment.

However, the most frequent use of marking for population estimation has probably been through the use of a uniform mark on a sample of animals collected and released on one occasion, followed by the application of a different mark at each subsequent sampling, of which there may be several. These capture-recapture methods have provided statisticians with the opportunity of devising numerous analytical techniques for determining densities at different times of sampling, and estimates of additions to, and losses from, the population since the previous assessment. These methods have particular applicability to insect populations, where the field worker is handling large numbers of relatively catchable animals.

In conclusion, it is appreciated that there can be overlap between the major research areas identified here; as a result, several different types of information may be simultaneously obtained from the one animal. The methodology is potentially highly productive of results, and its use as a research tool should not be underestimated.

Types of Marking

The papers of this symposium describe many of the marking methods available, their efficacy and how they can be used to greatest benefit. But is it possible to categorise these marking techniques in any generalised way? Should this prove feasible, it may help us more readily to identify the advantages and limitations of a particular technique if we can see into which broad category it fits. In attempting a classification of marking techniques I would suggest that the first division should be between experimental situations where there is no need to impose a mark, and those were one is necessary. The former would be suitable for those animals which, because of unique individual facial features, fur colouration and patterning or other obvious external characters, could be recognised individually without the need to introduce any form of marker. This technique has been applied to such mammals as giraffe, buffalo, several species of primate, lion and feral cats, but is inapplicable to species that cannot be readily observed from fairly close quarters. The main advantage of the technique is its relative simplicity.

Techniques involving the imposition of a mark could be divided into those where the mark is temporary and those where it is permanent. The removal of small patches of hair and the use of hair dyes are both methods of temporary marking: thus an experiment using them will be short. Permanent marks include those where a uniform mark is applied to all animals collected, and those where a mark is used that can identify each animal individually. The former has already been alluded to in the context of population assessment; also within this category is the use of the radioactive isotope which emits a uniform signal.

Marking which identifies an individual animal is probably the most widely used technique. Here are included numbered discs, clipped toes, numbered bird rings, coloured leg rings for birds, numbered tags and so forth. These obviously divide into two categories—those that permit recognition of an animal from a distance, and those for which it is possible only if the animal is caught or examined at very close quarters. The latter is more limiting to field study than the former, but there is frequently no alternative for certain types of animals.

This outline scheme has its shortcomings: for example, some marks are somewhere between the permanent and the temporary, and it is possible that temporary marking techniques may have a similar breakdown into subdivisions, as do the permanent marking techniques. Furthermore, two or more techniques can be applied to a population at the same time, to facilitate more efficient recognition of individuals.

Practical Considerations

Finally, some general comments on practical considerations in marking animals. Four criteria should be accepted before any programme of marking is begun.

First, it is essential that marking should only be undertaken for a definite scientific or educational purpose. It is frequently desirable that the work programme be co-ordinated with those of others so as to minimise duplication.

Secondly, marking should be undertaken only by those with training and skills in the technique to be used. For many techniques the training need not be long and elaborate but it should be sufficiently informative for the prospective marker to know precisely how to go about his work.

Thirdly, those marking should be fully conversant with the potential hazards, limitations and consequences of the techniques they are using, both to themselves and to their animals. For example, markers applied to young animals may cause severe discomfort as the animal grows; also special hazards are involved in the use of radioactive markers.

Fourthly, the most appropriate technique should be adopted for the problem to be solved. Precise definition of the problem should make clear what is required of the method. No purpose is served by using a method providing superfluous information. The most intricate method can waste time for the investigator, and increase the likelihood of the animal being subject to stress.

There are many recognition marking techniques to be considered, and I think it would be correct to say that the London meetings were the first to be held to consider recognition marking exclusively and comprehensively. The R.S.P.C.A. is to be congratulated on its initiative in sponsoring this symposium, which I am confident will be of ultimate help and guidance to the Society, as well as to a prospectively wider audience through publication.

Acknowledgements

I am grateful to my colleagues on the Wild Animals Advisory Committee for the assistance and advice they have given in the formulation of this symposium. Mr W. J. Jordan, the Committee Secretary, most helpfully co-ordinated the work of the Committee and the Society. Finally, I would like to record the Committee's appreciation of the very considerable efforts Miss Gillian Bishop of the R.S.P.C.A. has put into the administration of the symposium, and the most efficient way she dealt with the detailed work of preparing and organising the programme.

References

Calderwood, W. L. (1907). *Life of the Salmon*. Edward Arnold, London.
Chitty, D. (1937). A ringing technique for small mammals. *J. anim. Ecol.*, **6**, 36-53.
Dudley, J. E. and Searles, E. M. (1923). Color marking of the striped cucumber beetle (*Diabrotica vittata* Fab.) and preliminary experiments to determine its flight. *J. econ. Ent.*, **16**, 363-368.

Eisentraut, M. (1935). Ergebrisse des Fledermausberingung. *Ornith. Monatsber.,* **43**, 150.

Fisher, J. and Peterson, R. T. (1964). *The World of Birds*. Macdonald, London.

Hanks, J. (1967). The use of M99 for the immobilisation of the defassa waterbuck (*Kobus defassa penricei*). *E. Afr. Wildl. J.*, **5**, 96–105.

Hanks, J. (1969). Techniques for marking large African mammals. *Puku*, **5**, 65–86.

Hewer, H. R. (1974). *British Seals*. Collins, London.

Krassovskii, S. (1935). Experiments in marking the Arctic fox (*Alopex lagopus*) on Novaya Zemlya. *Bull. Arct. Inst. Leningr.,* **9**, 281.

Meder, O. (1926). Über die kennzeichnung von weisslingen zwecks Erfassung ihrer Wanderung. *Int. ent. Z.,* **19**, 325–330.

Millais, J. G. (1904–06). *Mammals of Great Britain and Ireland*. 3 vols, Longman Green, London.

Morris, F. O. (1857). *A History of British Birds*. 6 vols, George Bell, London.

Reyburg, O. (1947). *Studies on Bats and Bat Parasites*. Bokförlaget Svensk Natur, Stockholm.

Scheffer, V. B. (1950). Experiments in the marking of seals and sea lions. *Spec. scient. Rep. U.S. Fish. Wildl. Serv.,* **4**, 1–48.

Slijper, E. J. (1962). *Whales*. Hutchinson, London.

Southern, H. N. (1940). The ecology and population dynamics of the wild rabbit, *Oryctolagus cuniculus. Ann. appl. Biol.,* **27**, 509–526.

Walton, I. (1653). *The Compleat Angler.*

Section 1 *Methods of capture, and marking in captivity*

W. J. Jordan

We are in a period of change, the astrologers tell us; we are leaving the age of Pisces and entering the influence of Aquarius, and the two ages are very different. Whatever the reason, change is both profound and rapid, and three basic essentials are there for its continuation and acceleration.

First, the human population explosion, if it continues on its present course, will double world population between now and AD 2000. Secondly, we are approaching visible limits to natural resources, including the important resource of wilderness areas. Thirdly, the fundamental differences between the new religion of science and the old mysticism are now obvious; the former proclaims that all is knowable, and the latter that nothing is.

The R.S.P.C.A. subscribes to the Buddhist's prayer—at least so far as this Conference is concerned: 'Have courage to alter what can be altered, fortitude to endure what can't be, and wisdom to tell the difference.'

There is no doubt that natural wildlife areas are under great pressure, particularly in developing countries with burgeoning human populations. Man has become the supreme exterminator—witness the destruction of countless millions of American Passenger pigeons and the decimation of the great buffalo herds. Yet the Indians knew the value of nature to man—'If all the beasts were gone, man would die of a great loneliness of spirit.'

But man is also a conservationist; a great deal of money and effort has recently gone into the study of animals, both in the wild and in zoos, to see what steps can be taken to preserve and manage stocks for posterity. Our first contributor to this section of the symposium, Dr Keith Eltringham, is widely experienced in work of this kind. His paper draws attention to methods of capturing birds and mammals which, like good marking methods, leave the subject as little harmed as possible, and available intact for further study in the field.

Perhaps most zoos are a sort of living museum—a peep-show to distract the public for an hour or so. But there are some who believe that zoos can also be reservoirs—perhaps the only safe repositories—for endangered species. In zoos which take on this important conservation role, good management programmes based on knowledge of individual animals are essential. These depend on reliable methods of marking, a field in which our second contributor, D. G. Ashton, has much experience. Mr Ashton is a veterinary surgeon who, after qualifying at Cambridge and a spell in general practice, is now Veterinary Officer at Whipsnade Zoo. His paper stresses the importance of reliable marking methods in facilitating breeding programmes, inter-collection exchanges of breeding stocks, and other sound management practices.

Animals are used in enormous quantities in laboratory studies. Scientists and lay public alike are questioning the purpose of many experiments—have cosmetics, herbicides, pesticides and other industrial products contributed so substantially to human life that the suffering of so many animals is continually justified? Whatever the answer to this question, animals will still be used in laboratories for some time to come. Often they need to be marked individually, and the R.S.P.C.A. has an interest in promoting the most humane possible methods of marking. Our third contributor, Dr W. Lane-Petter, was for fifteen years Director at the Medical Research Council Laboratory Animal's Centre; from 1956 to 1969 he was Secretary General of the International Committee on Laboratory Animals, and he has written and edited many works on the welfare of laboratory animals and related subjects.

2 Methods of capturing wild animals for marking purposes

S. K. Eltringham*

This account of capture methods will be confined to birds and mammals because it is mainly with these groups that special techniques have been developed.

Birds

In many cases, commercial methods of catching birds for the market have been adapted for scientific purposes. Those which cause damage to the bird, such as liming, are obviously not acceptable for scientific work, while special techniques have to be developed for passerines and other groups not regularly exploited as food. The most widely used method for catching birds, whatever their species, is simply to take them from the nest when they have reached a size large enough to carry the mark without discomfort. The method can necessarily apply only to nidicolous species although precocious chicks can often be caught, while still flightless, by running them down on foot. However, most techniques for catching adult birds rely on driving or luring them into some form of trap.

Cage traps

Passerines and similar sized birds may be captured without much difficulty in cage traps, which rely on the bird being unable to find its way out of a chamber into which it has entered through a small opening—frequently at the end of a funnel as in a lobster pot. Large scale trapping often involves a device based on the Heligoland trap, originally designed on Heligoland to catch migrating song birds. Essentially, the trap is a large curved tunnel with a high wide opening, which gradually narrows down to a small catching box. Large square cage traps with funnelled openings at water level were used successfully to catch ducks at the edge of Abberton Reservoir in Essex by the late Major General C. B. Wainwright

*Dr Keith Eltringham took a PhD in marine ecology before joining the Wildfowl Trust in 1957. Later he became a lecturer in zoology at King's College, London, leaving in 1967 for Uganda where he was appointed successively Director of the Nuffield Unit of Tropical Animal Ecology, Director of the Uganda Institute of Ecology, and Chief Research Officer of the Uganda National Parks. Both at Slimbridge and in Uganda he was involved in the capture of animals for marking purposes. Since 1973 he has been a lecturer in wildlife biology at Cambridge University.

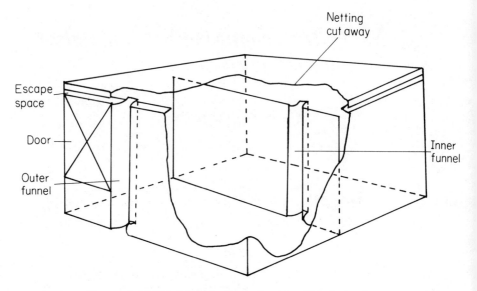

Figure 2.1 Modified Abberton trap, about 2 m high, for use in tidal waters to catch swans, ducks and other waterfowl. The escape space prevents the birds drowning should the trap become completely submerged by unexpected high tides. (After Garden, 1964).

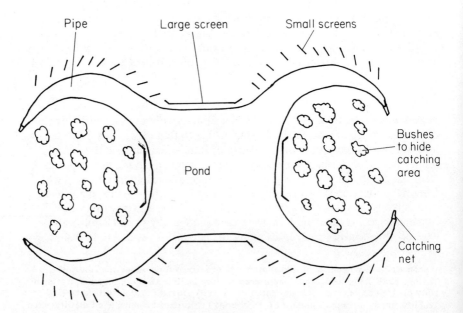

Figure 2.2 Plan of a typical duck decoy. The pond is roughly 50 m across.

(Wainwright, 1957). The trap design has been modified by Garden (1964) and Young (1964) for use in tidal waters to catch swans and other waterfowl as well as ducks (figure 2.1).

Duck decoys

Ducks have always been caught for food in this country; one of the principal methods of catching them was the duck decoy. Although no longer commercially viable, the decoy continues to be used for scientific purposes. A typical decoy (figure 2.2) consists of a central pond, with four curved canals or pipes extending from the corners, covered with netting on large metal hoops which progressively decrease in size until they end in a small catching bag. Ducks are enticed into the pipe. When they reach a certain point, the operator, who is screened from the ducks on the open pond, shows himself. The birds fly away from him towards the blind end of the pipe and into the catching net. A pipe at each corner is necessary to allow for wind direction, for ducks tend to take off into wind and it is important that they should fly up the pipe and not back down towards the open pond.

Capture of nesting ducks

American workers have used dogs, mainly retrievers, to catch incubating ducks on the prairies. Most female ducks sit tight on the nest, hoping to avoid detection by immobility. However, if the biologist has previously noted the position of the nest, he can approach quite closely before setting his dog at it. The female explodes from the nest before the dog reaches her, but she needs a few seconds to gather sufficient height to be out of range, and before she can do this the dog usually manages to leap up and pluck her out of the air. A well-trained dog with a 'soft' mouth can catch and hold a duck without disturbing so much as a feather.

Another ingenious method for catching incubating ducks is to dispense with the dog and cover the nest, after the bird has been flushed, with a length of netting held a few centimetres off the ground with sticks. The returning duck creeps under the netting—becoming hopelessly entangled in it when, on the following day, she is rushed and attempts to fly off. Other species have similarly been caught by placing cage traps over the nest. These admittedly drastic treatments do not appear to upset the bird unduly, for she will soon return to her nest on release.

Rocket nets

Rocket nets are similar to clap nets, which are large nets suddenly pulled over birds entering a trapping area. The nets have to be camouflaged and operated with ropes by hidden observers. More sophisticated designs have triggered springs for throwing the net. This type of trap has been greatly developed by the Wildfowl Trust for the capture of geese, through the use of rockets powered by cordite to propel the nets. Rocket nets have also been used to catch waders when they are driven off the shore into fields by high tides; very large catches have been made on the Wash (Ogilvie, 1965).

Round-up of flightless geese

Members of the family Anatidae, to which geese belong, are unusual in that all the flight feathers are moulted at once so that the bird becomes flightless. Advantage can be taken of their temporary incapacity to round them up and walk them into an enclosure. This technique, described by Gooch (1953) for lesser Snow and Blue geese *Anser caerulescens*, was developed from the traditional hunting methods of eskimos. The aim is to concentrate the birds into a milling throng by walking round the flock and dropping off a man at intervals until the whole group is encircled. One man then walks away towards the trap while the others slowly close in on the flock, which follows the retreating figure into the pen. The same technique of rounding up flightless Pink-footed geese *Anser brachyrhynchus* was rediscovered independently by Scott, Boyd and Sladen (1955), again from hearing of traditional hunting methods.

The Wildfowl Trust staff found that it is possible to round up birds fully capable of flight when 57 coots *Fulica atra* were gently walked into a funnel trap (Anon, 1961). Swans can also be caught in this way, despite their prowess in the air, if they are driven through an area with bushes or other obstacles which obstruct their take-off run. Nesting adults of the Mute swan *Cygnus olor* can easily be caught with a swan-hook, which is rather like a shepherd's crook, placed around the base of the neck. Despite its ferocious reputation, the swan can be readily overpowered by holding its wings to its body. Swans can be pulled out of the water into a boat in a similar fashion, as in swan-upping.

Mist nets

Although Heligoland traps are used principally to capture passerines, most small birds that are ringed are caught by mist nets. These are fine mesh, black nylon nets that are erected on poles in places where birds can be expected to pass, for example across flight lines leading to roosts. Dawn and dusk are the best times of day, for not only are the birds' movements more predictable at these times, but the reduced illumination probably makes it more difficult for the birds to notice the net. The bird is caught by becoming entangled in the mesh. Its release is sometimes difficult, and may require cutting the net. In Britain, mist nets may be bought by licensed ringers through the British Trust for Ornithology, Tring.

Stupefying drugs

Stupefying drugs can be used for birds which are attracted to bait. The major problem is one of dosage, for the amount of bait eaten cannot easily be controlled. Some birds may fly off only partially affected yet sufficiently so for them to fall easy victims to predators later on. Others may eat too much bait and be poisoned. The latter problem can sometimes be overcome, particularly with meat- or fish-eaters, by forcing them to disgorge their meal after capture. α-Chloralose is probably the most favoured drug and has been used with Canada geese *Branta canadensis* (Crider and McDaniel, 1967), wood pigeons *Columba palumbus* (Murton, Isaacson and Westwood, 1965) and wild turkey *Meleagris gallopavo* (Williams, 1966). Avertin (tribromoethanol) was used by Mosby and Cantner (1956) to catch wild turkeys and by Smith (1967) for the capture of gulls, cormorants and other sea birds. Vultures were caught in the Etosha National Park in South West Africa after they had fed on a zebra which had been killed by an overdose of phencyclidine (Ebedes, 1973).

Mammals

Bats

Mist nets are ideal for trapping bats, which usually have regular routes to and from their roosts, and it is a simple matter to string nets across their flight path. Again, care is essential in extracting the animals from the nets for they are perhaps more easily damaged than birds by rough handling. An alternative to mist netting if the roost is accessible is to scrape bats off the walls of caves into oversized butterfly nets. This is a smelly, messy business but can be highly effective where bats roost in large numbers. 'Lobster pot' traps have also been used to capture bats roosting in caves.

Small mammal traps

The most widely used live traps are the Sherman and Longworth models. The Longworth trap incorporates a nest box and if bedding is provided, most rodents when caught will go to sleep and come to no harm. Shrews are less likely to survive because the length of time that usually elapses between capture and inspection of the traps is longer than they can manage without food. Medium sized mammals such as stoats, mongooses and other of the smaller carnivores require a more spacious trap and the one commonly in use is the Havahart which is basically an open tunnel, square in cross section, with wire mesh sides and a sprung door at each end. It is manufactured in various sizes. Commercially produced traps may be bought through most laboratory suppliers.

Large mammal traps

Various forms of box trap have been constructed for the capture of bears, large cats and other carnivores. In most cases, the animal is caught when it takes the bait and trips the trigger mechanism of a trap door. The animal can then be immobilised by injection although it may first be necessary to calm it down by spraying the mouth with a suitable drug. A large cage trap was used by Rood (1975) to catch entire packs of Banded mongoose *Mungos mungo* in Uganda. Similar 'one-off' traps can be designed to meet particular requirements.

Modified gin traps have been used by biologists to catch large carnivores such as bears, wolves or foxes. The teeth of the traps are either filed down or covered with a thick layer of sacking to prevent laceration of the foot when the animal is caught. However, this method is not to be recommended for a certain amount of damage is inevitable if the trap is to be powerful enough to hold a large struggling animal (Nellis, 1968). For similar reasons snares in the form of a stopped noose are unacceptable on humane grounds as well as on grounds of inefficiency. Five

Animal marking

of twenty-six coyotes *Canis latrans* held in snares set by Nellis (1968) were found to be dead on inspection. Mammals which can be caught *in situ* or on running down may sometimes be immobilised by hooding; a method developed by Stirling (1966) for seals may have more general application. Covering the eyes often induces a restive animal to remain still for handling.

Drug immobilisation

The immobilisation of large mammals by means of the remote injection of drugs has been widely used in marking programmes. Many deer in Britain and the United States have been caught in this way, as well as a great variety of large mammals in Africa, North America, the polar regions and elsewhere. An account of the early drugs used and the methods of delivery is given by Harthoorn (1965) who has also published a more recent review (Harthoorn, 1976).

The projector
In the early days, the drugs were delivered by means of a crossbow firing a feathered shaft. In expert hands, the crossbow can be very effective but it has

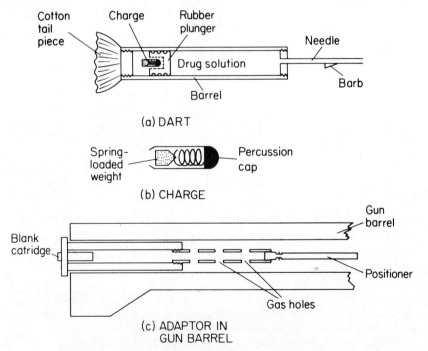

(a) DART

(b) CHARGE

(c) ADAPTOR IN
GUN BARREL

Figure 2.3 Diagrams of the apparatus manufactured by the Palmer Chemical and Equipment Co. Inc. which has been used in many drug immobilisation programmes. The dart, about 8 cm long, and adaptor are placed in succession in the breech of the gun. The positioner ensures that the dart is pushed the correct distance up the barrel. The propulsive force is provided by gas from the blank cartridge emerging at high pressure through the gas holes.

tended to be replaced by the more convenient and cheaper gun, the propulsive force being a blank cartridge or compressed CO_2.

The type of gun in general use today is exemplified by the popular model manufactured as the Cap Chur gun by the Palmer Chemical and Equipment Co. Inc., Douglasville, Georgia, USA. The Cap Chur gun is a shot gun which has been modified by the addition of a rifled sleeve to the barrel and a special adaptor for dispersing the gases from the blank cartridge. Figure 2.3 shows details of the gun and dart. An assessment of the various guns, crossbows and syringes in common use is given by Jones (1976).

The dart

Various types of dart have been used over the years and most are described by Harthoorn but one that is in common use is illustrated in figure 2.3. It consists of an aluminium or alloy barrel, containing the drug, threaded at each end so that the needle and tail piece can be screwed into it. The plunger and charge provide a device for injecting the drug once the dart has hit the target animal. The charge contains a spring loaded weight which travels forward under its own momentum at the time of the strike and fires the detonator. The resulting explosion drives the rubber plunger down the tube to inject the drug. Harthoorn (1976) maintains that the force of the explosion tends to damage the muscle tissues and he advocates a gentler injection brought about by the build-up of CO_2 gas behind the plunger. The gas is generated by the action of a weak acid on a carbonate tablet after the dart has struck the target. The injection is slower than with the explosive device and if the dart drops out prematurely, an insufficient dose may be given.

Problems in drug delivery

Various practical problems have arisen during the use of this apparatus in the field; some of these have been described by Woodford, Eltringham and Wyatt (1972). A common problem is the blockage of the needle point by a skin or bone plug after the dart has hit the target. If this happens, the drug solution cannot be injected and the dart usually blows apart. This difficulty can be overcome by brazing a bead of welding material on to the bevel of the tip of the needle (Harthoorn, 1976). A more serious problem is the frequency with which the needle bends or breaks off at its junction with the barrel. This is more likely to occur with thick-skinned animals; presumably the needle cannot penetrate the target quickly enough before the sudden deceleration throws an intolerable strain on its base.

A contributory factor in the breakage of needles is the high muzzle velocity of the dart. Accuracy in shooting requires a spinning, ballistic missile rather than a flighted arrow, and high velocity improves the chances of success. However, there is a real danger of the projectile acting as a bullet and over-penetration is a serious risk with thin-skinned animals such as antelope. These must not be fired from too close a range and accuracy must, therefore, give way to safety.

Failure of the animal to react after an apparently successful hit is a common experience. A possible cause of failure is that the drug has been injected sub-dermally or into some biologically inactive tissue such as fat. For successful immobilisation the drug needs to be injected intramuscularly.

A frequent (10 per cent) cause of failure noted by Woodford *et al.* (1972) was penetration of the plunger by the detonator. This results in only partial injection of the drug since the plunger does not travel fully down the barrel. Again, this is a design weakness which calls for a stronger plunger. Woodford *et al.* found that the use of two plungers overcame the problem, although there was a penalty in that the capacity of the barrel was thereby reduced.

Type of drug
Most immobilising drugs fall into one of two classes. First, there are the depolarising neuromuscular blockers. Drugs of this type have an action similar to that of the naturally occurring acetylcholine which is secreted at the nerve/muscle junction to cause depolarisation. Normally, the acetylcholine is immediately broken down by cholinesterase, thus allowing a further nerve impulse to pass. The artificial blockers, however, are decomposed only very slowly so that further passage of nerve impulses is prevented and the muscle is paralysed. The over-all action of the drug is to cause paralysis of the skeletal muscles, but an overdose will affect the respiratory muscles as well and death will follow from asphyxiation. For this reason, such drugs should not be used for the 'humane' killing of animals as has been proposed in the literature for culling operations (Pienaar and Van Niekerk, 1963). It should also be remembered that an animal immobilised by a paralysing drug is fully conscious and capable of feeling pain. In no circumstances should such drugs be used if any technique involving surgery, such as the implanting of electrodes under the skin, is to be used. The eyes should be covered with a cloth to prevent damage from the sun should the eyelid or iris muscles be incapacitated.

The advantages of paralysing drugs lie with the operator rather than with the animal. The drugs are inexpensive and are not classified as dangerous, so that they can be used by biologists without medical or veterinary qualifications. They are also convenient to use in the field being very stable in powder form yet readily soluble in water. They are safe to use as they do not penetrate unbroken skin, and have no effect when taken orally. The drug is destroyed by heat so that the meat of animals dying from an overdose can safely be eaten when cooked. Recovery from the drug is rapid and complete so that no long period of aftercare is necessary.

These drugs have their disadvantages, however. There can be distressing side effects including excessive salivary and bronchial secretion. There is no antidote (with one exception, flaxedil, which is not a depolariser but a paralysing drug) and the difference between the effective and lethal doses is small. They cannot, therefore, be used on young animals but only on adults whose average weights are known. Not surprisingly, mortality tends to be high; Short and Spinage (1967) report a 10 per cent loss during the capture of waterbuck *Kobus defassa* with succinylcholine chloride (scoline). On the other hand, Schaller (1972) experienced only one death with this drug during the capture of 166 lions *Panthera leo* in the Serengeti while Krunk (1972) safely immobilised some 255 Spotted hyaena *Crocuta crocuta* with scoline before losing three in one month. Nevertheless, such drugs are not desirable on humane grounds for there is evidence that they cause suffering in the animals concerned. In any case, they have tended to become replaced by drugs of the second category—the centrally acting compounds.

These drugs act predominantly on the central nervous sytem and their effects range from tranquillisation to complete anaesthesia. Tranquillisers are mainly useful in translocation work and are not very suitable for marking and release, but they can bring about a useful reaction when mixed with a small dose of narcotic. Instead of collapsing, the subject remains standing in a condition of extreme tractability. The one advantage of these drugs for marking programmes is that it is better for the animal to remain upright—particularly if it is a ruminant, which is at risk from bloat while lying on its side. Similar synergistic effects can be achieved by the mixing of various narcotic drugs.

Drugs which cause deep anaesthesia are popular in immobilisation work. Two widely used examples are M99 (etorphine hydrochloride) and fentanyl. M99, which is manufactured by Reckitt and Sons Ltd, Hull, is a synthetic morphine derivative many times more powerful than morphia. Like all narcotics, it has an antidote (M285 or direnorphine) which acts by competing with M99 for the receptor sites of the brain. It can, therefore, act as a narcotic itself so that an overdose of antidote will bring the animal round from the immobilising drug but immediately send it back to sleep.

Narcotic drugs have a wide safety margin with little risk of overdosing. Hence mortality is very low while graded doses of antidote can be administered to balance the drug and induce any desired level of unconsciousness during which the righting and postural reflexes of the animal are retained. Such drugs are humane since no fear or pain (narcotics are also analgesics) is experienced while under their influence.

Nevertheless, these drugs have their disadvantages. They are very expensive and extremely dangerous to handle. As they are on the Dangerous Drugs Register, they can be dispensed only by licensed practitioners. They are not always effective pharmaceutically. Thus M99 is not suitable for cats, in which it causes violent excitement rather than anaesthesia, and has tended to be replaced by phencyclidine (Sernylan) which is manufactured by Parke Davis. This is not a narcotic but a dissociative anaesthetic which does not normally cause unconsciousness but renders the animal indifferent to stimuli. It is particularly suitable for carnivores; Bertram (1976) used it to immobilise 67 lions with the loss of only two, neither of which died from the effects of the drug itself. Sernylan has many disadvantages, however, chief among them being the long period of anaesthesia which averaged from $5\frac{1}{2}$ to over 7 hours in Bertram's experience (there is no antidote). The need to protect the animal during this period seriously restricts the catching time available in a marking programme. Smuts, Bryden, De Vos and Young (1973) describe the use of ketamine Cl-581 (Parke Davis) for the immobilisation of lions. This has a wider safety margin, is quicker in action and does not cause the convulsions frequently found with Sernylan. An inconveniently large volume has to be administered, however, and a more potent drug is Cl-744 (Parke Davis) which was used by Bertram and King (1976) to immobilise 26 lions and 6 leopards. The mean time from darting to recovery was only 2 hours and 8 minutes, and there were no convulsions or deaths.

Mass capture

The driving of large numbers of ungulates into traps was developed in South Africa by Oelofse (1970) and the method has been used in Kenya (Swank, Casebeer, Thresher and Woodford, 1974). It relies on the fact that the animals are reluctant to leap over the plastic sheeting which forms the wings of the trap (Densham, 1974). The trap itself is a temporary paddock constructed of hessian and plastic. Once inside the trap, the animals can be moved individually through a squeeze crush into a chute for marking. The method has not come into general use because of expense and the large work force needed to operate it. Some species such as zebra and particularly wildebeest are aggressive towards each other in the trap. Eland do not fight, but cause problems by attempting to leap through or over the plastic walls. This was the only species which Swank *et al.* (1974) could easily drive into the trap; they had no success at all with gazelle, Impala *Aepyceros melampus* or Hartebeest *Alcelaphus buselaphus.*

Other methods of catching large mammals in quantity include drop nets (Ramsey, 1968) and cannon nets, which are similar to rocket-propelled nets (Hawkins, Martoglio and Montgomery, 1968).

References

Anon (1961). Ringing 1959-1960. *A. Rep. Wildfowl Trust*, **12**, 18-19.

Bertram, B. C. R. (1976). Lion immobilization using phencyclidine (Sernylan). *East Afr. Wildl. J.*, **14**, 233-235.

Bertram, B. C. R. and King, J. M. (1976). Lion and leopard immobilization using C1-744. *East Afr. Wildl. J.*, **14**, 237-239.

Cooch, G. (1953). Technique for mass capture of flightless blue and lesser snow geese. *J. Wildl. Mgmt.*, **17**, 460-465.

Crider, E. D. and McDaniel, J. C. (1967). Alpha-chloralose used to capture Canada geese. *J. Wildl. Mgmt.*, **31**, 258-264.

Densham, W. D. (1974). A method of capture and translocation of wild herbivores using opaque plastic material and a helicopter. *Lammergeyer*, **21**, 1-25.

Ebedes, H. (1973). The capture of free-living vultures in the Etosha National Park with phencyclidine. *J. southern Afr. Wildl. Mgmt. Ass.*, **3**, 105-107.

Garden, E. A. (1964). Duck-trapping methods. *A. Rep. Wildfowl Trust*, **15**, 93-95.

Harthoorn, A. M. (1965). Application of pharmacological and physiological principles in restraint of wild animals. *Wildl. Monogr.*, **14**, 1-78.

Harthoorn, A. M. (1976). *The Chemical Capture of Animals*, Ballière Tindall, London.

Hawkins, R. E. Martoglio, L. D. and Montgomery, G. G. (1968). Cannon-netting deer. *J. Wildl. Mgmt.*, **32**, 191-195.

Kruuk, H. (1972). *The Spotted Hyaena*, University of Chicago Press, Chicago.

Jones, D. M. (1976). An assessment of weapons and projectile syringes used for capturing mammals. *Vet. Rec.*, **99**, 250-253.

Mosby, H. S. and Cantner, D. E. (1956). The use of Avertin in capturing wild turkeys and as an oral-basal anaesthetic for other wild animals. *Southwestern Veterinarian*, **9**, 132-136.

Murton, R. K., Isaacson, A. J. and Westwood, N. J. (1965). Capturing columbids at the nest with stupefying baits. *J. Wildl. Mgmt.*, **29**, 647-649.

Nellis, C. H. (1968). Some methods for capturing coyotes alive. *J. Wildl. Mgmt.*, **32**, 402-405.

Oelofse, J. (1970). Plastic for game catching. *Oryx*, **10**, 306–308.

Ogilvie, M. A. (1965). Wader ringing by the Wildfowl Trust, 1959–64. *A. Rep. Wildfowl Trust*, **16**, 48–54.

Pienaar, U. de V. and Van Niekerk, J. W. (1963). Elephant control in national. parks. A new approach. *Oryx*, **7**, 35–38.

Ramsey, C. W. (1968). A drop-net deer trap. *J. Wildl. Mgmt.*, **32**, 187–190.

Rood, J. P. (1975). Population dynamics and food habits of the banded mongoose. *East Afr. Wildl. J.*, **13**, 89–111.

Schaller, G. B. (1972). *The Serengeti Lion*. University of Chicago Press, Chicago.

Scott, P., Boyd, H. and Sladen, W. J. L. (1955). The Wildfowl Trust's second expedition to Central Iceland, 1953. *A. Rep. Wildfowl Trust*, **7**, 63–98.

Short, R. V. and Spinage, C. A. (1967). Drug immobilisation of the Uganda defassa waterbuck. *Vet. Rec.*, **79**, 336–340.

Smith, N. G. (1967). Capturing seabirds with avertin. *J. Wildl. Mgmt.*, **31**, 479–483.

Smuts, G. L., Bryden, B. R., De Vos, V. and Young, E. (1973). Some practical advantages of Cl-581 (Katanine) for the field immobilization of larger wild felids, with comparative notes on baboons and impala. *Lammergeyer*, **18**, 1–14.

Stirling, Ian. (1966). A technique for handling live seals. *J. Mammal.*, **47**, 543–544.

Swank, W. G., Casebeer, R. L., Thresher, P. B. and Woodford, M. H. (1974). *Cropping, Processing and Marketing of Wildlife in Kajiado District, Kenya*. Working Document No. 6, FAO/UNDP Kenya Wildlife Management Project, Nairobi.

Wainwright, C. B. (1957). How to make and use duck traps. *A. Rep. Wildfowl Trust*, **8**, 44–47.

Williams, L. E. (1966). Capturing wild turkeys with alpha-chloralose. *J. Wildl. Mgmt.*, **30**, 50–56.

Woodford, M. H., Eltringham, S. K. and Wyatt, J. R. (1972). An analysis of mechanical failure of darts and costs involved in drug immobilization of elephant and buffalo. *East Afr. Wildl. J.*, **10**, 279–285.

Young, C. (1964). Shelduck trapping methods. *A. Rep. Wildfowl Trust*, **15**, 95–96.

3 Marking zoo animals for identification

D. G. Ashton*

Compared with techniques for marking wild animals in the field, the marking of zoo animals is relatively unstudied. Recent reviews of field marking methods for mammals and birds (Twigg, 1975; Marion and Shamis, 1977) cite 155 and 219 references respectively. Apart from papers in the International Zoo Year Book (especially Volume 8; see references), little has been written about marking methods for zoos. This chapter surveys existing literature and summarises reports which I have recently received from colleagues in other zoos.

There are three possible reasons why marking techniques have been neglected in zoos, all of them open to serious criticism. First, the relatively small numbers of animals of one kind typically held in early collections reduced recognition problems to a minimum; keepers might justifiably have claimed to know all their animals without marking. The modern trend toward larger groups of animals, combined with economic necessity of reducing staff as much as possible, makes this no longer possible. Secondly, zoo custodians who have needed to mark their animals have tended to accept the methods used in field studies. However, field methods of marking animals are seldom appropriate for zoo animals; much better methods, single or in combination, may be available.

The third and most important reason why zoo marking has not been studied seriously is that individual recognition has not generally been considered essential for good management. However, the changing role of modern zoos has emphasised the need for marking as an important aspect of management practice. Destruction of natural habitats, political instability and ambivalence over conservation, and the relentless demands of expanding human populations have made it difficult for some species to survive in their natural habitats; zoos are rapidly becoming repositaries for increasing numbers of rare and endangered species of animals. The European bison *Bison bonasus* and Hawaiian goose *Branta sandvicensis* already owe their existence to breeding in captivity, and more species will be added to the list. Producing healthy animals free from defects (for example reduced fertility and reduced viability of offspring due to inbreeding; Falconer, 1960), in numbers sufficient to replace zoo stocks and to repopulate the wild as new, safe habitats become available, demands a very high standard of zoo management. Co-operation between zoos in breeding-exchange programmes is essential to make the best use of limited gene pools, and biological research into the nutritional requirements,

*David Ashton, MA, VetMB, MRCVS, graduated from Clare College Cambridge and qualified at the Cambridge University School of Veterinary Medicine. After four years in general practice, two in Yorkshire and two in London, he became Veterinary Officer with the Zoological Society of London at Whipsnade Park.

physiology and behaviour of species is needed to fill gaps in our knowledge (Jarvis, 1969).

Good management, co-operative breeding programmes and research all set a premium on sound techniques for marking individuals. Day-to-day management including veterinary treatment, health and insurance certification, and the maintenance of health and breeding records, is more effective when marked animals are involved (Jarvis, 1969); studbooks and other records compiled for unmarked animals are suspect and may be positively misleading. Some governments already require permanent marking of certain species to comply with health regulations—for example ungulates imported into the United States must be tattooed—a practice which is likely to spread. Identity marking also prevents any disputes which may arise in breeding exchange programmes or loans of animals between collections. Natural marks or patterns may be used for positive individual recognition in a very few species, but need to be entered in permanent records so that people who are unfamiliar with the animals can identify them unambiguously.

Both humanitarian and aesthetic considerations exclude several forms of marking from general practice in zoos; heat branding and all but the most minor mutilations are rejected, and every effort is made to reduce handling stresses during marking. It is usually impractical and undesirable to immobilise valuable animals solely for marking or identification purposes, and marking is best done while an animal is being handled for some other reason—for example foot trimming or transfer from one location to another. Timing of marking may, however, be critical. In many species the first few hours or days after birth provide the best opportunity. In the herd of Pere David's deer *Elaphurus davidianus* at Whipsnade, fawns are tagged as a matter of routine within a few hours of birth, before flight reactions develop. Care must be taken with some species which tend to reject newborn offspring if they are handled (Oosterhuis, personal communication); in these, it is better to wait until the young animal is several days old and the mother well accustomed to it.

Great care must always be exercised in providing tags or markers of the right size and appropriate materials, and in applying them properly (Bell, 1968). Bird bands, especially, must be of the correct size, to allow for movement and growth (see Spencer, chapter 5 in this volume). Bands which are too tight may cause constriction, especially if the wearer is still growing, and lead to injury or loss of the limb. Bands which are too loose may fall off, or settle over toes and joints to the discomfort and disablement of the wearer. Careful vigilance and corrective action will prevent serious injury; negligence can result in suffering and the possible loss of valuable animals.

Criteria for Recognition Marks in Zoo Animals

Ideally, the system should be (a) harmless to the animals, (b) permanent, allowing recognition at any time from a few days after birth to post-mortem examination, (c) recognisable from a distance without need for restraint, (d) unobtrusive and aesthetically acceptable, and (e) cheap, quick and simple to apply. These criteria may differ from those of farmers, field zoologists and laboratory workers, who are seldom concerned (for example) with aesthetics, or may be able to handle their animals repeatedly without difficulty. No one system at present fulfils all these criteria.

Within the limitation of the methods commonly in use, there are two basic requirements: (1) permanent identification of an individual for long-term management and records, for example tattoos; and (2) relatively short-term identification of an individual, recognisable at a distance, for day-to-day management, for example ear tagging.

If a particular system is unsuitable for either one of these requirements, it should not be ruled out for the other if there is no better alternative.

Identification of Mammals

Techniques for identifying mammals include tagging, ear notching, toe clipping, tattooing, freeze branding, horn branding and use of natural markers. Field techniques such as dyeing or clipping of fur have little application, but see chapters 4 and 12 for further details.

Ear tagging

This is probably the most commonly used method, especially for ungulates. *Monel metal tags*, available in a range of sizes for agricultural stock, are inconspicuous but cannot usually be read on an unrestrained animal. *Coloured plastic tags* include the commonly-used 'Rototag' (Dalton Supplies Ltd, Nettlebed, Henley on Thames, Oxon., U.K.), which is available in eleven colours. Tags may be numbered, though the numbers cannot usually be read from a distance; colours are usually visible but dirt and fading may reduce their effectiveness after a time. Round plastic tags include 'Stig tags' (Alfred Cox Ltd, Edward Road, Coulsden, Surrey, U.K.); these are less obtrusive than Rototags and fit more snugly. This makes them useful in Suoidea (pigs and peccaries) and the Equidae, though granulation reactions have been noted in about 10 per cent of horses and in White rhinoceros *Ceratotherium simum*, necessitating removal. Deer and antelope wear metal or plastic tags with equal durability, but plastic tags have proved less durable on White rhinoceros, camels and the tribe Bovinae. A recently introduced 'Reise tag' (Dalton Supplies Ltd), larger and more flexible than standard Rototags, should last longer although only three colours are currently available. A few species are intolerant of ear tags; there was a 60 per cent loss in Barbary sheep *Ammotragus lervia* in London Zoo due to chewing. They are unsatisfactory in such long-haired animals as European and American bison.

Polar bears *Thalarctos maritimus* have been ear tagged in the wild by Larsen (1971) and Lentfer (1968); plastic tags fared better than metal ones, and after 2½ years had caused no local reaction.

None of the zoos using ear tags reports adverse comment from the public. They are useful for day-to-day management, but need to be used in conjunction with more permanent methods of identification such as tattooing or freeze branding.

Ear notching

Most useful in large-eared ungulates and some carnivores, this technique involves

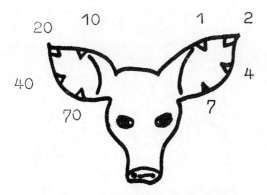

Figure 3.1 An ear notching code.

cutting one or two notches at any of four predetermined coded sites (figure 3.1); up to 99 animals can be distinguished. Identification is often easier with notches than with ear tags, though coloured tags are easier to see at a distance. Notches usually last longer than tags, though they can be distorted by infection, growth, or damage due to fighting. They are more difficult and time consuming to apply than tags, but may be more acceptable aesthetically (Schmidt, 1975). Oosterhuis (personal communication) reports that notching has now replaced routine tagging in ungulates at San Diego Zoo. Slightly more skill is required, for example in judging appropriate notch size; any bleeding which occurs can usually be controlled with clips which fall off after a time.

Tattoos

This is a widely used method of permanent marking. Special tattooing pliers from agricultural suppliers can be used to imprint letters and numbers, or identifying marks can be made with an electric tattooing pencil (Holborn Surgical Instrument Co., Ltd, Dolphin Works, Margate Road, Broadstairs, Kent). Ears, axilla, medial thigh, ventral abdomen or chest, foot and inside lip have been used in a range of species (Ogilvie, 1968; Dietlein, 1968; Oosterhuis, personal communication). Green ink seems preferable to black or red, especially in dark-skinned animals. Ogilvie (1968), Graighead *et al.* (1960), Lentfer (1968) and Larsen (1971) used tattoos in field studies of Grizzly and Polar bears. A code of tattoo marks above the eyes has been used in Patas monkeys *Erythrocebus patas* and Hamadryad baboons *Papio hamadryas* (figure 3.2), and around the eyes in Squirrel monkeys *Saimiri sciureus*; visibility varies with the size of the marks, skin colour and amount of facial hair, but Banks (personal communication) mentions that marks of this kind may be clearly visible at a distance of three metres. The marks must be neat and straight to avoid confusion with dirt spots. Correct tattooing techniques and practice are stressed by several zoos (Davis, 1968; Ulmer, 1968; Oosterhuis, personal communication) otherwise fading and complete disappearance may occur. Except in species which are easy to handle, or where the marks are readily visible, tattooing may best be used in conjunction with more obvious markers for purposes of day-to-day management.

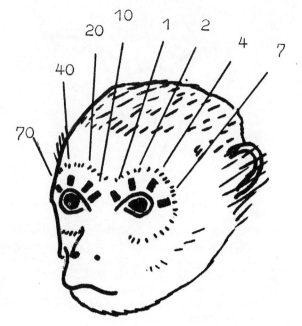

Figure 3.2 An eye tattoo code.

Freeze branding

This relatively new technique is discussed more fully by Newton in chapter 15. It is not yet generally used in zoos, though Egoscue (1975) mentions its application in Prairie dogs *Cynomys ludovicianus*. Trials on Przewalski horses *Equus przewalskii* at Whipsnade have produced easily visible hairless brands on an adult, and white-hair brands on foals which show up less clearly against the pale summer coat. The site used was the caudal thigh, which is discretely hidden by the tail at rest but shows up when the animal moves or flicks its tail. Freeze brands are permanent and easily visible on dark-skinned animals; overbranding may be used to produce bare patches on paler coats. The marks tend to be rather coarse and may become blurred by the growth of long winter coats. An unalterable code of angle marks has been developed by Farrell *et al.* (see chapter 15). Special equipment and skill are required, but are becoming readily available through increasing agricultural use. A wide variety of animals from hairless elephants to hairy mice, and including beavers, cetaceans and seals, have been freeze branded successfully (Pienaar, 1970; Haddow, 1972; Zurowski, 1970), and the method is likely to be of increasing use in zoos as it becomes more widely known.

Horn branding

This is the only form of heat branding now used in most zoos. The area of horn subject to least wear, usually the inner curvature, is branded (Aldous and Craig-head, 1958; Tijskens, 1968). The mark is discreet, can be read at 5 metres with the naked eye, and may last for eight or more years (Banks, personal communication). On European bison and other hairy species it shows up better than ear tags, but cannot be applied until the horns are fully grown; temporary tags may be needed up to this stage.

Natural marks

Variations in the following natural marks have been used to identify individuals: stripe patterns on hind legs of zebras (Klingel, 1965), blotch patterns on necks of giraffes *Giraffa camelopardalis* (Foster, 1966) stripe and spot patterns on tigers *Panthera tigris*, cheetahs *Acinonyx jubatus* (Oosterhuis, personal communication) and Okapi *Okapia johnstoni* (Okapi stud book). Also used are vibrissae patterns on the muzzles of lions *Panthera leo* (Pennycuick and Rudnai, 1970), and wrinkle contours on the snouts of Black rhinoceros *Diceros bicornis* (Goddard, 1966). Natural marks provide reliable permanent identification for suitable species, provided the mathematically predictable possibility of two or more identical individuals occurring is realised (see Pennycuick, chapter 16). A difficulty is that rapid identification of animals grouped in a paddock may not be possible without diagrams and a key; coloured tags or numbers are easier to record. Facial features of the great apes are often recognised easily, and can be linked with an appropriate and memorable name.

Some appropriate methods of marking rodents and other small mammals will be found in the chapters by Lane-Petter and by Twigg (chapters 4 and 12). Leg rings, often used in field studies, tend to fall off or cause local damage (Twigg, 1970). Toe rings are recommended by Cooley (1948), who used round Monel metal rings 0.5 mm in diameter and 3 mm wide above the interphalangeal joint of the inside hind digit of fox squirrels. Coded toe clipping is a permanent and easy method of marking, but aesthetically unacceptable for use in zoos; loss of digits by fighting and other injury may cause misidentification. For methods of marking bats see Stebbings (chapter 9). Rototags (see above) have lasted 3½ years on dorsal fins of dolphins in the wild (Norris and Pryor, 1970) and would be equally applicable to captive animals; freeze branding has also been used on cetaceans (Newton, personal communication). Pinnipeds (seals and sea lions—see Summers and Witthames, chapter 7) can be tagged, but the rate of loss of tags is high. Freeze branding (Newton, chapter 15) is a technique with good potential for use on these animals in zoos. Implant tags—small cylindrical nylon tags with number codes— were implanted subcutaneously in a standard site behind the ear in deer by Barnes and Longhurst (1960), providing a permanent marker which could be read only on removal. A possible improvement would be an implanted magnetic strip, coded and readable through the surface skin.

Identification of Birds

Two standard and widely used methods of marking birds in zoos are leg banding (Flipper banding in penguins) and patagial tagging. Other temporary markers used for short-term identification of particular individuals include neck collars for geese and swans, and various plumage paints and dyes.

Leg banding

Originally developed for use in the field, leg banding is discussed at length by
Spencer in chapter 5. Standard metal or plastic bands are used in zoos, usually
applied around the tarso-metatarsus; banding the tibio-tarsus may be preferable
in long-legged ciconiids, cranes and some waders, though nesting birds occasionally
suffer rubbing and pressure injuries from bands in this position. Cranes (Sauey,
personal communication) are adept at removing overlapping plastic bands, and
where these are used sealing the ends with acetate cement helps to lengthen their
life (Kear and Duplaix-Hall, 1975). In the larger species, even with metal rings, a
self locking type is much preferred to prevent ring loss or damage to the leg by a
partially opened band (Berger and Mueller, 1960; Griswold, 1968). Small psitta-
cines can be marked with butt-ended metal bands, but macaws, large parrots and
cockatoos need a stronger design. Miniature 'bull-rings' of round-section stainless
steel, hinged and locking with a recessed screw, have been found effective at
Philadelphia Zoo (Griswold, 1968). Great care is necessary in selecting bands of
the right shape and size, to avoid injury. Plastic and metal bands may be used in
combination, but two metal bands on the same leg may damage each other and
injure the wearer (Reed, 1953; Ogilvie, 1968). Faecal matter may build up on
flat leg bands on falcons and other birds of prey, and vultures can remove butt-
ended designs. Griswold (personal communication) suggests that the parrot 'bull-
rings' (mentioned above) may be an effective alternative in birds of prey. Wacher-
nagel (1968) noted a problem in Whydas, due to a build-up of leg scales, and
recommends banding male peafowl above the spur.

    Small cable ties—'Panduits' (marketed in the United States but similar designs
are available from electrical wholesalers in Britain)—are used for banding at San
Diego Zoo in certain species; they consist of strips of thin but tough coloured
plastic with an adjustable ratchet lock— once threaded the bands cannot be opened
without cutting. Trimmed and heat sealed, they form excellent leg bands, or flipper bands for penguins. Small ones measure 2 mm wide by 0.8 mm thick; larger
sizes measure 5 mm wide, 1 mm thick and up to 18.5 mm long, with an expanded
area 13 x 25 mm for labelling.

Patagial tags

The patagial membrane, a thin fold of skin extending from the scapular (shoulder)
to the carpal (wrist) joint, is a convenient site for tagging birds, free of muscles,
tendons and large nerves and blood vessels. Small metal or plastic tags (for example
Rototags—see above) are an attractive, often invisible alternative to leg bands.
Reuther (1968) reported their use for all species larger than thrushes at Cleveland
Zoo. Grisewold (1968) at Philadelphia Zoo marks gallinaceous, anserine and
young ratite birds in this way with aluminium locking tags, and Oosterhuis (per-
sonal communication) uses patagial Rototags on storks, cranes and ratites; small
Rototags have marked Secretary birds *Sagittarius serpentarius* successfully at
Whipsnade. Parrots and large ratites tend to remove patagial tags.

Flipper bands

Leather bands with engraved plastic discs are used to identify penguins at Amsterdam Zoo (Dekker, 1968). Griswold (personal communication) uses large, self-locking cattle ear tags on Humboldt penguins *Spheniscus humboldti* with Panduits as an alternative. Flat bands of Monel metal or aluminium are also available from commercial suppliers. Care must be taken with flipper bands, especially metal ones, to ensure that they do not become too tight and occlude blood supply during the moult.

Other methods of marking zoo birds

Parrots in Washington Zoo are identified by underwing tattooing (Dietlein, 1968). Reuther (1968) records the use of web punching, but damage through fighting and other causes often destroys identification marks of this kind. Freeze branding has been used in field studies of ducklings (Greenwood, 1975) but the marks did not last. Metal tags can be given temporary colour by use of Scotch-lite and other adhesive tapes.

Identification of Reptiles and Amphibia

Snakes often carry individually distinctive scale patterns which can be photographed or sketched for permanent record. Ventral caudal scales can be removed in coded patterns (Ogilvie, 1968); a system used at Oklahoma Zoo identifies 99 individuals. with results lasting for several years. Clipping of anal or belly scales in coded patterns is also effective; see Spellerberg and Prestt, chapter 14. Weary (1969) used a hot needle to remove scales, reducing incidence of scale regeneration and infection; the technique was especially favoured for small snakes. Clarke (1971) branded ventral and caudal scales using a hot chrome–nickel wire; the resulting distortion provided a permanent mark.

Tortoises and turtles are readily marked by notches cut or holes drilled in the carapace edges; the results are durable but not permanent. Pough (1970) threaded tags through drilled holes, and metal tags are similarly used at New York Zoo (Dowling and Gilboa, 1968). Ogilvie (1968) reports branding individual scutes down to the bone, according to a code. Painted numbers are used on shells of Aldabra tortoises *Geochelone gigantea* at San Diego Zoo.

Natural marks, ventral scale branding, and toe clipping may be used to identify lizards and other reptiles. Crocodiles are tattooed on the ventral surface in the femoral region at Oklahoma Zoo. Dowling and Gilboa (1968) report the use of metal tags for large lizards and crocodiles in New York Zoo; sites of tagging are not specified.

Amphibia are rarely marked in zoos; techniques reviewed by Nace *et al.* (1974) are worth considering. Natural marks, coupled with measurements, prove suitable in some species. Tattooing, using either an infiltration technique or multiple needle puncture, tends not to be permanent because of skin changes. Freeze branding (ineffective in juveniles) and chemical branding with 0.5 per cent amido black in 7 per cent acetic acid outlast tattooing. Toe clipping is ineffective because of regeneration in some species.

Discussion and Conclusions

There is no single ideal method of marking zoo animals for individual identification. Field research methods may be applicable, but usually require modification; there is considerable scope for the development and evaluation of new methods which will overcome the disadvantages of those already in use. Techniques which may be more widely used in the future include freeze branding, implanting inert tags with magnetic codes, and blood typing—a recent development with possible applications as more information becomes available. A major stumbling block to the widespread acceptance of marking in zoos has been—and still is—the aesthetic consideration of disfigurement. Fear of public reaction to disfiguring marks has probably been over-rated (Banks, personal communication; Dekker, 1968; Griner, 1968; Jarvis, 1968; Van den Sande, 1968; Wackernagel, 1968; Sauey, personal communication). The public do not seem to notice or, if they do, they accept that marking is an important aspect of management.

Artificial marks should not be used if natural marks, coupled with a proper record, provide a reliable and practical alternative. Unfortunately this is often not the case. It should be remembered however, that an efficient marking system made with miminal discomfort and disturbance to the animal is basically humanitarian in that it enables individual animals to be identified rapidly, and the necessary action to be taken for their welfare. Marking systems must be coupled with efficient record systems, from which data can easily be retrieved (Jarvis, 1969). Both are of paramount importance in furthering our knowledge of zoo animals and their good management, and must be major considerations in any approach to the keeping of animals in zoos.

Acknowledgements

I thank those individuals whose personal communications are mentioned in the text, and Lieutenant Colonel V. W. Tregear who is working on a more detailed study of the marking of zoo animals. I thank also Mrs Deveney and Mrs Morris, who typed the manuscript.

References

Aldous, M. C. and Craighead, F. C. (1958). A marking technique for Bighorn sheep. *J. Wildl. Mgmt,* 22, 445–446.

Barnes, R. D. and Longhurst, W. M. (1960). Techniques for dental impressions, restraining and embedding markers in live-trapped deer. *J. Wildl. Mgmt,* 24, 224–226.

Bell, J. (1968). Bird banding at New York Zoo. *Int. Zoo Yb.,* 8, 402.

Berger, D. D. and Mueller, H. C. (1960). Band retention. *Bird-Banding,* 31, 90–91.

Clark, D. (1971). Branding as a marking technique for amphibia and reptiles. *Copeia 1971,* (1), 148–151.

Cooley, M. E. (1948). Improved toe-tag for marking fox squirrels. *J. Wildl. Mgmt,* 12, 213.

Craighead, J. J., Hornocker, M., Woodgerd, W. and Craighead, F. C. (1960). Trapping, immobilising and colour-marking Grizzly bears. *Trans. 25th North Am. Wildl. nat Resour. Conf.*, 347-363.

Davis, J. A. (1968). Marking large animals at New York Zoo. *Int. Zoo Yb.*, **8**, 395.

Dekker, D. (1968). A note on bird banding at Amsterdam Zoo. *Int. Zoo Yb.*, **8**, 404.

Dietlein, D. R. (1968). Notes on marking and identification of individual animals at the National Zoological Park, Washington. *Int. Zoo Yb.*, **8**, 393-394.

Dowling, H. G. and Gilboa, I. (1968). A Zoo record system: the method used in the Department of Herpetology at New York Zoo. *Int. Zoo Yb.*, **8**, 405-408.

Egoscue, H. J. (1975). The care, management and display of Prairie dogs in captivity. *Int. Zoo Yb.*, **15**, 45-48.

Falconer, D. S. (1960). *An Introduction to Quantitative Genetics.* Oliver and Boyd.

Foster, J. B. (1966). The giraffe of the Nairobi National Park: home range, sex ratios, the herd and food. *East Afr. Wildl. J.*, **4**, 139-148.

Goddard, J. (1966). Mating and courtship of the Black rhinoceros (*Diceros simus*). *East Afr. Wildl. J.*, **4**, 69-75.

Greenwood, R. J. (1975). An attempt to freeze-brand Mallard ducklings. *Bird-Banding*, **46**, 204-206.

Griner, L. A. (1968). A note on marking animals for identification at San Diego Zoo. *Int. Zoo Yb.*, **8**, 392-393.

Griswold, J. A. (1968). A bird banding and recording system. *Int. Zoo Yb.*, **8**, 398-401.

Haddow, H. H. (1972). A permanent marking technique for pigmented mammals. *J. Wildl. Mgmt*, **36**, 645-649.

Jarvis, C. (1969). Studying wild mammals in captivity: standard life histories with and appendix on zoo records. *Int. Zoo Yb.*, **9**, 317-328.

Kear, J. and Duplaix-Hall, N. (1975). *Flamingos.* Poyser Ltd, Berkhamsted.

Klingel, H. (1965). Notes on the biology of the Plains zebra (*Equus quagga boehmi*) Matschie. *East Afr. Wildl. J.*, **3**, 86-88.

Larsen, T. (1971). Capturing, handling and marking Polar bears in Svalbard. *J. Wildl. Mgmt*, **35** (1), 27-36.

Lentfer, J. W. (1968). A technique for immobilising and marking Polar bears. *J. Wildl. Mgmt*, **32**, 317-321.

Marion, W. R. and Shamis, J. D. (1977). An annotated bibliography of bird-marking techniques. *Bird-Banding*, **48** (1), 42-61.

Nace, G. W., Culley, D. D., Emmons, M. B., Gibbs, E. L., Hutchison, V. H. and McKinnell, R. G. (1974). *Amphibians: Guidelines for the Breeding, Care and Management of Laboratory Animals.* I.L.A.R. (NAS/NRC). Washington, D.C. 108-114.

Norris, K. S. and Pryor, K. W. (1970). A tagging method for small cetaceans. *J. Mammal.*, **51**, 609-610.

Ogilvie, P. W. (1968). Animal marking techniques used in Oklahoma City Zoo. *Int. Zoo Yb.*, **8**, 390-392.

Pennycuick, C. J. and Rudnai, J. (1970). A method of identifying individual lions (*Panthera leo*) with an analysis of the reliability of identification. *J. Zool. Lond.*, **160**, 497-508.

Perkins, J. E. (1945). Biology at Little America III. *Proc. Am. phil. Soc.,* **89,** 270-284.

Pienaar, U. de V. (1970). A lasting method for the marking and identification of Elephant. *Koedoe,* **13,** 123-126.

Pough, F. H. (1970). A quick method for permanently marking snakes and turtles. *Herpetologica,* **26,** 428-430.

Reed, P. C. (1953). Danger of leg mutilation from the use of metal colour bands. *Bird-Banding,* **24,** 65-67.

Reuther, R. T. (1968). Marking animals in zoos. *Int. Zoo Yb.,* **8,** 388-390.

Scheffer, V. B. (1950). Experiments in the marking of seals and sea-lions. *United States Department Int. (Fish and Wildlife Service) Special Science Report (Wildlife),* No. 4. Washington D.C.

Schmidt, G. R. (1975). In *Breeding Endangered Species in Captivity* (ed. R. D. Martin), Academic Press, New York, p. 277.

Tijskens, J. (1968). A note on the marking of horned animals at Antwerp Zoo. *Int. Zoo Yb.,* **8,** 398.

Twigg, G. I. (1975). Marking mammals. *Mammal Rev.,* **5** (3), 101-106.

Ulmer, F. A. (1968). The marking of Philadelphia Zoo mammals. *Int. Zoo Yb.,* **8,** 396-397.

Van den Sande, A. P. (1968). Marking penguins for identification. *Int. Zoo Yb.,* **8,** 403.

Wackernagel, H. (1968). A note on bird banding at Basle Zoo. *Int. Zoo Yb.,* **8,** 404.

Weary, G. C. (1969). An improved method of marking snakes. *Copeia 1969,* (4), 854-855.

Zurowski, W. (1970). Marking beavers. *Acta theriol.,* **15,** 520-523.

4 Identification of laboratory animals

W. Lane-Petter*

Laboratory animals are used for scientific investigations, and also for special breeding programmes. In all cases the need for an accurate and unmistakable means of identification is self-evident. The smaller laboratory animals, such as rats and mice, are used in rather large numbers, and to identify all individuals positively might raise serious practical problems were it not for the fact that the animals are caged, either singly or in small groups. It is much easier to put a label on a cage than to ask a small animal to carry an identity disc, and if the animal is very small the marker has also to be so small that it can carry very little information.

Birds, even small ones, have thin legs and relatively large feet at the ends of them. This arrangement makes it easy to put on a ring in a choice of colours that can carry letters or digits for positive identification. The anatomy of most small mammals is not so convenient, and other methods need to be considered.

Identification by Cage Label

A single animal in a cage needs no marking, for the label on the cage can carry all the identification that can possibly be needed. It is only necessary to ensure that when the animal is moved to a new cage the right label goes with it. However, labels can fall off cages, become illegibly dirty, or be eaten by the animal, so that careful attention has to be paid to designing a good label holder. Most cage manufacturers supply efficient label holders.

A group of animals in a single cage can be identified as a group by the label on the cage. This may be sufficient, because the animals may—as in toxicity tests, for example—be treated as identical experimental units, and any information being sought is about the response of the group in the statistical sense. If there is a group of ten animals in the cage, and eight show a certain response to experimental treatment, two remaining unresponsive, it does not matter which eight respond,

*W. Lane-Petter, MA, MB, BChir, FIBiol, Hon MPS, is a graduate of Cambridge University and after a time in general practice served throughout the war in the RAMC. After the war he spent three years as a Home Office Inspector under the Cruelty to Animals Act of 1876, and fifteen years as Director of the MRC Laboratory Animals Centre. He spent some years in the laboratory animals industry before returning to Cambridge in 1972. He was Secretary General of the International Committee on Laboratory Animals (ICLA) from 1956 to 1969, and is now an honorary member of ICLA, as well as a vice-president of the Institute of Animal Technicians (formerly president) and of the Institute of Science Technology. He has written extensively, and also edited a number of works, about laboratory animals and related subjects.

only that eight out of ten did so. Thus, in such cases no marking of individual animals is needed.

In maintaining inbred strains—that is, animals subject generation after generation to brother × sister or other very closely related mating—or other colonies where the control of pedigree is all-important, identification must always be positive and proof against error. But a pair, male and female, in a cage are identified by their sex and the label on the cage, while their offspring usually need no further identification until they are weaned and moved to other cages. Thus marking of individual animals is seldom necessary.

Natural Markings

Although most laboratory animals seem to be albinos, and therefore not easily distinguishable by their natural appearance, some such as guinea pigs are multicoloured and the pattern of markings is often, like fingerprints, unique to each animal. This is particularly the case when the animals are from an outbred colony, where no attempt has been made to standardise coat colour. Positive, permanent and easily read identification can then be made on natural markings alone. It is useful to have a rubber stamp, in the shape of the animal's outline, stamped on the animal's identity card and to mark on this—not on the cage label—its individual colours and their distribution. Tortoiseshell and other tri-coloured, spotted or banded animals are particularly amenable to this method, but it is no use for self-coloured animals or albinos.

A special case of identification by natural markings is that of nose-prints. These have been used with dogs, and probably could be used with other species. They are always unique, like fingerprints, but reading them requires some skill; they are probably more valuable for forensic purposes than in the laboratory.

Painting the Fur

In the absence of distinctive natural markings the fur of an animal can be coloured with a variety of stains or dyes. These last only as long as the hairs that are dyed, but the period is measured in weeks, and the dyes are easily renewed or touched up. A dab of dye on different parts of the body—neck, shoulders, back, flanks, haunches, tail—and the use of, say, four distinctive colours makes a code easy to devise.

Useful dyes are (Short and Woodnott, 1969) yellow—saturated picric acid, chrysoidin: red—fuchsins: violet—gentian or methyl violet: green—brilliant, ethyl or malachite green: blue—trypan blue.

Painting the Skin

Fur dyes will also colour the skin, but soon disappear. Special cases, however, are the rat and the mouse, which have long naked tails. The rat's tail in particular accepts colouring very well; the mouse's tail being smoother is less easily coloured.

Black, blue, green and red are the most useful colours. Ordinary thick felt marker pens, with waterproof ink, are suitable for marking tails. The rat's tail may be marked in rings about 1 cm wide, and three such rings in different colours, plus the tip, can be accommodated on a single rat's tail. The colour will last for three weeks or so, and is easily touched up. The mouse's tail is not so easy to band, and it is often necessary to colour the whole tail; it will wear off in two or three weeks, but can be touched up before all the colour has disappeared.

Clipping

Hairs, and especially the whiskers or vibrissae, may be clipped, but soon grow again. Clipping may also entail a variety of minor mutilations, such as slitting the ears of rats or mice, removing parts of claws (including the nail-bed) or digits, or docking the tail, and such mutilation is permanent and lends itself to an identification code. Some healing may occur, especially of ear slits, and obscure the mutilation. This method can be aesthetically distasteful, and often needs to be done under an anaesthetic, but if it is not extensive the animal probably does not miss what has been taken away. Toe clipping is often the most useful method of identifying very young animals, before they are weaned.

Punching

Punching entails making a hole in a suitable part of the body, such as the ear, the skin of a bird's wing or the web of the foot. It is another form of mutilation, not always requiring an anaesthetic to apply. The site and number of holes punched, often combined with ear slitting, makes it easy to devise an identification code, of which many have been published.

The above methods of marking all depend on placing a mark (other than a number or letter) on a part of the animal's body. The number of possible combinations is a function of the type of mark (for example the colour) and the location (for example left or right ear), and if zero marking is included the possible number is doubled. With one mark, zero included, and two locations, four combinations are possible. With two marks, zero included, and two locations, nine combinations are possible, and so on.

The choice of a code will thus depend on how many combinations are required. Some codes go up to as high a figure as one thousand, but the complicated pattern of marking or mutilation, especially in smaller animals, raises the possibility of misreading the number and thus introducing errors. With all such methods the maximum number of identifications needed should be decided in advance and the simplest and most foolproof code devised to meet it.

Tattooing

Tattooing is a means of depositing a pigment in the dermal layer of the skin, and is thus a permanent mark. It has to be done on a hairless part of the body, large

enough to accept letters or figures that can be conveniently read. A mouse's ear
can be tattooed with a single letter or digit, but this is not recommended. Suitable
sites for tattooing are the ears of dogs, cats, rabbits and guinea pigs (possibly also
of rats); the front of the chest, the abdominal wall or the forehead of monkeys,
and any suitable area on larger animals. Black and green are the most useful
colours, blue and red being sometimes harder to read subsequently. Green will
often stand out well in a pigmented skin.

Tagging

Many types of tags, of different colours and carrying numbers of figures, are
made, from very small ones for the ears of mice or the wings of chicks, to large
ones for pigs and cattle. Many are in the form of metallic strips bent double,
with a sharp point on one limb and a slot on the other. The tag is placed on the
ear or other part of the body, the sharp end being bent at a right angle and pushed
through the skin to engage in the slot on the other limb and be bent over.

Normally no anaesthetic is needed to apply tags, if the appropriate size for
the animal is chosen. In groups of animals tags may be torn out by fighting or
playing, but if chosen properly they are usually permanent.

Buttons or studs are a special type of tag, and may carry numbers or letters.
Either they may be like a bachelor's button that is pushed through a punch
hole in the ear or web and secured by a keeper on the other side, or they may be
fixed in place by a nylon stitch inserted with a needle and tied off. An
anaesthetic is usually required to fix buttons. Small buttons, or a sequence of
coloured glass beads, may be stitched on to the skin of the dorsal lymph sac of frogs
(no anaesthetic is needed), to provide easy identification.

Ringing

In addition to birds' legs, which could have been specially designed for carrying
rings, the rabbit's leg above the hock can also be ringed. Care must be taken to
choose exactly the right size of ring: too large a ring will fall off or may chafe,
too small a ring will bite into the flesh and may do serious damage.

Collars and Belts

By law, dogs carry collars specifically for identification purposes. Cats may also
have collars, and tolerate them well. Sheep and cattle have suitable necks for
collars. Collars may also be used for monkeys, but equally convenient in many
species—such as rhesus—is a belt or collar round the waist. A wire pipe cleaner,
carrying a disc or other label, makes a useful collar for a guinea pig, the ends being
twisted together. The correct fit is when one finger can be inserted comfortably
under the collar when it is round the animal's neck, but not two.

For larger animals leather or chain collars are best, with plates or discs to
carry the identification. For cats a type of flat, transparent, tubular plastic is

available: the identification is written or typed on light card and slipped inside the tube; this is then put round the cat's neck and stapled on at exactly the right tension for comfort.

Conclusion

All methods of identification must meet certain criteria. They must be positive and reliable, without the possibility of being misread. They must not cause the animal any discomfort and, if they are painful to apply, the animals must first be anaesthetised. They must be as durable as the need dictates, which may not always be for the lifetime of the animal.

Lastly, they must not affect the animals in such a way as may interfere with experimental observations. This is particularly important in cases where the animals' behaviour is to be studied. Small mutilations, the application of paints or dyes, or the wearing of tags, rings or collars, might in some circumstances obtrude upon the animals' consciousness or be noticed by its companions. If such a possibility exists it is for the experimenter to satisfy himself that the method of marking chosen is one that will not in any way influence the behaviour or responses of the animals, or affect the experimental observations he wishes to make.

No one method meets all these criteria with every animal, but one or two methods are especially liable to fail on one or other ground. Mutilation and tagging can be inhumane, and if they are used great care needs to be taken to see that they are not so. But, provided proper care is taken to choose the right method in any particular case, identification of laboratory animals can always be achieved with certainty and humaneness.

Reference

Short, D. J. and Woodnott, D. P. (1969). *The IAT Manual of Laboratory Animal Practice and Techniques,* Crosby Lockwood, London, p. 96 *et seq.*

Section 2 Tagging

Lord Medway

A tag in the context of this symposium is any device attached, generally but not always externally, to an animal to be identified. Tags have a long history (see chapter 1) during which they have proved their value in marking many different kinds of animals. Bearing serial codes of letters and figures, tags can provide individual recognition marks, effectively for limitless numbers of subjects. They are versatile, durable, decipherable by the uninitiated and—if properly designed and carefully applied—cause negligible injury or inconvenience to the animals carrying them.

With little doubt the most successful tagging projects—measured by numbers of individuals marked, non-traumatic effects of markers, or diversity and productivity of research projects—have involved birds. The first two chapters in this section, by Mr Spencer and Dr Patterson, are justifiably devoted to the variety of tags devised for use on birds. Tags have also been used satisfactorily on many kinds of mammals; chapter 7 (Dr Summers and Miss Whitthames) discusses tagging in comparison with other methods of marking seals, chapter 8 (Mr Brown) deals with the special problems of tagging whales, and chapter 9 (Dr Stebbings) shows tagging to be perhaps the most successful method of marking bats. The simple application of bird rings to mammals is seldom effective. Fogden (1974) placed bird rings successfully on the elongated tarsal joint of Western tarsiers *Tarsius bancanus*, but most leg, toe or tail rings are too loose, too tight, or quickly defaced by gnawing. The variety of devices applied under field conditions to large and small mammals has been reviewed by Giles (1969), Hanks (1969) and Twigg (1975). Ear tags have proved of limited value on small mammals but successful on many larger mammals, and identifying collars have also been used with varying degrees of success. For further discussion of tags applied to large mammals in zoos, and smaller animals in laboratories, see especially chapters 3 and 4.

Tags have also been applied with great success to both freshwater and marine fish (Dr Laird, chapter 10), and tagging as a method of marking reptiles is mentioned in chapter 13: see also Harrisson (1956). The marine environment involves particular problems of wear and corrosion, but tags of Monel and other special alloys, and more recently of heavy plastic, have been developed by manufacturers for this special need (see plate 1). Even on terrestrial animals tag materials are subject to stresses of kind and degree rarely encountered in other circumstances. The development of successful tagging programmes in zoological research has been notable for the co-operation between manufacturers and users. The interchange between the British firm of Lambournes and the British Trust for Ornithology (and other bird-ringing organisations around the world) has been

Plate 1 Green turtle *Chelonia mydas*, flipper-tagged with Monel tag supplied by the National Band and Tag Co., U.S.A.

especially productive, and the National Band and Tag Co., has achieved a similar reputation in the United States. Dalton tags—designed primarily for agricultural use—have been applied successfully in research projects involving wild creatures as diverse as kob in the African savannah and turtles in tropical seas.

Animals which are too small to carry numbered tags effectively may still be tracked (though not always identified as individuals) by use of radioactive tags—see chapter 19. Small animals in general present particular problems to the biologist who seeks to mark them, especially if—like insects— they also shed their skin periodically. Some special techniques of invertebrate marking are discussed by Professor Southwood in the final chapter of this section.

References

Fogden, M. P. L. (1974). A preliminary field study of the Western Tarsier *Tarsius bancanus*. In *Prosimian Biology* (eds. R. D. Martin, G. A. Doyle and A. C. Walker) Duckworth, London, pp. 151–165.

Giles, R. H. (ed.) (1969). *Wildlife Management Techniques*. 3rd edn, revised, Wildlife Society, Washington D.C.

Hanks, J. (1969). Techniques for marking large African mammals. *Puku,* **5,** 65–86.

Harrisson, T. (1956). Tagging green turtles. *Nature,* **178,** 1479.

Twigg, G. I. (1975). Marking mammals. *Mammal Rev.,* **5,** 101–116.

5 Ringing and related durable methods of marking birds

Robert Spencer*

Of all the methods of marking birds, the close ring is certainly the most ubiquitous in Britain and Ireland. Its use, however, is almost entirely confined to birds reared in captivity. The chief reason for this is that the close ring has to be passed up over the part-grown foot to its final position on the tarsus and this operation has to be carried out before the bird, if it is a passerine, is six or seven days old at the latest. The reason for this early ringing is that a ring which will pass over a fully grown foot can equally well come off again or, what is far worse, may slip down sufficiently to trap the toes without actually coming off, thus rendering the foot useless.

Close rings are expensive to manufacture and, due to technical limitations, it is possible to mark them with only a short inscription. These are not disadvantages in the field of cage birds and aviculture, where close rings find their chief use, for most aviculturalists use rings in small quantities, and are primarily concerned with proving identity to the initiated.

An essential feature of most marking of wild birds is that it should be intelligible to the uninitiated public, on whose co-operation it usually depends, and much the commonest device is the split ring. This is a band of metal which is wrapped round the tarsus, and in some parts of the world, notably the United States, is known as a bird band. Because it can be fitted to both nestlings and fully grown birds it is much more flexible in application than the close ring. Furthermore, because it is manufactured flat it is cheaper to make and can carry a big inscription.

A split ring which is intended to be meaningful only to the person who fitted it need carry no more than a code number. In practice, the common use of split rings is to mark wild birds as individuals in such a way that any person finding a bird wearing one is able, if he chooses, to co-operate with the person fitting the ring. To permit this co-operation, each split ring is stamped not only with a unique serial number but also an address. The length of that address and of the serial number tend to determine the minimum ring size which it is practicable to use: there is no point in so reducing the size of the letters and the figures that they can be read only by the aid of a magnifying glass. Nor is it sensible to so abbreviate the address on the ring that a finder doubts whether it is postally adequate. Thus in practice the lower size limit for a ring carrying a postal address and a six figure serial number is an inside diameter of about 2.0 mm.

*Robert Spencer is a Senior Research Officer in the Ringing and Migration Section of the British Trust for Ornithology. He has administered the British Bird Ringing Scheme since 1954 and is General Secretary of the European Union for Bird Ringing.

Judged by even the rather crude standard of whether or not the ring will stay on the leg, a graded series of some nine or ten different sizes would be required to mark the bird species which occur wild in Europe. Such a series would, however, often lead to a rather poor fit and in practice a series of perhaps seventeen sizes is required. The largest ring in use in Europe today has an inside diameter of 26 mm. The better the fit one aims at, the more complex the position becomes, especially in sexually dimorphic species. For example, in most of the birds of prey it is possible—and preferable—to ring the male with a ring one size smaller than that used for the female. This is easy if the birds are ringed when fully grown and therefore readily sexable but we are only now learning how to sex nestlings. In addition to variation of tarsus thickness due to sex, diameters may also differ from one individual to another, and also with age. At the time when a young passerine leaves the nest its tarsus is usually significantly thicker than it will be later in life. An example of the importance of this 'puppy fat' is that one may ring an adult Tree sparrow *Passer montanus* with a 2.3 mm ring, whereas a nestling requires a 2.8 mm ring.

Split rings are customarily supplied open, in the shape of a letter C. This is true of all small-sized rings and it is of course possible to manufacture even the largest sizes to this format. However, as the diameter increases so is it necessary to increase the gauge of the metal used and, very often, also the 'height' of the ring in order to provide increased mechanical strength. Even then the two ends of the ring may tend to gape apart with the passage of time, due to metal fatigue, and so it is not unusual for large rings to incorporate some clip or locking device to prevent this happening (figure 5.1). The clip type of ring has a long history and in some countries the design has been used for even quite small rings. However, in the belief that any projection from a ring might be just that bit more likely to become trapped in vegetation, so handicapping or injuring the bird, most countries confine the use of clip rings to large birds which would have no difficulty in freeing themselves should the clip become entangled.

Figure 5.1 Split ring with locking device.

Two processes operate to limit the useful life of bird rings—abrasion and corrosion. The extent to which either occurs varies enormously from species to species. For example swifts *Apus apus* have feathered tarsi and spend much of their lives on the wing. Probably the only time that a swift ring comes into contact with hard objects is when a bird visits its nest. As a result, abrasion is absolutely minimal. Rings from owls, which also have feathered tarsi, similarly wear very little. At the opposite extreme are birds like gulls and waders which are constantly paddling through a highly destructive mixture of small mineral grains and water—the latter often saline. Abrasion obviously affects the external surfaces of bird rings; less obviously it is often the inside surface which is most affected. The constantly renewing scales of the bird's leg clearly act as a gentle abrasive, although a snugly fitting ring, which moves little on the leg, greatly reduces this process.

Saline water, coupled perhaps with guano, can lead to very serious corrosion. Thus a ring made of aluminium, after being worn by a Kittiwake *Rissa tridactyla* for no more than two or three years, may be completely illegible. It was not until some forty years after the start of bird ringing that critical examination cast doubt on the suitability of the bird rings then in use to measure the life spans of the birds which wore them. Attempts to plot survival curves produced improbable results, and it was obvious that in some species the birds were long outliving the life of the rings they wore. To obtain better survival figures it was necessary to re-capture and re-ring some species such as the Manx shearwater *Puffinus puffinus* every three or four years, but this expedient was costly and troublesome and it was clear that more research into metals was required.

Traditionally, bird rings have been made of commercially pure aluminium, the advantages of this metal being that it is light, malleable and cheap. However it is soft, mechanically rather weak, and corrodes readily so that it is not suitable for large, long-lived species, nor for those in which corrosion and abrasion are likely to occur. Some marginal improvement can be achieved by increasing the temper of the aluminium, though this reduces ease of handling.

From the pure aluminium many ringing schemes have therefore turned to alloys of aluminium. That used by the British Trust for Ornithology incorporates 3 per cent magnesium and 0.5 per cent manganese, and the resultant rings exhibit much improved wearing properties, at least on land birds. The problem for waders, herons, ducks, terns and seabirds in general is scarcely solved by the use of aluminium alloy and subsequent research led to the selection of Monel, an alloy of nickel and copper. Laboratory tests on this alloy were remarkably encouraging, establishing that it was many times more resistant to abrasion than the aluminium alloys. Unfortunately extensive field use revealed that in tropical saline waters it was subject to a form of destruction known as 'crevice attack'. In this the two ends of the ring act as electrodes, the saline water as electrolyte, and a minute electrical current carries away particles of metal—a process which quickly renders the inscription illegible (figure 5.2). Thus the two hard metals in use today, which appear to offer maximum resistance to abrasion, corrosion and crevice attack are Incoloy—used extensively in Britain—and stainless steel—used by one of the main ring manufacturers in Europe. Although the introduction of these harder metal has led to greatly improved performance, it has proved difficult technically. Fortunately the species most requiring durable rings are all of medium or large body-size so that the weight of the ring is not a crucial factor. Nevertheless because the metals used are heavier than aluminium it has been policy to reduce the gauge to a minimum commensurate with mechanical strength and this has involved increasing temper. Increased temper in turn leads to increased springiness and the phenomenon of 'spring-back', in which

Figure 5.2   Corrosion of the ring as a result of 'crevice attack'
quickly renders the inscription illegible.

the two ends of the ring, after being brought together, spring back again by
small amounts, leaving a crack which could be dangerous. It has therefore
been necessary to examine critically ring shape, and to design pliers suitable
for closing rings made of these hard metals, and indeed capable of bringing
the two ends together under tension.

Stainless steel, Monel and Incoloy share one unfortunate property. Aluminium
is a pale metal, and the surface remains pale due to oxidisation so that the ring
is always conspicuous. The harder metals are naturally darker and tend to
remain dark and are therefore less conspicuous. The result is that a rather
higher proportion of aluminium bird rings are spotted by members of the public
and reported than is the case with the more durable rings. Bearing in mind
that the recovery rate for small birds is generally very low, rarely exceeding
2.0 per cent, it will be appreciated that any factor which reduces the chances of
ring recovery should be avoided as much as possible.

Although the introduction of harder metals has done much to extend the
working life of rings, abrasion, possibly aggravated by corrosion, remains a serious
problem in a few species, mainly seabirds. On a bird whose tarsus is roughly
circular in cross section the closed ring is circular and therefore revolves freely.
As a result any wear which occurs tends to be distributed evenly round the entire
circumference of the ring. On the other hand there are seabirds such as the
Razorbill *Alca torda* and Manx shearwater with highly elliptical tarsi. On these
species the ring has to be fitted elliptically and is thus not free to revolve (figure
5.3). The situation is greatly exacerbated by the fact that the legs on these
two species are set far to the back of the body so that when the birds are ashore
the tarsi are held almost horizontal and the ring may be constantly in touch
with an abrasive rock or sand surface. An early attempt to overcome this abrasion,
involving the use of aluminium, was to produce an overlapped ring, twice as
long as necessary, with the inscription repeated twice. Thus, when the ring was
closed on the leg, the inner inscription was completely protected by the outer
one, and its life considerably extended (figure 5.4). More recently, using Incoloy,
which is not suitable for a long overlap, it has been possible to redesign the ring
so that the inscription appears twice, once on either 'side' of the leg while the

rear portion, which is unavoidably in contact with the ground, carries no inscription.

Figure 5.3 Elliptically fitted ring.

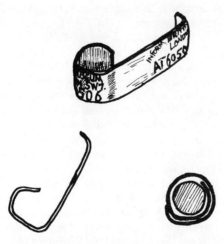

Figure 5.4 Overlapping ring with repeated inscription extends the useful life of the band.

A different approach to the problem of abrasion has been tried with success on some wading species. This involves marking the bird on the tibia rather than on the tarsus so that the ring is clear of mud and sand, and often clear of water as well. An important factor limiting the use of this ring position is that on most species the ring is much less conspicuous and it is therefore much less likely to be seen and reported by members of the public.

In some species of birds such as swifts and the Kingfisher *Alcedo atthis* the tarsus is so short in length that a ring of conventional design is too tall to fit comfortably without pressing on the joints above and below. To meet such situations it is necessary to design a very 'short' ring. This may involve positioning the address beside, rather than above or below, the serial number, and the resulting long piece of metal has to be overlapped in fitting until the ring has an appropriate diameter.

While it is possible, and indeed ideal, to ring most nestling passerines at the age of six or seven days, in the case of a number of other orders including all the wildfowl, the diameter of the tarsus—or more strictly speaking the size of the foot—is not big enough to retain the ring in position until the bird is three quarters grown, by which stage it is highly mobile and very difficult to catch. Russian ornithologists have succeeded in overcoming this problem by temporarily reducing the inside diameter of rings with the aid of Plasticine or florist's wax. The ducklings can thus be ringed while they are much smaller, and as the tarsus grows the Plasticine or wax yields. So far as is known the technique has not been used in Britain, but a number of birds ringed this way have subsequently been shot by wildfowlers in Britain and reported to us, and we have received no reports of leg damage, either from them or from the Russian ornithologists.

So far, this chapter has dealt with marking systems which render birds recognisable as individuals once they are in the hand, but there is also a vital research need to be able to recognise individual birds in the field and various systems to do this have been developed. They fall into two main categories: those which attempt to make use of a single numbered metal bird ring and those which require the use of supplementary marks. An interesting early approach to the problem was developed in Germany in the 1930s for use with White storks *Ciconia ciconia*. These birds invariably nest in positions where they are conspicuous and may be observed on the nest platform from fairly close proximity. A clip ring was therefore introduced which was conventional in so far as it carried a unique serial number and an address, but which was also coded uniquely by means of notches of different shapes located in varying positions on the clip (figure 5.5). Enough permutations of shape and position were available to allow individual recognition of many birds, but at a later stage large figures were introduced with the object of allowing the ring number to be read from a distance with the aid of binoculars or a telescope.

It was this use of large figures, rather than of recognisable silhouettes, which survived the test of time. In Britain the Wildfowl Trust were among the first to use rings with figures so large that they could be read in the field (figure 5.6): this was in connection with their detailed study of the Pink-footed goose *Anser brachyrhynchus*. Since then, particularly for intensive university studies, special rings with large figures have been developed for various seabird species including the Cormorant *Phalacrocorax carbo* and Shag *Phalacrocorax aristotelis*.

Figure 5.5 A clip ring showing the notch.

Figure 5.6 Ring with numbers large enough to be read in the field.

Figure 5.7 Ring made from Darvic. The outer coat of this plastic is engraved so that the darker layer below shows through.

More recently, for Mute swans *Cygnus olor* and Canada geese *Branta canadensis* rings have been made from a laminated plastic known by the trade name of Darvic. This material cannot be given an inscription by a dyepress but has to be engraved, the process cutting through the pale outer layer to reveal a contrasting dark layer beneath (figure 5.7). Large figures can be used and—a great time saver—the code number may be repeated two or three times on the circumference of the ring, thus avoiding the long periods of field observation which are otherwise often necessary to ensure that the entire number has been read. It is essential to bond the overlapped ends with glue to prevent the ring from coming undone. Fortunately the plastic is available in various colours, thus increasing the number of permutations, so that it is possible to mark a large number of birds as individuals without using code numbers which exceed three digits. In this device numbered ringing is combined with colour ringing (to be mentioned later in this chapter). It should, however, be noted that these engraved Darvic rings do not carry a return address so that they are meaningful only to the initiated. Thus, in studies which also seek the co-operation of the public, they must be used in conjunction with conventional metal rings.

Mention has already been made of the problems associated with marking young wildfowl while they are still small enough to be captured easily, and of a recent Russian approach to the problem. An older technique, still used, though mainly by wildfowl breeders, is the patagial clip. This vaguely resembles a safety-pin in which the pin is of stainless steel while the metal cap carries a unique serial number and return address (figure 5.8). The pin is passed through the patagium, closed as one would fasten a safety-pin, and then clamped in a pair of pliers to prevent it from coming undone accidentally. There is a slight risk of the clip becoming hooked on some foreign body, in which circumstances a tiny duckling would be unlikely to be strong enough to free itself, but the chief limitation to the usefulness of this marking technique is that it is not conspicuous enough. There is little chance of a tag being noted on a bird which is found dead and often it is only when a shot bird is being plucked for the table that the tag is noticed.

Figure 5.8 A patagial clip.

In Antarctica experience showed that the short stout tarsi of penguins, coupled with the propensity of some species for 'toboganning' meant that conventional rings were impracticable. As a result, flipper bands were developed, fitted closely round the base of the flipper (figure 5.9). Here they are out of harm's way, but the great merit is that the serial number can be read easily on the sitting bird without disturbing it—an advantage in any circumstances and particularly so in a cold climate.

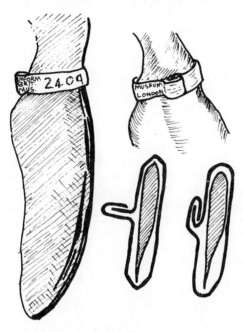

Figure 5.9 Flipper band for use on penguins.

For intensive studies, particularly of bird behaviour, the paramount need is to be able to recognise instantly the bird in the field as an individual. For many years the conventional method of doing this has been to use colour rings. It is possible to obtain self-coloured rings in up to about ten different shades, and if these are used in combination a large number of permutations is available. Commonly, colour rings are made of celluloid and are very light and small. Thus, depending on the length of the tarsus and on the size of the bird, it is possible to fit several on each leg without handicapping the wearer in any way. The late Dr David Lack, in his classical study of the Robin *Erithacus rubecula* used up to four rings on one leg without detecting any signs that the birds wearing them were adversely affected. Of course, complex codes in which the precise sequence of colours on each leg is significant are likely to be read accurately only by the research scientist himself or by his associates. Colour marking programmes which invite the co-operation of the public, as for example in tracing the dispersal of birds from a roost or colony, should sensibly be limited to one or two colours.

Unfortunately the pigment used in celluloid colour rings is not light fast and some colours tend to fade quickly, dark blue becoming light blue, red turning to pink etc. Thus for studies expected to last several years, the number of colours available is much reduced. Furthermore the celluloid itself rapidly becomes brittle so that even if the rings do not fade they are liable to disintegrate in three or four years. More recently Darvic has been used. This plastic has proved admirably durable as well as light-fast, but it is tedious to work and it is believed that no Darvic rings are available commercially.

Colour rings are only as valuable as the amount of effort devoted to subsequent observation, and even then for certain species there may be grave limitations. For example, colour rings on the legs of pipits and wagtails may seem conspicuous enough when the birds are perching on rocks or tops of walls, but in even quite short grass the rings are lost to view. In a similar way, although it is technically possible to fit colour rings on the legs of ducks it is of very limited value, for so much important behaviour in these species takes place on the water, in circumstances where the legs are completely out of sight.

In short, conventional colour rings, and leg rings bearing large figures designed to be read in the field, are useful only on those species which occupy habitats, or carry out crucial activities such as foraging and courtship, in positions offering the field workers a reasonably unimpeded view of the ring. So many species are excluded by this definition, including members of important groups such as the Anatidae, seabirds and raptors, that much time has been devoted to developing marking devices which may be attached to the dorsal surfaces of birds—wings, back, neck, head and beak. Some of them have the major advantage that they may be 'read' accurately while the bird is in flight. Such techniques include the dyeing of the portions of the bird's plumage, imping, back tabs, wing tabs, streamers, neck collars and bill discs, all of which are dealt with by Dr Patterson in his contribution. Here it is necessary only to comment that sightings of all such markings are meaningful only to the initiated. If the co-operation of the public is to play any part in the study it is essential to publicise the study, and it is customary to add a conventional numbered ring.

The British Trust for Ornithology, which is responsible for running the national bird ringing scheme, has for many years also acted as an unofficial clearing house for reports of distinctively marked birds. A register of all known colour ringing and marking schemes is maintained which does help in the tracing of marks, but the primary purpose of which is to try to prevent research workers from inadvertently spoiling each other's studies by using colour combinations or marks which duplicate, or might be confused with, others already in use on the same species. It is in their own best interests that research workers consult the register maintained by the B.T.O. *before* they finalise their colour marking programme.

Acknowledgement

I thank Kevin Baker for the illustrations.

References

Coulson, J. C. (1963). Improved colour-rings. *Bird Study*, **10**, 109–111.
Coulson, J. C. and White, E. (1955). Abrasion and loss of rings among sea birds. *Bird Study*, **2**, 41–44.

Coulson, J. C. (1976). An evaluation of the reliability of rings used on Herring and Lesser Black-backed Gulls. *Bird Study*, **23**, 21–26.

Dorst, J. (1962). The Migrations of Birds. Heinemann, London.

Harris, M. P. (1964). Ring loss and wear of rings on marked Manx Shearwaters. *Bird Study*, **11**, 39–46.

Kadlec, J. A. (1975). Recovery rates and loss of aluminium, titanium and Incoloy bands on Herring Gulls. *Bird-Banding*, **46**, 230–235.

Lockley, R. M. and Russell, P. (1953). *Bird Ringing: the Art of Bird Study by Individual Marking.* Crosby Lockwood, London.

Mead, C. J. (1974), *Bird Ringing.* B.T.O. Guide No. 16, 1–64.

Marrion, W. R. and Shamis, J. D. (1977). An annotated bibliography of bird marking techniques. *Bird-Banding*, **48**, 42–61.

Poulding, R. H. (1954). Loss of rings by marked Herring Gulls. *Bird Study*, **1**, 37–40.

Rydzewski, W. (1951). A historical review of bird marking. *Dansk Orn. Foren. Tidsskr.,* **45**, 61–95.

Sales, D. I. (1973). A ring address experiment. *Bird Study* **20**, 313–314.

Smith, A. J. M. (1966). Colour marking of Sandwich Terns. *Seabird Group Bull.,* **2**, 49–51.

Spencer, R. (1959). Progress and prospects in ringing. *Ibis*, **101**, 416–424.

Spencer, R. (1970). The role of bird ringing in conservation. *Bird Study*, **17**, 104–110.

6 *Tags and other distant-recognition markers for birds*

I. J. Patterson*

Marking birds for recognition at a distance poses special problems due to small body size, delicate plumage and the possibility of affecting flight. In many species, colours and plumage features are important in recognition and display, which may be disrupted by additional markers. Tarsal ringing (Spencer, chapter 5) has been used very successfully for many years on large numbers of birds, and other marking methods should be considered only when research would be unduly hampered by the limitations of ringing. The chief drawback of tarsal marking is that the legs of many species are hidden for much of the time—when they are swimming, in long vegetation, or in flight—and this has led to attempts to mark birds higher on the body. This chapter reviews the main methods used, concentrating on factors affecting the choice of the best marker for a particular study, and dealing with the materials used, the means of attachment, visibility, durability and any reported effects of the marker on the bird. Only a few key references to each method are given, since a recent bibliography (Marion and Shamis, 1977) lists the species on which each marker has been used and gives an exhaustive list of papers which can be consulted for details of the construction of markers and the techniques for attachment.

There are two main approaches to marking birds: (a) marking the plumage itself with dye or paint, and (b) attaching marker tags to the bird.

Dye Marking

Dyes have been used on a very wide range of species, particularly those with light-coloured areas on the plumage. The dye must give an easily recognisable colour but be non-toxic, resistant to fading, effective in a cool solution with a wetting agent, and of course be harmless to the plumage. Many commercial dyes are excluded by their requirement for hot treatment or irritant solutions, and some effective bleaches may affect the structure of the feather. Dyes which have been

*Dr Ian Patterson is a graduate of Aberdeen (BSc) and Oxford (DPhil). His research degree study was on the social organisation of colonies of Black-headed gulls and the function of nesting in a colony. After two years as a research fellow working on social behaviour, dispersion and populations of the Rook at Aberdeen University, he was appointed to his present post there of Lecturer in Zoology. Since 1970 his research has been on social behaviour and limitation of population size in Shelducks.

used include alcohol-soluble dyes in a variety of colours (Boyd, 1951), picric acid which gives a strong permanent yellow, human hair dye and lighteners (Ellis and Ellis, 1975) various colours of cellulose paint (Swank, 1952) and food dyes (Evans, 1951). The water-based picric acid solution and hair dyes must be used with a wetting agent to penetrate the waterproofing on the feather.

Application of dyes may be by dipping of large feather areas for gross marking to detect movement (Boyd, 1951) or by combinations of small spots for recognition of individuals. In my own study of Shelducks *Tadorna tadorna*, five distinct areas of the plumage (figure 6.1) were used to give 31 individual combinations in each colour of dye. With all dyes, the colours are strongest if the bird is not released until the plumage has dried. As an alternative to dyeing plumage *in situ*, larger feathers can be cut near the base and replaced by imping (Wright, 1939), using waterproof glue and a thin splint inside the shaft of the feather. This is laborious but allows thorough dyeing of feathers in advance, including the use of hot treatments. Dyes may be applied without the trauma of capture by remote operation of a spray (Hansen, 1964) or by placing dye-soaked pads on the nest rim, but the placement of the dye on the plumage is fairly haphazard. Ducklings have been dyed by injection of food dyes into the egg just before hatching (Evans, 1951) but great care is required to avoid infection.

Figure 6.1 Male Shelduck showing dye spot positions.

The visibility of dye marks is usually good while the colours remain bright. Geese dyed with large patches were visible in flight up to about 2 km and on the ground up to about 1 km (Boyd, 1951). Eagles marked with hair dye were identifiable up to about 2 km (Ellis and Ellis, 1975) and I can identify individually dyed Shelducks up to about 1 km.

The durability of dye is ultimately limited by the moult of the feathers marked, but in practice it usually fades or washes out earlier. The worst fading occurs in food dyes and alcohol-soluble dyes, especially in birds which bathe a lot; picric acid and hair dye last longest, usually for the life of the feather. Cellulose paint is also resistant to fading but tends to clog the feathers and may be removed during preening. With all dye marking the results tend to be rather variable, even when using the same technique, since several factors such as dryness and cleanliness of the feathers may affect penetration of the dye.

There have been very few reports of adverse effects of dye marking on the bird, even when these have been looked for (Boyd, 1951 and my own observations on Shelduck). Yellow paint on the heads of Mourning doves *Zenaidura macroura* disrupted pair bonds; other colours, and yellow elsewhere on the body, had no effect (Goforth and Baskett, 1965). The painting of male moustache markings on female Flickers (*Colaptes auratus*) affected sex recognition (Noble, 1963) so that there is a need for care not to disrupt existing important display or recognition features.

Neck Tags

Neck markers, used in early attempts to identify gamebirds in the United States (Taber, 1949) were made from flexible plastic or thin rubber, marked with a pattern or number, and attached by a stainless steel surgical safety pin passed through a small pinch of skin at the back of the neck. Visible up to about 300 m, they were not very durable and have now been superceded by other markers. The mean period of retention on Coots *Fulica americana* was 3 months (Gullion, 1951) and one-third to two-thirds of tags on Pheasants *Phasianus torquatus* were lost in the first year (Taber, 1949). The tags tended to catch on obstacles and to be pulled at by other birds. There was some tissue reaction to the pin (Gullion, 1951) and a report of weight loss after marking (Taber, 1949) so that this type of marker does not seem to have been satisfactory.

Back Tags

Developed mainly for gamebirds, tags designed to lie in the middle of the back (figure 6.2) are useful on any large bird which stands fairly upright, or where the commonest view is a rear one. They are rather cumbersome for small birds and rarely used on them. Back tags are usually made from flexible PVC or PVC-coated nylon fabric, marked with numbers or letters, and attached by a soft leather or nylon cord harness with straps which pass round each wing base. They are easy to see, and readable up to about 100 m in Partridges *Perdix perdix* (Blank and Ash, 1956) and up to about 660 m in Pheasants (Labisky and Mann, 1962).

Durability is usually limited by the harness, leather in particular becomes brittle. Mean retention times of 12 months on Waterhens *Gallinula chloropus* (Anderson, 1963), 6.5 months (maximum 33) on Ruffed grouse (Gullion, Eng and Kupa, 1962), 15 months on Partridges (Blank and Ash, 1956) and up to 18 months on Pheasants (Labisky and Mann, 1962), have been recorded. The newer nylon cord harnesses should greatly improve durability.

There is little indication of adverse effects on the bird. A potential danger is breakage of the harness on one side, with a risk of entanglement, though it is likely that the second side would break soon after, freeing the bird. The survival of back-tagged Red grouse *Lagopus lagopus* is the same as that of ringed birds (Boag, Watson and Parr, 1973) so the method seems to be reasonably safe.

Figure 6.2 Red grouse with a back tag.

Collars

Neck collars have been used almost exclusively on waterfowl (figure 6.3), especially geese and swans in the United States, but they could possibly be used on other long necked birds. Made from rigid PVC, acrylic resin or aluminium, they are marked with patterns or large numbers and letters; they fit loosely on the base of the neck and are too small for the head to slip through. Their visibility is usually very good, with colours distinguishable up to about 2 km (Ballou and Martin, 1964). Numbers were readable up to about 15 m on Whistling swans *Cygnus columbianus* (Sladen, 1973), and up to about 400 m on Blue geese *Chen caerules-*

Figure 6.3 Goose with a neck collar.

cens (MacInnes, Prevett and Edney, 1969). Over 80 per cent of collared Whistling swans were re-recorded during a year, compared to only 8 per cent of birds with coloured rings only.

Durability is also good, with retention of 90 per cent of collars on Canada geese *Branta canadensis* over the first year, and of 80 per cent over the second year (Ballou and Martin, 1964). Fjetland (1973) reports similar results on Canada geese, with retention of 30 per cent of tags to the sixth year.

Some adverse effects of collars have been reported. Ducks tend to trap their beaks in the collars (Helm, 1955), which should not be used on smaller waterfowl. There are several reports of ice forming on the collar in severe weather conditions (Ballou and Martin, 1964; Craighead and Stockstad, 1956 and MacInnes *et al.*, 1969) but the more conductive aluminium collars may prevent icing. Ankney (1975) suggested that collars increased mortality by starvation in breeding Lesser snow geese *Chen caerulescens.* His data were criticised by Raveling (1976) but in his reply Ankney (in Raveling, 1976) presented revised data which still suggested some increase in mortality of collared geese. Lensink (1968) showed some inhibition of reproduction in Brent geese *Branta bernicla* wearing collars; MacInnes *et al.* (1969) described how Blue geese pull at collars a great deal, but considered that adverse reports are rare in relation to the very large numbers of these conspicuous collars used.

Nasal Markers

Nasal discs and saddles for ducks and geese have been used extensively in the United States and also in Australia. They are made from rigid or flexible PVC with patterns or numbers, and are attached by a short nylon or stainless steel pin through the nostrils, which in these groups has a naturally-occurring hole passing right through (figure 6.4). Because of their small size nasal markers are only moderately visible; numbers have been read up to about 80 m on various ducks (Bartonek and Dane, 1964) and up to about 100 m on Shoveller *Spatula clypeata* (Sugden and Poston, 1968). Their durability on ducks is good, with 75 per cent retaining their markers for one year (Bartonek and Dane, 1964). Poor results have been noted on Canada geese, with only 20 per cent retention for one year and none for a second year (Sherwood, 1966).

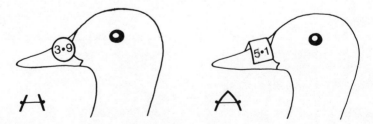

Figure 6.4 Nasal discs and saddle for ducks.

There are reports of nasal discs snagging on vegetation and injury to the beak above the nostrils in Canada geese (Sherwood, 1966), and increased mortality of

diving ducks fitted with discs (Bartonek and Dane, 1964). The dangers of entanglement seem to be much less in nasal saddles which prevent vegetation becoming
wrapped around the pin (Sugden and Poston, 1968). These authors report that
courtship behaviour in Shoveller was unaffected by nasal saddles, and Bartonek
and Dane (1964) suggest that pair formation in Blue-winged teal *Anas discolor*
was unaffected by nasal discs.

Wing Tags

Wing markers, lying on the top surface of the wing between the carpal joint and
the body, have been used on a range of species. When the bird is at rest the tag
hangs vertically down the side of the body (figure 6.5).

Figure 6.5 Eider with wing tag.

The tags are made from rigid PVC or flexible PVC-coated nylon fabric marked
with colour patterns or large numbers and letters. They are attached by a stainless
steel or nylon pin passing through the patagium, a web of very thin skin with few
nerves or blood vessels. A small nylon washer spreads the load on the underside
of the patagium (Anderson, 1963). Each bird is normally marked on both wings.
   The visibility of wing tags is good even on fairly small birds. Using a telescope,
Anderson (1963) read tags on Waterhens up to about 150 m; I have identified
colour-patterned tags on Rooks *Corvus frugilegus* up to about 200 m, and numbered or lettered tags up to about 400 m. Using only 7x binoculars Hester (1963)
was able to read numbered tags on small birds such as Starlings *Sturnus vulgaris* at
about 110 m and Knowlton *et al.* (1964) identified colour strip tags on Turkeys
Meleagris gallopavo up to about 200 m. In tests with rook tags at a range of 400 m,
with several different observers using a 60x telescope in good light, correct identifications were made in 88 per cent of white tags with black characters (*n* = 74), in
80 per cent of pale green tags with black characters (*n* = 20) and in 31 per cent of
tags marked with combinations of three colour strips (*n* = 16).
   The durability of wing tags is also good. In tests of early versions Anderson
(1963) found that tags were retained for up to 24 months on Mallards *Anas platyrhynchos* and up to 18-24 months on Eiders *Somateria mollissima* and Waterhens,
but the rate of loss was not measured. Knowlton *et al.* (1964) found that on turkeys less than 1 per cent of tags were lost in the first year, but 20 per cent of birds
lost at least one tag by entanglement in netting during trapping operations. I have
measured the rate of loss of tags in a breeding population of rooks by regular observation of tagged birds both in the colony and the feeding grounds. Whenever a

marked bird was seen I recorded whether both tags were present, to detect the loss of the first tag of the pair while the bird could still be identified by its second tag. Just over 5 per cent of tags were lost in the first year but this rate increased gradually in subsequent years (figure 6.6). One rook still retained one of its tags after 12 years. There were probably several causes of loss including breakage of the tag, especially around the pin hole, but the principal cause was almost certainly wear of the pin by the tag. Most older tags had their pins partly worn through. Although the pins were replaced if the bird was recaptured, this wear probably explains the increasing likelihood of loss with the age of the tag.

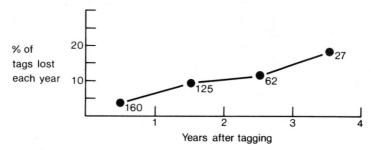

Figure 6.6 The proportion of wing tags lost by rooks each year, in relation to the age of the tag.

Few adverse effects of wing tags have been reported. Anderson (1963) found a higher rate of nest desertion in female eiders caught on the nest and wing tagged, compared to those given only leg rings. He attributed this difference to the greater handling time required for tagging. He also reported that 3.4 per cent of tagged eiders became solitary and showed erratic escape behaviour. However, Hewitt and Austin-Smith (1966) found no obvious behavioural changes in any of the passerine species they tagged, and no difference between the recapture rates of tagged and leg-ringed birds. Knowlton *et al.* (1964) report little or no change in the behaviour of tagged turkeys, and I have watched newly-tagged rooks returning to their mates in the colony without seeing any unusual reaction. Injury is unlikely since, if the tag became entangled, the pin is usually pulled through the very thin patagium, leaving only a small slit.

Conclusions

There are some problems, however slight and infrequent, or adverse effects on the bird and limited durability of most tagging methods for birds. Consequently leg rings should be used for marking whenever possible, unless the legs are visible so little that the research would be unduly hindered. Most problems have been experienced with neck tags, collars and nasal markers, and these methods should be avoided. None of them has been used on any scale in Britain. Fewest problems exist with dye, back tags and wing tags. Of these, dye marking is least likely to cause adverse effects; it is the best method for short-term studies, and for those where the birds can be retrapped regularly to have the dye renewed. For more permanent marking and for species which are difficult to catch, wing tags can be used with few problems on a wide range of species. Back tags are useful on birds in which a back view is commonest or where harness attachment is preferred to the use of pins.

References

Anderson, A. (1963). Patagial tags for waterfowl. *J. Wildl. Mgmt,* **27**, 284-288.

Ankney, C. D. (1975). Neck bands contribute to starvation in female Lesser snow geese. *J. Wildl. Mgmt,* **39**, 825-826.

Ballou, R. M. and Martin, F. W. (1964). Rigid plastic collars for marking geese. *J. Wildl. Mgmt,* **28**, 846-847.

Bartonek, J. C. and Dane, C. W. (1964). Numbered nasal discs for waterfowl. *J. Wildl. Mgmt,* **28**, 688-692.

Blank, T. H. and Ash, J. S. (1956). Marker for game birds. *J. Wildl. Mgmt,* **29**, 328-330.

Boag, D. A., Watson, A. and Parr, R. (1973). Radio-marking vs back tabbing Red grouse. *J. Wildl. Mgmt,* **37**, 410-412.

Boyd, H. (1951). Notes on colour marking of Geese. *Wildfowl. Severn Wildfowl Trust Annual Report 1950-51,* 14-16.

Craighead, J. J. and Stockstad, D. S. (1956). A colored neckband for marking birds. *J. Wildl. Mgmt,* **20**, 331-332.

Ellis, D. H. and Ellis, C. H. (1975). Color marking Golden eagles with human hair dyes. *J. Wildl. Mgmt,* **39** (2), 446-447.

Evans, C. D. (1951). A method of color-marking young waterfowl. *J. Wildl. Mgmt,* **15**, 101-103.

Fjetland, C. A. (1973). Long-term retention of plastic collars on Canada geese. *J. Wildl. Mgmt,* **37**, 176-178.

Goforth, W. R. and Baskett, T. S. (1965). Effects of experimental color marking on pairing of captive Mourning doves. *J. Wildl. Mgmt,* **29**, 543-553.

Gullion, G. W. (1951). A marker for waterfowl. *J. Wildl. Mgmt,* **15**, 222-223.

Gullion, G. W., Eng, R. L. and Kupa, J. J. (1962). Three methods for individually marking Ruffed grouse. *J. Wildl. Mgmt,* **26**, 404-407.

Hansen, C. G. (1964). A dye spraying device for marking desert Bighorn sheep. *J. Wildl. Mgmt,* **28**, 584-587.

Helm, L. G. (1955). Plastic collars for marking geese. *J. Wildl. Mgmt,* **19**, 316-317.

Hester, A. E. (1963). A plastic wing tag for individual identification of passerine birds. *Bird-Banding,* **34**, 213-217.

Hewitt, O. H. and Austin-Smith, P. J. (1966). A simple wing tag for field-marking birds. *J. Wildl. Mgmt,* **30**, 625-627.

Knowlton, F. F., Michael, E. D. and Glazener, W. C. (1964). A marking technique for field recognition of individual turkey and deer. *J. Wildl. Mgmt,* **28**, 167-170.

Labisky, R. F. and Mann, S. H. (1962). Back tag markers for Pheasants. *J. Wildl. Mgmt,* **26**, 393-399.

Lensink, C. J. (1968). Neckbands as an inhibitor of reproduction in Black Brant. *J. Wildl. Mgmt.,* **32**, 418-420.

MacInnes, C. D., Prevett, J. P. and Edney, H. A. (1969). A versatile collar for individual identification of Geese. *J. Wildl. Mgmt,* **33**, 330-335.

Marion, W. R. and Shamis, J. D. (1977). An annotated bibliography of bird marking techniques. *Bird-Banding*, **48** (1), 42-61.

Noble, G. K. (1963). Courtship and sexual selection of the Flicker (*Colaptes auratus luteus*). *Auk,* **53** (3), 269-282.

Raveling, D. G. (1976). Do neckbands contribute to starvation of Lesser snow geese? *J. Wildl. Mgmt,* **41**, 571-572.

Sherwood, G. A. (1966). Flexible plastic collars compared to nasal discs for marking geese. *J. Wildl. Mgmt,* **30**, 853-855.

Sladen, W. J. L. (1973). A continental study of Whistling Swans using neck collars, *Wildfowl,* **24**, 8-14.

Sugden, L. G. and Poston, H. J. (1968). A nasal marker for ducks. *J. Wildl. Mgmt,* **32**, 984-986.

Swank, W. G. (1952). Trapping and marking of adult nesting doves. *J. Wildl. Mgmt,* **16**, 87-90.

Taber, R. D. (1949). A new marker for game birds. *J. Wildl. Mgmt,* **13**, 228-231.

Wright, E. G. (1939). Marking birds by imping feathers. *J. Wildl. Mgmt,* **3**, 238-239.

7 The value of tagging as a marking technique for seals

C. F. Summers and Susan R. Witthames*

Seals are difficult animals to study because they are inaccessible for much of their life cycle. However, the offspring are born synchronously on land, often in densely populated breeding assemblies. In many species this offers an opportunity to mark them, particularly the young, in large numbers. Marking studies on the Northern fur seal *Callorhinus ursinus* began over a century ago in Alaska, and since then many techniques have been used (Scheffer, 1950). Tagging was first used to mark Weddell seals *Leptonychotes weddelli* in 1903 (Hickling, 1962) but was not used in the United Kingdom until 1951. The very first seal tagged, a Grey seal pup *Halichoerus grypus* born on the Farne Islands, England, was recovered from Norway—a result which led to sustained enthusiasm for marking schemes at all the major British Grey seal breeding assemblies (see Hewer, 1974).

The Method

One of the first types of tag used was made of aluminium, and of the sort commonly used as ear tags for domestic livestock. Later tags were made of stainless steel or Monel metal. There have been several variations of this design, which essentially consists of a flat strip of metal pointed at one end and with a slot at the other (figure 7.1a). When the strip is bent round, the pointed end pierces the skin of the seal and engages in the slot at the other end of the tag. Some required slits to be cut in the skin before they could be applied, while others were applied with pliers and had a sharpened point so that they were self-piercing. The size of tags used varied from cattle ear tags to poultry wing clips. On the Northern fur seal they were applied to the ear, the fore-flipper and both in the interdigital web and over a digit of the hind-flipper. Ear tags were unsuccessful and those in the interdigital web were lost more quickly than tags applied either over a digit or to a fore-flipper (Scheffer, 1950). A version of this type of tag is still in use; some have remained in position on the hind edge of the fore-flipper of Antarctic fur seals *Arctocephalus gazella* for 16 years (Payne, 1977).

*Dr Summers is a graduate of the Universities of London and Aberdeen. He joined the Seals Research Division in 1972 to study the ecology of Grey and Common seals with particular reference to the assessment and management of British stocks.

Susan Witthames is a graduate of the University of London. She joined the Seals Research Division in 1971 and until recently co-ordinated records of all seal tagging activities undertaken in the British Isles.

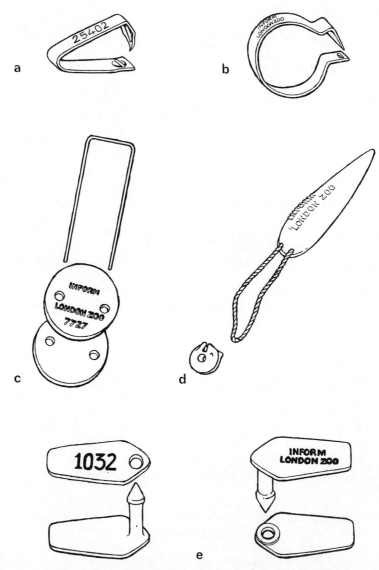

Figure 7.1 Types of tags used on seals (for explanation, see text).

An unsuccessful variant of the metal tag was the flipper ring (figure 7.1b) designed by Hewer (1955). This was of Monel metal and, with the use of special pliers,
was intended to enable a single operator to tag young Grey seals. However, there
was a high loss rate because the ends of the tag often failed to engage, and their
use was discontinued after a short while.

Tags applied to the Northern fur seal have been recovered in the course of sealing operations but, since there is no comparable industry in the United Kingdom,

the recovery of British marked seals has depended, for the most part, on casual observations. A metal disc tag used by Sivertsen (1941) was modified by replacing the metal with brightly coloured plastic (Rasmussen and Øritsland, 1964), and used on Grey seal pups at the Farne Islands, North Rona, Shetland and Orkney, colour-coded yellow, green, blue and red respectively. The tags (figure 7.1c) consist of two discs about 30 mm in diameter. One disc is placed on top of the flipper or tail and one on the underside. They are held together and attached to the seal by stainless steel or Monel wire. The thickness of the discs and the wire has varied. It is necessary to keep the tag as light as possible, but if the wire is too thin it is likely to cut through the skin. Another design of plastic tag, used to mark young Grey seals in Orkney, was shaped like a carrot (figure 7.1d) to reduce drag when the seal was swimming. Made of conspicuous red polypropylene it had a nylon loop which was passed through an incision made in the tail or flipper and secured underneath by a small polypropylene grommet. Applying the tag took a long time and, although the tag itself was durable, the nylon frayed at the junction with the plastic and many tags were lost. Carrot tags were used only in 1961.

Rototags (figure 7.1e), first adopted in 1961, combined rapid application with conspicuously coloured plastic marks. Made entirely of plastic, the Rototag consists of two flat interlocking components which are attached with pliers so that they make a loose sandwich of, for example, the interdigital web. The male part of the tag has a sharpened end to penetrate the tissue. Rototags are made in several sizes, and are currently used on phocid seals by biologists in Canada, Europe and the United Kingdom with varying degrees of success depending on several factors. First, the quality of the plastic appears to vary and, at very low temperatures, some batches have been liable to crack (Brodie, personal communication). The tag must be prevented from rotating about its peg or it will wear a hole in the web large enough for it to fall through. This can be avoided by placing the tag as close as possible to the proximal part of the web. Application of the tag is made easier if the web is stretched taut before the pliers are closed on to it. The peg should point upwards when the tag is in position, to avoid unnecessary abrasion on land. It is clear that species which spend time hauled out on ice keep such tags in position for much longer than those which haul out on land, because of differences in the rate at which the plastic is abraded.

As tagging schemes often depend for their success on the co-operation of the non-scientist, it is important that this co-operation is effectively invited either through some publicity exercise directed towards the relevant people (for example hunters, coastguards, fishermen, holidaymakers) or through a suitable inscription on the tag itself, or both. Tags applied to seals in the British Isles have a unique number on one side and the inscription 'Inform London Zoo' on the other. The zoo does not itself take part in tagging programmes, but acts as a return address and passes the information to the Seals Research Division, where a register of British tagging statistics is maintained.

The effect of tagging on survival is difficult to measure. It is likely that, in some circumstances, the component of a population which is catchable for tagging is not representative. Where various types of mark have been compared, by multiple marking, it appears that tagging may reduce survival to some extent (Scheffer, 1950) but this may not be measurable with small samples (Bonner and Vaughan, 1972; Vaughan, 1978).

The Results

Despite the large number of seals marked for study purposes there are, in the literature, many more papers which describe the effort invested in tagging schemes compared with those which interpret the results from such schemes. Where results are discussed, they are often necessarily speculative and, in some cases, the objectives of the scheme remain obscure or unstated. However, over the years tagging programmes have contributed information about seal movements, population parameters and behaviour.

The dispersal of young animals from their birthplace has been investigated in the British Isles. Hewer (1974) reviews the results obtained from tagging Grey seals at assemblies in Wales, the Hebrides, Orkney and the Farne Islands. He concludes that dispersal, which occurs radially from birth sites, is passively brought about by wind action on surface water, and that there is considerable overlap of movement of seals from different localities. Although some recoveries have been from places as distant as Iceland, Norway and Spain, these constitute only a small proportion of total recoveries and are not thought to be involved in the establishment of new colonies. Bonner and Witthames (1974) have published data showing a similar dispersal of young Common seals *Phoca vitulina* from the Wash, England.

Tagging programmes have provided information about the birthplace of seals which cause damage to fishing gear. It has, for example, been demonstrated that Grey seal pups found dead in fixed-engine salmon fishing gear along the Scottish east coast originate from the Farne Islands, Orkney and, to a lesser extent, North Rona.

In population studies tagging has provided animals of known age against which methods of age determination have been tested (Scheffer, 1950). It has also allowed cohorts of known age to be observed over long periods (Payne, personal communication). Mark–recapture studies using tags have been used to estimate pup production of the Common seal in the Wash (Summers and Mountford, 1975) and of the Fur seal, *Arctocephalus pusillus,* in South Africa (Best and Rand, 1975). They have also been used to investigate natural mortality of Fur seals in the North Pacific (Scheffer, 1950) and of Grey seals in the Baltic (Söderberg, personal communication), and in population studies of Weddell seals *Leptonychotes weddelli* in Antarctica (Stirling, 1971).

Tags, if numbered, provide a unique mark and consequently yield incidental information about the behaviour of individuals. In some cases they have been used primarily for behaviour studies in which continuous observations of individuals has been possible (Kaufman *et al.,* 1975; Anderson, personal communication).

Alternatives to Tagging

Tagging, as a marking technique, provides a unique mark which is relatively cheap and easy to apply. If done by trained operators it causes minimal stress to the seal. However, it is not a universally suitable technique. It normally requires that the animal be restrained while the tag is applied and the mark is by no means permanent, particularly when applied to a species which spends much of its time on land. While ideal for short-term behaviour and mark–recapture studies, tagging does not give quantitatively rigorous data when used for longer-term studies of movements and survival.

If the animal to be marked can be restrained, there are simple techniques available such as shaving the fur or punching holes in the interdigital web. Chapman and Johnson (1968) and Payne (in press) have used shaving in a mark–recapture study to estimate pup production in Fur seals. This is clearly only useful in the short term. Scheffer (1950) pointed out that by varying the position and number of holes punched in the interdigital web several hundred individual marks can be applied. This has the disadvantage that the holes are inconspicuous, and they may become indistinct.

If a permanent mark is required for information on (for example) stock relations, long-term behaviour studies, evaluation of age-specific life-table parameters etc., there is, at present, no substitute for branding. Scheffer (1950) concluded that hot iron branding was slower and more difficult to carry out than tagging and that it did not lend itself to the marking of a large series of uniquely marked individuals. Hot iron branding has been carried out at a number of Grey seal breeding assemblies in the British Isles. The most extensive series is that branded by the Nature Conservancy at North Rona from 1959 to 1968 (Boyd and Campbell, 1971), where each year class was uniquely marked. Moulted pups branded at this locality were subsequently discovered as breeding adults at the Monach Isles in the Outer Hebrides (Harwood, Anderson and Curry, 1976) demonstrating at least some mixing of stocks from these two assemblies. Mansfield and Beck (1977) report that from 1969 to 1974 1845 moulted Grey seal pups were individually marked at Sable Island in the West Atlantic by hot iron branding using a combination of four characters. This marked stock is therefore of very great value and affords excellent opportunities to study the ecology and behaviour of the Grey seal in Canada.

The objective of hot iron branding is to promote the formation of scar tissue which does not contain hair follicles. In the relatively aseptic conditions on sea ice the risk of infection of the brand wound is probably low. However, in situations where the animal is likely to stay on land after the brand is applied, presumably this risk is higher and survival may be adversely affected. Nevertheless this is poorly quantified even in Northern fur seal studies; Scheffer (1950), reporting on a stock of 15 000 marked animals branded in 1940 and 1941, thought that branding might affect the growth rate of the animal and detract from its value as a study specimen, but found no tangible evidence of the effect.

An alternative to hot iron branding is cryogenic or freeze branding, the object of which is to destroy pigment cells in the skin to produce an area of white hair in the shape of the brand cypher. Although established as a technique for use on domestic livestock, it has not been used on seals for a long enough period to be regarded as a replacement for the hot iron method. Keyes and Johnson (1971) reported the start of a four year programme to freeze brand Northern fur seals at the Pribilof Islands. By using a system of identification symbols they were able to mark individually 775 pups in 1969. The disadvantage of the technique is the difficulty of maintaining an adequate supply of the freezing agent in remote field situations.

Studies of movements and activities of seals in the sea have always been particu-

larly difficult. Recent developments in radio and ultrasonic tracking have prompted some workers to apply the techniques to studies on marine mammals (International Whaling Commission; Sub-Committee on small cetaceans, 1975; Leatherwood, Caldwell and Winn, 1976; Siniff, Reichle, Hofman and Kuehn, 1975). But,
as Wartzok, Ray and Martin (1975) point out, radiotelemetry, as used for terrestrial mammals and birds, is not appropriate because the attenuation of electromag-
netic waves increases with conductivity of the medium. Ultrasonic telemetry, as
used for studying fish, is not suitable either because marine mammals are sensitive
to high frequency sounds. For studying the physiology and behaviour of animals
in the sea they have used an instrument package capable of recording data transmitted from sensors in and on the submerged animal. In the example cited, they
attached the apparatus, consisting of sensors, an electronic transmitting device
and a recorder, to the back of a Steller sea-lion *Eumetopias jubatus* to investigate
changes in body temperature during diving. Disadvantages of telemetry, even using
short range transmission to a recording package, are the high cost of information
about relatively few animals, the possibility that behaviour is influenced by the
presence of the package and the difficulties of recovering the package.

Techniques for marking unrestrained animals include the use of dyes, paints
and bleaches. These do not last beyond the following moult but for many purposes are highly suitable. For example, censuses of Grey seal pups at densely populated breeding assemblies are best done by dyeing the pups to avoid counting
errors (Boyd, Lockie and Hewer, 1962; Coulson and Hickling, 1964; Summers,
Burton and Anderson, 1975) and paint and bleach marks have been used to identify Elephant seals during the breeding season (Laws, 1956). A further technique
for use on unrestrained animals has been described by Homestead, Beck and
Sergeant (1971). It is a method of branding using a mechanically detonated explosive device attached to a modified spear-fishing gun. Their paper shows photographs of brand marks applied in this way to several species of seals but there is no
information on the long-term quality of the brand.

It will be apparent that the type of mark selected for studying seals will be
determined by the kind of information required. An example of a current problem
is that to maintain a large number of permanently marked animals in a population
requires their capture at some stage in order to apply the mark. Since, for most
species, adults are difficult to handle in large numbers, it is usual to mark pups.
This, of course, is inefficient because, in the case of the Grey seal, only about 50
per cent of the animals marked can be expected to survive to breeding age at least
5 years later. Clearly, a method of applying permanent marks to unrestrained
adults is required. An explosive branding technique may, in time, provide this
need. Alternatively, the development of a technique for administering a bone
labelling substance such as tetracycline, which fluoresces under ultraviolet light
(Frost, Villanueva, Roth and Stanisavljevic, 1961), to unrestrained adult seals
would provide valuable information in situations where the researcher has access
to large collected samples. This type of label has been successfuly applied to restrained seals (Yagi, Nishiwaki and Nakajima, 1963) and dolphins (Best, 1976) and
the technology for administering such labels to unrestrained animals should not be
difficult to develop.

References

Best, P. B. (1976). Tetracycline marking and the rate of growth layer formation in the teeth of a dolphin (*Lagenorhynchus obscurus*). *South Afr. J. Sci.* **72**, 216-218.

Best, P. B. and Rand, R. W. (1975). Results of a pup-tagging experiment on the *Arctocephalus pusillus* rookery at Seal Island, False Bay, South Africa. In *Biology of the Seal* (ed. K. Ronald and A. W. Mansfield). Rapports et Proces-Verbaux des Reunions, Conseil International pour l'Exploration de la Mer **169**, 267-273.

Bonner, W. N. and Vaughan, R. W. (1972). *Sealing and Common seals* (Phoca vitulina) *in the Wash, England.* International Council for the Exploration of the Sea, CM 1972/N:10.

Bonner, W. N. and Witthames, S. R. (1974). Dispersal of Common seals (*Phoca vitulina*) tagged in the Wash, East Anglia. *J. Zool.*, **174**, 528-531.

Boyd, J. M. and Campbell, R. N. (1971). The Grey seal (*Halichoerus grypus*) at North Rona, 1959-1968. *J. Zool.*, **164**, 469-512.

Boyd, J. M., Lockie, J. D. and Hewer, H. R. (1962). The breeding colony of Grey seals on North Rona, 1959. *Proc. Zool. Soc. Lond.*, **138**, 257-277.

Chapman, D. G. and Johnson, A. M. (1968). Estimation of Fur seal pup populations by randomized sampling. *Trans. Am. Fish. Soc.*, **97**, 264-270.

Coulson, J. C. and Hickling, G. (1964). The breeding biology of the Grey seal, (*Halichoerus grypus*), on the Farne Islands, Northumberland. *J. Anim. Ecol.*, **33**, 485-512.

Frost, H. M., Villanueva, A. R., Roth, H. and Stanisavljevic, S. (1961). Tetracycline bone labeling. *J. New Drugs*, **1**, 206-216.

Harwood, J., Anderson, S. S. and Curry, M. G. (1976). Branded Grey seals at the Monach Isles, Outer Hebrides. *J. Zool.*, **180**, 506-508.

Hewer, H. R. (1955). Notes on marking of Atlantic seals in Pembrokeshire. *Proc. Zool. Soc. Lond.*, **125**, 87-95.

Hewer, H. R. (1974). *British Seals.* Collins, London.

Hickling, G. (1962). *Grey Seals and the Farne Islands.* Routledge and Kegan Paul, London.

Homestead, R., Beck, B. and Sergeant, D. E. (1971). A portable instantaneous branding device for permanent identification of wildlife. In *Biological Sonar and Diving Mammals. J. Wildl. Mgmt*, **36** (3), 947-949.

International Whaling Commission, Scientific Committee, Sub-Committee on Small Cetaceans (1975). Report of the meeting on Smaller Cetaceans, Montreal, April 1-11, 1974. *J. Fish. Res. Bd. Can.*, **32**, 889-983.

Kaufman, G. W., Siniff, D. B. and Reichle, R. (1975). Colony behaviour of Weddell seals, *Leptonychotes weddelli*, at Hutton Cliffs, Antarctica. In *Biology of the Seal* (ed. K. Ronald and A. W. Mansfield). Rapports et Proces-Verbaux des Reunions, Conseil International pour l'Exploration de la Mer **169**, 228-246.

Keyes, M. C. and Johnson, A. M. (1971). Cryogenic marking. U.S. Department of Commerce, National Oceanic and Atmospheric Administration, National Marine Fisheries Service, Special Scientific Report-Fisheries, No. 628, 11-12.

Laws, R. M. (1956). The Elephant seal (*Mirounga leonina* Linn.) II. General, Social and Reproductive Behaviour. Falkland Islands Dependencies Survey, Scientific Reports No. 13.

Leatherwood, S., Caldwell, D. K. and Winn, H. E. (1976). Whales, dolphins and porpoises of the Western North Atlantic. National Oceanic and Atmospheric Administration, Technical Report NMFS CIRC-396.

Mansfield, A. W. and Beck, B. (1977). The Grey seal in eastern Canada. Environment Canada, Fisheries and Marine Service Technical Report No. 704, 81 pp.

Payne, M. R. (1977). Growth of a fur seal population. *Phil. Trans. R. Soc., B,* **279**, 67-79.

Payne, M. R. (1978). Population size and age determination in the antarctic fur seal, *Arctocephalus gazella. Mammal Rev.*, **8**, (1 and 2), 67-74.

Rasmussen, B. and Øritsland, T. (1964). Norwegian tagging of Harp seals and Hooded seals in North Atlantic waters. *FiskDir. Skr.,* **13**, 43-55.

Scheffer, V. B. (1950). Experiments in the marking of seals and sea-lions. U.S. Fish and Wildlife Service, Special Scientific Report, Wildlife, **4**.

Siniff, D., Reichle, R., Hofman, R. and Kuehn, D. (1975). Movements of Weddell seals in McMurdo Sound, Antarctica, as monitored by telemetry. In *Biology of the Seal* (ed. K. Ronald and A. W. Mansfield). Rapports et Proces-Verbaux des Reunions, Conseil International pour l'Exploration de la Mer, **169**, 387-393.

Sivertsen, E. (1941). On the biology of the Harp seal, *Phoca groenlandica* Erxl., Investigations carried out in the White Sea 1925-1937. *Hvalråd. Skr.,* **26**.

Stirling, I. (1971). Population dynamics of the Weddell seal (*Leptonychotes weddelli*) in McMurdo Sound, Antarctica, 1966-1968. *Antarctic Research Series,* **18**, 141-161. American Geophysical Union, Washington, D.C.

Summers, C. F., Burton, R. W. and Anderson, S. S. (1975). Grey seal (*Halichoerus grypus*) pup production at North Rona: A study of birth and survival statistics collected in 1972. *J. Zool.,* **175**, 439-451.

Summers, C. F. and Mountford, M. D. (1975). Counting the Common seal. *Nature,* **253**, 670-671.

Vaughan, R. W. (1978). A study of Common seals in the Wash. *Mammal Rev.*, **8**, (1 and 2), 25-34.

Wartzok, D., Ray, G. C. and Martin, H. B. (1975). A recording instrument for package use with marine mammals. In *Biology of the Seal* (ed. K. Ronald and A. W. Mansfield). Rapports et Proces-Verbaux des Reunions, Conseil International pour l'Exploration de la Mer, **169**, 445-450.

Yagi, T., Nishiwaki, M. and Nakajima, M. (1963). A preliminary study on the method of time marking with lead salt and tetracycline on the teeth of Fur seals. Whales Research Institute, Scientific Report, **17**, 191-195.

8 *Whale marking techniques*

Sidney G. Brown*

The world-wide development of modern whaling in the late nineteenth and early twentieth century, using an explosive harpoon fired from a cannon mounted on a steam-powered catching boat, led to an increasing need for information on the distribution of whale stocks and the relation of the catches to the size of the stocks. Some method of marking living whales so that the marks might be recovered from them after capture could clearly provide an important source of such information. Several people apparently had the idea of marking whales at about the same time (Brown, 1977) but the first actual experiment in marking whales at sea appears to be that of Captain Amano, a Japanese whaling captain, who fired a 'marking rod' into a Blue whale *Balaenoptera musculus* off the Japanese coast in February 1910, and captured the same whale two years later in June 1912 (Omura and Ohsumi, 1964).

In 1924, Hjort in Norway and Harmer with the Discovery Committee in England began new experiments in marking whales, and from their work arose the first large-scale marking programme, undertaken by the Discovery Committee in the Southern Hemisphere.

Discovery Type Whale Marks

'Drawing-pin' mark

The first mark used by the Discovery Committee resembled a large drawing-pin. It consisted of a hollow barbed metal head 6.5 cm in length arising from the centre of a flat metal disc of 4.5 cm diameter. The disc bore an inscription and address for the return of the mark, together with a serial number. The mark was mounted on a wooden shaft which fitted into the barrel of a modified 12-bore shotgun (Kemp, Hardy and Mackintosh, 1929).

The mark was designed to penetrate just below the surface of the blubber of the whale, leaving the disc flush with the skin, with the wooden shaft disengaging and falling away. The mark would thus be visible on the body surface of the whale

*Mr Sidney Brown is a graduate of the University of London. He has worked with the Whale Research Unit on the biology of large whales since 1951, with field work in the Antarctic and at whaling stations in South Georgia, South Africa and Iceland. A member of the Scientific Committee of the International Whaling Commission, he is especially interested in whale distribution and migrations, and he co-ordinates the Commission's whale marking programme.

if it was later captured and processed on board a factory ship or at a land station. Many whales were marked on the whaling grounds around South Georgia but no marks were ever recovered. The mark penetrated no more than 6.5 cm into the blubber and there is no doubt that it was quickly rejected by the whales, since it is now known that blubber suppurates readily and that whales can rid themselves of deep-rooted external parasites.

Standard Discovery mark

When it was realised that the 'drawing-pin' external mark was a failure, several other designs were considered and the present internal mark finally adopted. It consists of a metal tube 1.5 cm diameter and approximately 23 cm in length fitted with a conical, bluntly pointed, leaden ballistic head, and with a shotgun cartridge crimped to the open end of the tube. The tube was originally made of aluminium, but this was found to corrode and was replaced with stainless steel. Engraved on the tube are a serial number and a legend and address for return. Fired from a modified 12-bore shoulder shotgun, the mark is designed to bury itself completely in the body of the whale, and to be found when the animal is later captured and processed. It was first used during the 1932/33 Antarctic whaling season. When marks had been successfully fired and recovered during this season, and in the following year, an extensive marking programme was undertaken by the Discovery Investigations (Rayner, 1940).

Since Discovery marks first appeared, the following modifications have been introduced:

Streamer modification
Discovery marks are intended to be recovered from the body of the whale during the processing of the carcass, and they are often found in the meat of the dorsal muscles, adjacent to the backbone. However, returns showed that many marks were not detected during the flensing and lemming (butchering) operations on the flensing deck but passed with the meat or blubber into the factory machinery where they were later recovered from Kvaerner cookers and other apparatus when these were emptied at regular intervals. It is usually not possible to trace the individual whale from which the mark came in these cases so that the value of the recovery is reduced. To improve the chances of marks being detected at an early stage in the processing of the carcass, standard marks were modified to include six coloured nylon threads, each approximately 0.5 mm thick and 2 m long. These were designed to stream from the open end of the tube and indicate the presence of the mark to the flensers, so that there would be an opportunity for the collection of biological samples (for example ovaries, baleen plates, ear plugs) of value in age determination and other studies, from the marked whale (Clarke and Ruud, 1954). Nylon streamers visible on the surface of the whale after a hit would also help to reduce the possibility of double-marking of individuals.

In practice, while many streamer marks have been recovered, there is no evidence that they have facilitated the recovery of the marks on the flensing deck. In some cases the streamers had been severed and lost by abrasion at the open end of the mark. They were also too fine to be easily visible on the back of the swimming whale, and their manufacture in this form has been discontinued.

Increased charge modification
The standard 12-bore mark was designed to mark all species of large whales, including Sperm whales *Physeter catodon*. In studies of Sperm whales off the west coast of South America, where a large marking programme was undertaken, it soon became apparent that the propellant charge of the cartridge of the standard mark was not always sufficiently powerful to allow effective hits; at the usual marking range of approximately 40 m the marks did not completely penetrate the tough blubber of adult sperm whales. An increased charge cartridge was therefore made up for marks intended for use on sperm whales (Clarke, 1962). This mark is still in production and use.

Small whale modification (.410 mark)
The use of the standard 12-bore mark is properly limited to animals measuring at least 11 m in total length, since there is evidence that smaller sized whales may be seriously injured or killed if hit by the 12-bore mark at close range (Clarke, 1971). Although some species of small whales have been marked with the standard mark (Brown, 1975), it is clearly not suitable for the smaller species in general, nor for small calves of the large whale species. A smaller version of the standard 12-bore mark was therefore developed in 1955 by Sergeant in Canada for use on small whales and calves. Approximately 15 cm long, it is fired from a .410 shotgun, and has been used in marking Minke whales *Balaenoptera acutorostrata* in the North Atlantic and Antarctic Oceans. A version of the .410 mark incorporating a single white streamer has also been used to facilitate recognition of marked animals, and avoid double-marking.

Visual streamer marks

The standard Discovery mark is an internal mark and can only be recovered from a whale when it is killed and processed by the whaling industry, or if a marked animal should die from other causes and be washed ashore and the carcass examined (Mitchell, 1970). With the decline of the whaling industry, the total protection of some species and the decreased catch quotas set by the International Whaling Commission on those species still subject to whaling, the number of mark returns reported has been drastically reduced in recent years. It has therefore become important to consider other means of carrying out research on large whales using mark–recapture methods without killing large numbers of animals. The development of an externally visible mark which can be seen at long range on the living whale is listed as a matter of high priority in Schevill (1974) and elsewhere, and attempts have been made to modify the standard Discovery mark to include some form of streamer visible at a distance.

Mitchell and Kozicki (1975) have described such a prototype mark in which the streamer consists of a strip of coloured nylon-coated vinyl approximately 1 cm wide and 90 cm long. This is attached to an anchor rivet behind the head of the mark by a length of braided Dacron, Teflon-coated line, the line and streamer being coiled in the tube and released when the mark is fired. The mark has been tested on Fin whales *Balaenoptera physalus* and Blue whales.

It functions correctly but there is no information yet on the duration of the streamer. Best and Brown (unpublished) have carried out field trials with a similar mark on Southern right whales *Eubalaena australis*, again with inconclusive results.

An associated development of the Mitchell and Kozicki prototype is its modification to carry a chemical (Quinacrine) for the permanent 'marking' of the laminae in the ear plugs of baleen whales. These are counted in age determination studies and there is still doubt as to their rate of formation. This could possibly be resolved by a marking project using these marks (Kozicki and Mitchell, 1974).

Marking Techniques for Large Whales

The standard Discovery mark has a maximum range of approximately 65 m and most marking is carried out at 35–45 m range. Marking programmes have generally concentrated on marking large whales on the high seas, either on the polar feeding grounds or in warmer waters. This involves the use of a suitable vessel and a commercial whale-catching boat has usually been employed on marking cruises. The *William Scoresby,* used in the Discovery Committee marking programme, was built on the lines of a whale-catcher, especially for whale marking (Rayner, 1940). A whale-catcher has the sea-going qualities, speed and manoeuvrability required to chase large whales successfully. Chartered with a whaling crew, the necessary expertise in the sighting, identification and hunting to within marking range, is also available. However, in inshore waters it may be possible to use other suitable vessels. Whale chasing motor launches of 11 m or less over-all length have been very successfully used by Dawbin (1956) in New Zealand coastal waters for marking Humpback whales *Megaptera novaeangliae* and among the South Pacific islands he has even used a sailing yacht only 4.3 m long.

Whales may be chased by *luse-jag* in which the animal is stalked as in big-game hunting, or by *prøyser-jag* in which the whale is deliberately made to run and show itself by chasing it at full speed. The former method allows greater accuracy in shooting; a combination of the two probably works best on marking cruises (Clarke and Ruud, 1954).

The marks are fired from a shoulder gun, or from a Morris tube mounted in the barrel of the harpoon cannon. Where possible, the region around the dorsal fin should be aimed at in baleen whales, and the region behind the dorsal fin in sperm whales. In all species, the region around and behind the flipper should be avoided (Clarke, 1971). The results of shots are classified as: hit, hit protruding, possible hit, ricochet, miss, or no verdict. A hit means that the mark is completely embedded in the whale and only whales with hits are recorded as effectively marked. Protruding marks may fall out of the blubber later, or be worked out by the healing process.

The serial number of the mark fired, and the result of the shot, the species marked, and estimated length of the whale should be immediately recorded to avoid error. These 'rough log' records should be transferred to the principal records at convenient intervals with the marks listed in chronological order of firing and the geographical position of firing and date added.

Most whale marking schemes pay a reward to the finder for each mark returned with information on the date and position of capture, together with the species, sex, length and other data relating to the animal in which the mark was found. After checking, marks can be returned as souvenirs to finders if desired, together with information on the species, position and date of the original firing. It is important to keep whalers informed of the likelihood of finding marks in whales. Posters describing the marking scheme, illustrating the mark, and advertising the reward, can be displayed at whaling stations. The regular publication of lists of recovered marks with notes on their significance, and the names of finders is useful. It is also important that whale biologists are kept informed of the various marking schemes in operation, since returns may come in from widely scattered localities.

The Effects of Discovery Type Marks on Whales

The standard Discovery mark has been in use since 1932. In the Discovery Committee marking programme, reports on marks recovered after an interval of two or three years indicated that the tissue around the embedded mark was usually well healed. There were, however, some reports of pus around marks and there was no proof that lethal injury never took place. With the prospect of large-scale international marking programmes being undertaken, a detailed investigation of the problem of possible serious injury to whales from marking was carried out in Norway in 1953 (Ruud, Clarke and Jonsgård, 1953).

Marks were fired into harpooned whales at sea, and into dead whales at a whaling station. The marking on shore was mostly at very short range (3–10 m), which allowed the effects of maximum impact and penetration to be examined. The position of each hit and the eventual position of the mark in the carcass was carefully recorded for the 38 marks used on the nine Fin whales, one Blue and one Sei whale *Balaenoptera borealis* involved in the trials.

The results showed that in normal marking at normal ranges (35–45 m) most marks are not likely to cause any obvious injury. A mark normally penetrates the blubber and embeds in the dorsal muscle, above the level of the transverse processes of the backbone and well outside the body cavity so that damage to the internal organs is avoided. To reduce the possibility of a mark going astray, the marksman should if possible aim at a specific target area as already noted in the description of marking methods. Experience in an Antarctic whale-marking cruise immediately following the trials confirmed the conclusions and recommendations (Clarke and Ruud, 1954).

The trials were carried out on whales measuring from 14.6 to 22.0 m in length, and it is strongly recommended that use of the standard mark be restricted to animals measuring at least 11 m (Clarke, 1971). There are records of smaller Sei and Sperm whales being killed by this mark, and the .410 mark should therefore be used for marking smaller animals. As with the standard mark, there will be a lower size limit below which the .410 mark may cause serious injury. This will

Animal marking

vary with the species and circumstances of marking and has not yet been clearly defined, but a lower limit of 4.6 m for all species has been suggested by Brown (1975).

It was originally suggested (Ruud, Clarke and Jonsgård, 1953) that marks be smeared with a bacteriocidal ointment before firing in order to prevent infection of the wound after penetration. Penicillin ointment was used on some marking cruises, but there has been no evidence that the practice has been of value in preventing possible infection, and it has been discontinued.

Present Situation of Marking Large Whales

Almost all whale marking before the Second World War was carried out by Discovery Investigations, and mainly confined to Blue, Fin and Humpback whales in Antarctic waters. After the war, with the expansion of interest in research on whales and whaling, several organisations and whaling companies in Japan, The Netherlands, Norway, South Africa and the United Kingdom co-operated in whale-marking programmes in the Antarctic, and in 1955 an international marking scheme was launched under the auspices and with the support of the International Whaling Commission. This scheme is co-ordinated by the Whale Research Unit of the Natural Environment Research Council in England. It has developed to embrace all marking in the Southern Hemisphere with the exception of that carried out by the Soviet Union. With the increased effort, substantial additional numbers of Blue, Fin and Humpback whales

Table 8.1 Numbers of the large whale species, including the Minke whale, marked throughout the world with Discovery type marks* (from Brown, 1977)

	Blue	Fin	Humpback	Sei	Bryde's	Minke	Right	Grey	Sperm	Total
Antarctic (1932–39)	695	3673	566	12	3	6	–		33	4988
Antarctic (1945–75 International and U.S.S.R.)	290	2040	1090	400	31	68	–		551	4470
Southern Hemisphere outside Antarctic (1949–75)	5	24	2251	106	4	7	–		1274	3671
North Pacific (1949–72)	148	992	514	592	–	34	40		4160	6480
North Atlantic (1950–75)	20	342	210	30	219	8	–		135	964
All regions	1158	7071	4631	1140	257	123	40		6153	20573

*Antarctic U.S.S.R. scheme to 1972 only; North Pacific U.S.S.R. to 1966 and Japan to 1972 only.

have been marked. The latter especially in Australian and New Zealand waters. Sperm whales have also been marked in the Antarctic and in South African, South American and Australian waters.

Outside the scope of the international scheme is substantial marking in the North Pacific by Japan, the Soviet Union, United States, and Canada. Marking has also been carried out in the North Atlantic, especially by Canada and Norway. Brown (1977) includes tables of the numbers of the different species of large whales, including the Minke whale, marked in these different regions. Table 8.1 reproduces his table of the world total of large whales effectively marked using Discovery type marks, compiled from the available figures up to and including the 1975 season. The largest numbers of whales have been marked in the Antarctic in the pre-war and post-war years, and in the North Pacific. Fin (34 per cent), Humpback (22 per cent) and Sperm whales (30 per cent) account for 86 per cent of the total of 20 573 whales marked.

The percentage of marks recovered varies widely according to species and region, reflecting the numbers of animals marked and the intensity of whaling on the species concerned. For all species combined, the percentages range from 5.7 per cent in the North Atlantic to 14.8 per cent in the Antarctic in the post-war period.

Some Results of the Marking Programmes

Migrations and movements of whales

Direct evidence has come from marking for the annual migrations of Humpback, Fin and Sei whales between warm-water breeding grounds and polar feeding grounds in Southern Hemisphere populations, and also in North Pacific populations (Brown, 1962; Dawbin, 1966; Ivashin, 1971; Ohsumi and Masaki, 1975). In the Antarctic and North Pacific some Blue, Fin and Sei whales are shown to return year after year to the same region of the feeding grounds, while others disperse from the marking area (Brown, 1954, 1968; Ohsumi and Masaki, 1975; Rayner, 1940). Long-distance movements in Sperm whales have been demonstrated in the North Pacific, and the North and South Atlantic (Best, 1969; Ivashin and Rovnin, 1967; Mitchell, 1975). Ivashin (1967) reports a mark from a sperm whale marked in the North Atlantic and captured off South Africa which is the only record to date of the movement of any species of whale from one hemisphere to the other.

Longevity and age determination

The oldest marks to date from the different species have been returned after the following intervals of years; Blue 14, Fin 37, Humpback 17, Sei 11, Sperm 22. More important are marks returned after a period of years from whales for which biological collections are also available. These marks can provide important checks on methods of age determination, for example, those using counts of laminae in ear plugs from baleen whales or teeth from sperm whales (Best, 1970; Ohsumi, 1962).

Animal marking

Visual Marking of Small Cetaceans

The increasing interest in the smaller cetaceans in recent years has led to attempts to mark them in order to trace their movements and to provide biological data from recognised individuals. Since most species are not subject to fisheries from which internal marks can be returned, various types of visual marks have been used. A review of marking methods for small cetaceans is given in Evans, Hall, Irvine and Leatherwood (1972) and a number of visual marks are illustrated in Leatherwood, Caldwell and Winn (1976).

Various designs of nylon button tags, either colour-coded, or bearing letters or numbers visible at a distance, have been attached to the dorsal fins of captured animals prior to their release. These are visible when the animal surfaces to breathe, or if it rides the bow wave of a vessel. Spaghetti tags, first developed for use on fish, have been adapted for use on dolphins and have been extensively used in studies of the species of *Stenella* caught in the purse seine fishery for tuna in the tropical Pacific (Perrin, 1975). The dolphins were marked either during release from capture with the tuna, or while they rode the vessel's bow wave.

Freeze brands have been used on the dorsal fin or back of Bottlenose dolphins *Tursiops truncatus*, briefly captured and released, without apparent pain or discomfort to the animals (Irvine and Wells, 1972). Watkins and Schevill (1976) have experimented with underwater paint as a highly visible, variable, and easily applied method for marking cetaceans.

In conclusion, though not strictly visual marks, radiotelemetry data packages should be mentioned. These have been successfully used on small cetaceans (Evans, 1974a) and are now being experimented with on the calves of large whales which have been captured alive and later released (Evans, 1974b).

References

Best, P. B. (1969). The sperm whale (*Physeter catodon*) off the west coast of South Africa 4. Distribution and movements. *Investigational Report Division of Sea Fisheries South Africa*, No. 78, 1–12.

Best, P. B. (1970). The sperm whale (*Physeter catodon*) off the west coast of South Africa 5. Age, growth and mortality. *Investigational Report Division of Sea Fisheries South Africa*, No. 79, 1–27.

Brown, S. G. (1954). Dispersal in blue and fin whales. *Discovery Rep.*, **26**, 355–384.

Brown, S. G. (1962). A note on migration in fin whales. *Norsk Hvalfangsttid.*, **51**, 13–16.

Brown, S. G. (1968). The results of sei whale marking in the Southern Ocean to 1967. *Norsk Hvalfangsttid.*, **57**, 77–83.

Brown, S. G. (1975). Marking of small cetaceans using 'Discovery' type whale marks. *J. Fish. Res. Bd Can.*, **32**, 1237–1240.

Brown, S. G. (1977). Whale marking: a short review. In *A Voyage of Discovery* (ed. M. Angel), Pergamon Press, Oxford, pp. 569–581.

Clarke, R. (1962). Whale observation and whale marking off the coast of Chile in 1958 and from Ecuador towards and beyond the Galapágos Islands in 1959. *Norsk Hvalfangsttid.*, **51**, 265–287.

Clarke, R. (1971). The possibility of injuring small whales with the standard *Discovery* whale mark. *Twenty-First Report of the International Whaling Commission.*, 106-108.

Clarke, R. and Ruud, J. T. (1954). International co-operation in whale marking: the voyage of the *Enern* to the Antarctic 1953. *Norsk Hvalfangsttid.*, **43** 128-146.

Dawbin, W. H. (1956). Whale marking in South Pacific Waters. *Norsk Hvalfangsttid.*, **45**, 485-508.

Dawbin, W. H. (1966). The seasonal migratory cycle of humpback whales. In *Whales, Dolphins and Porpoises* (ed. K. S. Norris), University of California Press, Berkeley, pp. 145-170.

Evans, W. E. (1974*a*). Radio-telemetric studies of two species of small odontocete cetaceans. In *The Whale Problem. A Status Report* (ed. W. E. Schevill), Harvard University Press, Cambridge, Mass., pp. 385-394.

Evans, W. E. (1974*b*). Telemetering of temperature and depth data from a free ranging yearling California gray whale *Eschrichtius robustus, Mar. Fish. Rev.*, **36**, 52-58.

Evans, W. E., Hall, J. D., Irvine, A. B. and Leatherwood, J. S. (1972). Methods for tagging small cetaceans. *Fish. Bull.*, **70**, 61-65.

Irvine, B. and Wells, R. S. (1972). Results of attempts to tag Atlantic bottlenosed dolphins (*Tursiops truncatus*). *Cetology,* No. 13, 1-5.

Ivashin, M. V. (1967). The whale-traveller. *Priroda,* No. 8, 105-107.

Ivashin, M. V. (1971). Some results of whale-marking carried out from Soviet ships in the southern hemisphere. *Zool. Zh.*, **50**, 1063-1078.

Ivashin, M. V. and Rovnin, A. A. (1967). Some results of the Soviet whale marking in the waters of the North Pacific. *Norsk Hvalfangsttid.*, **56**, 123-135.

Kemp, S., Hardy, A. C. and Mackintosh, N. A. (1929). Discovery Investigations. Objects, equipment and methods. *Discovery Rep.*, **1**, 141-232.

Kozicki, V. M. and Mitchell, E. (1974). Permanent and selective chemical marking of mysticete ear plug laminations with Quinacrine. *Twenty-fourth Report of the International Whaling Commission,* 142-149.

Leatherwood, S., Caldwell, D. K. and Winn, H. E. (1976). Whales, dolphins and porpoises of the Western North Atlantic. A guide to their identification. *National Oceanic and Atmospheric Administration Technical Report* NMFS CIRC-396, Seattle, pp. 1-176.

Mitchell, E. (1970). Request for information on tagged whales in the North Atlantic. *J. Mammal.*, **51**, 378-381.

Mitchell, E. (1975). Progress report on whale research, Canada. *Twenty-fifth Report of the International Whaling Commission,* 270-282.

Mitchell, E. and Kozicki, V. M. (1975). Prototype visual mark for large whales modified from 'Discovery' tag. *Twenty-fifth Report of the International Whaling Commission,* 236-239.

Ohsumi, S. (1962). Biological material obtained by Japanese expeditions from marked fin whales. *Norsk Hvalfangsttid.*, **51**, 192-198.

Ohsumi, S. and Masaki, Y. (1975). Japanese whale marking in the North Pacific, 1963-1972. *Far Seas Fish. Res. Lab. Bull.*, No. 12, 171-219.

Omura, H. and Ohsumi, S. (1964). A review of Japanese whale marking in the North Pacific to the end of 1962, with some information on marking in the

Antarctic. *Norsk Hvalfangsttid.,* **53**, 90–112.

Perrin, W. F. (1975). Distribution and differentiation of populations of dolphins of the genus *Stenella* in the Eastern Tropical Pacific. *J. Fish. Res. Bd Can.*, **32**, 1059–1067.

Rayner, G. W. (1940). Whale marking. Progress and results to December 1939. *Discovery Rep.,* **19**, 245–284.

Ruud, J. T., Clarke, R. and Jonsgård, A. (1953). Whale marking trials at Steinshamn, Norway. *Norsk Hvalfangsttid.,* **42**, 429–441.

Schevill, W. E. (ed.) (1974). *The Whale Problem. A Status Report,* Harvard University Press, Cambridge, Mass.

Watkins, W. A. and Schevill, W. E. (1976). Underwater paint marking of porpoises. *Fish. Bull.,* **74**, 687–689.

9 Marking bats

R. E. Stebbings*

This chapter briefly outlines the history of marking bats to the beginning of the modern era (*c*. 1952). The subsequent scale of this activity world wide is described, together with details of the methods. Particular emphasis is given to tagging, because this has been the most widely adopted practice and remains the most convenient method.

History

Harting (1889) referred to an experiment in which Pipistrelle bats were captured at a roost, taken a little distance away, released and apparently flew off towards the roost. He suggested that bats, like birds, could be marked by placing silver wire around the hind feet.

The first known marking of bats was in the United States in 1916 when Allen (1921) banded four *Pipistrellus subflavus* loosely on the leg using small aluminium bird bands. Although he released these a short distance from the point of capture he recovered three of them in the same roost in 1919. Howell and Little (1924) leg-banded five bats in 1921 and released them 20 miles from their roost. Two bats were retaken there in 1923. One bat had extensively scratched the band (by biting) and with the other the band had pierced membranes either side of the tibia.

Sherman (1937) leg banded 76 young *Tadarida brasiliensis cynocephala* a few days after birth in 1929 and recovered one female a year later with an embryo, demonstrating that maturity was reached within a year for that species. The cipher was totally obliterated, which was the first indication of the difficulty of banding *Tadarida*.

In 1931 Poole (1932) stained several *Myotis lucifugus* and demonstrated hom- ing over 10 and 18 miles in 4 days. Mohr (1934) continued these experiments, at first staining wing membranes with haemotoxylin, but later using aluminium bird

*Dr R. E. Stebbings became interested in bats at the age of 10, and 7 years later was concerned about the damage bands caused. During the following 10 years he was involved with developing bands in the United Kingdom that would not cause damage. For the first 9 years of his professional career he studied the ecology of salt marshes and reptiles, as well as work on oil pollution at sea and controlled environmental systems. During the past 6 years he has worked professionally on the population ecology of bats. He is Chairman of the bat group of the Survival Service Commission of the International Union for the Conservation of Nature.

bands applied to legs by slitting the interfemoral membrane and passing the band around the tibia. Mohr in this study was the first to experiment with numbered 'fingerling' tags attached to the ears (normally used for marking young fish). These were carried successfully for a year. With both bands and tags he recorded successful homing in a few days from 30 miles.

At this time Eisentraut (1934) began a substantial banding programme in Germany, using flanged aluminium bands applied around the forearm. He was mostly marking the large *Myotis myotis;* this sustained programme gave rise to many papers on bat biology during the 1930s and a total of 10 887 bats were banded by 1943 (Eisentraut, 1943).

As a result of Eisentraut's lead, a number of small banding programmes began in several European countries, but the only other substantial study began in 1936 in the Netherlands (Bels, 1952). This involved the wing banding of 17 335 bats of 14 species in 15 years. As a result Bels made substantial advances in our knowledge of bat behaviour and biology.

In the mid-1930s Griffin (1934, 1936) began his extended studies by tattooing numbers on wing membranes using black ink. Principally because of the time involved in marking each bat he soon changed to aluminium bird bands, mostly applied dorsally to the leg without slitting membranes. He banded 3000 bats of 6 species and was able to demonstrate homing and annual return of colonies to the same roosts. By 1945 (Griffin, 1945) he had banded 13 000 bats and had many cases of illegible ciphers and flesh overgrowth which also made it difficult to read numbers.

Because of these problems Griffin and others had experienced, Trapido and Crowe (1946) banded 5000 bats (mostly *M. lucifugus*) on the forearm. They intended to close all bands on to the membrane tightly, but noticed that those which were free to slide along the membrane caused fewer injuries. From this experience they advocated loose banding which forms the basis of most bat banding practice to the present day.

Mohr (1952) provides a detailed history of banding in the United States and reports the major findings from nearly 70 000 bats banded to that time.

Why Mark Bats?

Initially bats were marked to ascertain whether they had a homing instinct and then whether they migrated. Information on persistence and faithfulness to roosts was obtained and later the existence of 'family' groups. In the United States these aspects received most attention for the first 20 years but in Europe more effort was devoted to understanding the biology and ecology of bats. All studies tended to be based on hibernating populations rather than summer or nursery colonies.

During the 1950s, particularly in the United States when rabies was identified in bats, emphasis changed to understanding population dynamics, distribution and ecology of bats (see, for example, Davis, Herreid and Short, 1962). Although much is now known about the broad distributions of temperate species in North America and Europe, and classifications have been made as to their migratory or stationary habits (for example Gaisler and Hanak, 1969; Strelkov,

1969), little work has been done on the role of the individual in populations, family groups and associations with other species. There is still a great need to be able to identify individuals or groups and in the absence of natural markings, artificial aids are required.

Marking Methods

Short duration marks

The following are methods that may be used only for short periods (less than one year) and are generally applied as group marking. Some are useful for individually marking small numbers of bats with as little disturbance as possible.

Fur clipping
Fur, usually dorsal, can be cut with scissors. Often up to four distinguishable patches may be cut. This is a useful, harmless technique for identifying an individual or group temporarily. No known inconvenience is shown by the bats, but the mark may grow out rapidly (in 2–3 weeks) when bats are moulting (usually mid-summer for temperate species). Clipped fur is often visible without handling the bat.

Punch marking
Small holes are punched through wing membranes using either a tapered needle or, more conveniently, a tattoo outfit of the type used on rabbit ears. This outfit allows the rapid punching of numbers of four or five digits (Bonaccorso and Smythe, 1972). I have found that best results are obtained if 5 mm thick foam rubber is placed on the plain side of the tongs so that the tapered needles penetrate membranes to their full diameter. Holes are normally punched in the plagiopatagium between the fifth digit and the body. Punch marking results in white scar tissue forming in 10 days. The main advantage of this method is that large numbers of bats can be marked individually without causing any inconvenience to the bats. The most serious drawback is the short time the scars are visible. Bonaccorso, Smythe and Humphrey (1976) in marking *Corollia perspicillata* found scars lasting up to 5 months, but nothing discernible remained after 6 months. In June 1961, I punch marked and banded several *Plecotus* sp. and found the scars had gone within 2 months. Further disadvantages are that the bats need to be examined very carefully by hand and naturally occurring holes, scars and pigment blemishes can cause confusion. Nevertheless, punch marking is a useful short-period method.

Tattooing
Griffin (1934) marked wing membranes of *Myotis lucifugus* using a rabbit tattooing outfit together with black tattooing ink. He found the marks remained clear for at least 12 months. The main disadvantage to him was the slowness of tattooing each bat, compared to using aluminium bands.

Colour marking

A number of methods have been tried but no indications as to the effectiveness and merits were recorded. Mohr (1934) stained membranes with haemotoxylin and later (Mohr, 1952) referred to a study of *Tadarida* in which 2004 bats were painted with whitewash. Some of these bats homed 30 miles. Ryberg (1947) colour marked ears, and stated it was useful for short-period experiments, but did not mention the material.

Providing non-toxic colour materials are used, this method could be used for studies requiring group recognition without observer disturbance. Bats marked with fluorescing or reflecting materials could be detected while foraging. Highly-reflective plastic tape strips glued to head fur were used to mark *Phyllostomus hastatus*, and these lasted about 5 days. Spotlights and binoculars were used to recognise marked bats (Williams, Williams and Griffin, 1966; Griffin, 1970).

Adhesive tags

Daan (1969) marked hibernating bats (mostly small *Myotis*) by glueing a 5 mm diameter plastic-covered tape on to the top of the head. Each disc had a two-letter code allowing up to about 500 individual markings per species. It was thought that this method caused no inconvenience to the bats, since most did not wake when being marked. The main disadvantage is that a proportion (estimated to be 10 per cent by Daan) soon lost their discs, presumably because of inadequate glueing to the fur. Also this method would probably be effective only during hibernation because of the need to be close to the disc for reading numbers, and since discs would be lost in summer when the bats moult.

Lights

Buchler (1976) used a chemical light source attached to bats. The light is obtained by mixing two liquids (Cyalume manufactured by American Cyanamid Co.) and sealing them in glass spheres (5–10 mm diameter, 0.2–1.8 g). The spheres were stuck to the dorsal fur of bats. The brightness and duration of light emission could be controlled by varying the proportions of the mixture. Light was emitted for up to 3 hours and spheres easily fell from bats during grooming. Nevertheless this is a very useful method of obtaining detailed information about the local foraging behaviour of bats. These lights were visible from 225 to 475 m.

A more convenient light source would be 'Betalights' (Saunders–Roe Developments Ltd), which consist of a phosphor excited by tritium gas in glass capsules. These have an effective light emission life of up to 20 years and can be produced in almost any shape or size. Useful visible range can be from about 50 m to 1 km, depending on the shape, size and viewing method. Different colours are available, but effective range would be variable. If these were glued to bands, bats could carry them for life. However, possible drawbacks may be increased likelihood of predation and stress caused to the bat by the ever-present light.

Griffin (in Buchler, 1976) and Barbour and Davis (1969) used small 'Pinlights' attached to batteries taped to the bats, but with the advent of Betalights this cumbersome method is no longer useful.

Radio transmitters
Transmitters have been little used in bat studies because of their relatively large size and weight. With small devices (down to 1 g) now available the great disadvantage is their short range and the difficulty in following flying bats. However, for a large species such as *Phyllostomus hastatus* (70–100 g) studies using transmitters are much more practical. Williams and Williams (1967) used a 7 g transmitter with a 25 cm trailing wire antenna, strapped to a nylon net glued with Perlodion to the lower back fur of this bat. These were carried for up to 9 days without known ill effects and the maximum 'in sight' range was about 5 km. After a few days the bats were able to remove the net together with some fur.

Long duration marking methods

To date over 90 per cent of all marked bats have carried permanent marks. Most have been marked with rigid metal tags, but small numbers were given other kinds of tags, and some were marked by tissue modification.

Toe clipping (and claw clipping)
The terminal phalange and claw from one or two hind foot toes are removed using sharp scissors. This method should be confined to small species (maximum weight 30 g) and not involve any of the large-footed bats (for example *Myotis dasycneme*) that use their feet for catching and manipulating food. Dwyer (1965) toe clipped a maximum of two toes per foot and with sexual differences up to 510 combinations were possible per species. I have cut claws off juvenile bats in nursery roosts when too young to be banded. This allows subsequent recognition two to three months later when bats are old enough for banding, even if recaught away from the original roost. Toe clipping is a permanent mark, but claw removal often only lasts a few weeks, depending on how much is cut.

Ear tags
Fingerling tags, originally devised for marking small fish, have been used on several species of bat since the early 1930s (Mohr, 1934). They are usually made from stainless steel, measuring 2×7 mm when applied and have numbers but no return address. Fingerling tags are applied to the pinna using special pliers. Although relatively little used, ear tagging has several advantages over other tags. Being on the ear a bat is unable to bite or deform the tag, although they do sometimes scratch it vigorously. Tagged bats are readily visible even when in tight clusters. The main disadvantages are that they are relatively difficult to apply, particularly for a struggling bat, and being small only a small number can be used before duplication in cipher occurs. No return address is possible. Hitchcock (1965) found ear tags unsatisfactory but did not give reasons, while Griffin (1970) found them as satisfactory on *Myotis lucifugus* as wing or leg bands. He stated that they caused 'no appreciable injury or irritation nor any significant interference with echolocation'. However, I suspect that ear tags would not be suitable for marking species having rapid ear movements synchronised to their echolocation emissions (for example species of *Rhinolophus*), nor for large-eared bats (for example *Plecotus*).

Ear tags were used to mark the large *Phyllostomus hastatus* (Williams, Williams and Griffin, 1966) and although they were useful, gradually worked their way to the edge of the pinna and eventually were lost after several months. New tissue regenerated, and only a thin linear scar remained to indicate the previous position of the tag.

Thus, although fingerling tags can be regarded as permanent for the small species, they tend not to last on medium and large bats.

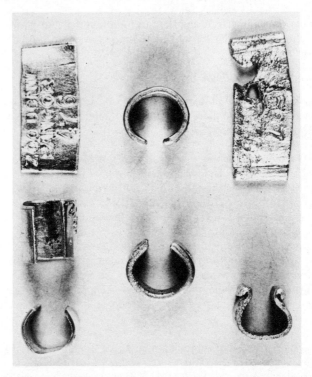

Figure 9.1 Examples of old styles of bands used in Britain. All were made from aluminium.

Top row: Bird band type, cut from sheet metal. Note sharp sheer edges and distorted shape due to stamping the cipher on to cut blanks. The flattened band is 12 X 6 mm.

Centre row: Bands made by hand from aluminium tape of the type used by Ransome (1971). Note smooth rounded edges to tape. Left, a used band that did not have the sharp ends filed smooth before application. Many injuries were caused. Bite marks are clearly visible. Right, the same band but with ends smoothed. Many *Rhinolophus ferrumequinum* have carried these over 20 years without injury.

Bottom row: Bands issued by the Mammal Society in the 1950s and early 1960s. Sharp edges caused much irritation and the chewed band was worn only for 3 weeks. Note distorted shape, due primarily to stamping the cipher.

Table 9.1 Examples of the scale of bat banding in selected countries. (Large numbers of bats have been banded in many other countries but often figures have not been published)

Country	National scheme	Band type	No. of species	No. of bats banded	Period	Reference
Australia	+	F & B	17	64 900	1957–74	Anon. (1976)
Belgium	+	?	15	18 343	1939–64	Fairon (1967)
Bulgaria	+	B	13	3 296	1940–62	Beron (1963)
Czechoslovakia	+	F	21	27 411	1948–67	Gaisler and Hanak (1969)
Denmark	–	B	6	3 828	1954–61	Egsbaek and Jensen (1963)
France	?	?	?	110 000*	1936–59	Saint-Girons H and M–C (1968)
Hungary	+	F	17	21 983	1951–61	Topal (1962)
Italy	+	?	7	5 943	1956–64	Dinale and Ghidini (1966)
Netherlands	–	F & B	14	17 335	1936–51	Bels (1952)
South Africa	+	?	14	8 548	1958–65	Coetzee (1965)
Sweden	–	F	13	1 000+	1938–46	Ryberg (1947)
Switzerland	+	?	12	300	1958–60	Aellen (1961)
United Kingdom	+	F & B	15	24 050*	1955–77	Stebbings, this paper
United States	+	F & B	40	1 931 333*	1936–77	Wilson, personal communication

*These totals are numbers issued and therefore some bands may not have been used.
F = Flanged bands   B = Bird bands.

Table 9.2 Bat banding in the United States showing the large increase in the mid-1960s. (Also shown are two individual studies)

Period	No. of years	Total banded	National scheme	Reference
1932–51	20	67 279*	+	See below
1952–56	5	92 844*	+	See below
1957–62	6	339 877*	+	See below
1963–66	4	1 000 000*	+	See below
1967–76	10	431 333*	+	See below
1960–63	4	73 816 (a)		Davis and Hitchcock (1965)
1952–67	15	162 892 (b)		Cockrum (1969)

(a) *Myotis lucifugus*   (b) *Tadarida brasiliensis*
* These figures have been taken or derived from Cockrum (1956); Hitchcock (1957); Manville (1962); Paradiso and Greenhall (1967); and Wilson (personal communication).

Metal bands

Bat bands have been manufactured mainly from aluminium, with some from Monel and (recently in Britain) from magnesium–aluminium alloy. A few have been made of steel for the largest species. The scale of bat banding world wide is indicated in tables 9.1 and 9.2. Most bands were cut from thin sheet or tape leaving sharp edges. Irrespective of whether the bands were placed on the leg or forearm, this resulted in the sharp edges rubbing on membranes (figure 9.1), causing irritation which was worsened by the bat biting the band, scratching

the surface and closing the ends tight to the membranes. Severe injuries sometimes resulted.

Choice of metal.   Leaving aside steel which has been little used, the three
other metals have the following characteristics. Aluminium bands are soft,
lightweight, easily applied without pliers, but tend to deform during application
when thin material is used. Easily deformed and defaced by biting, aluminium
bands lack springiness, but are shiny and easily seen. Monel is a tough dense
alloy that requires pliers for good application. It cannot be defaced by biting,
and is springy, so over-closing is not possible, but removal is difficult if bands
are causing irritation. Monel soon discolours (1-2 months) making banded bats
difficult to see in clusters (Dwyer, 1965). Magnesium alloy is of similar density
and shinyness to aluminium but is tough and slightly springy. Pliers are required
if large numbers are to be applied but bands can be fixed with the fingers.
Bats cannot distort or deface them.

Site of banding—leg versus forearm.   Griffin (1945) and Ryberg (1947)
preferred leg banding, though Griffin recorded extensive overgrowth of bands.
Most bands were placed dorsally around the tibia without slitting membranes,
although the latter were often penetrated by the sharp ends. Ryberg used flanged
bands, which minimised that problem. Forearm banding, which was always
predominant in Europe, was mostly adopted in the United States after 1946.
However, the use of bird bands with sharp edges resulted in large numbers of
bats receiving injuries of various kinds. Hitchcock (1957) described the problems
of using bird bands, especially if too small a band is applied. This can cause
swelling beneath the band and subsequent oedema and associated circulation
problems. Hitchcock found it was essential to ensure ends were parallel and
smooth if injury was to be minimised. *Tadarida* was cited as being one of the most
difficult species to band. Of 190 banded, 104 were injuried after one month,
33 so badly that they were killed. Perry and Beckett (1966) banded 10 000
neonatal *Tadarida brasiliensis*, 400 with a small band (No. 1) which caused severe
skeletal damage to forearm and manus and the others with a larger band (No. 2).
The latter tended to cause injury only when badly applied—for example flatten-
ing of band on to membrane.

Carefully applied bands to the forearm generally caused no problems and many
bats in Europe and North America have carried bands over 20 years. The greatest
longevity recorded is 24 years, for a *M. lucifugus* (Griffin and Hitchcock, 1965).

Bird band versus flanged bat band.   Herreid, Davis and Short (1960)
assessed the merits of these two types of band, but both bands had sharp edges
or burrs. Bird bands caused injuries to 76 per cent ($n = 114$) of bats within
21-50 days, whereas 57 per cent ($n = 92$) were damaged with bat bands.
Embedded bird bands (severe injury) averaged 40 per cent ($n = 113$) of
recoveries after six months while only 6 per cent ($n = 69$) of bat bands were
embedded. In Britain the Mammal Society designed and tested a number of
variations of flange shape and size, and an adopted pattern has been in use
since 1969 (see figure 9.2).

Bands currently issued by the Mammal Society in Britain.   The bands are
manufactured by Lambournes (Birmingham) Ltd to Mammal Society specifica-
tions. They are produced from magnesium–aluminium alloy, fully finished
without any sharp edges or burrs. Bands are supplied in batches of 50 in an open

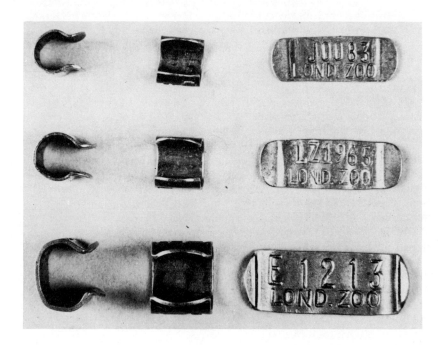

Figure 9.2 Three sizes of flanged bands currently used in Britain.
All are manufactured from magnesium–aluminium alloy and are
supplied fully-finished and ready to use. Note the lack of sharp
edges or burrs.

'ready to apply state' threaded on plastic tubing in numerical order. Currently
3 sizes are made: 2.5 mm internal diameter for bats up to 7 g; 3.0 mm for bats
7-12 g; 4.0 mm for bats 12-35 g. Larger sizes are available for tropical species.

Bels (1952) described the extreme difficulty he had in marking *Rhinolophus
ferrumequinum* (14-30 g); Topal (1962) who banded 293 of this species, found
almost all were injured by flanged bands. Dwyer (1965) banded 446 *R. megaphy-
llus* with bird bands and recovered 88 per cent with severe injuries in the first
9 months. I have banded *R. ferrumequinum* in Dorset since 1970. Of 279 banded,
150 (54 per cent) were recaught after one year, 105 (37 per cent) after two and
82 (29 per cent) after 3 years and none has had any injury or blemish of any
kind caused by the band.

Method of application. As reported above (p. 82) the importance of loose
banding (that is, the band being free to slide over membranes) was discovered
accidentally. For *R. ferrumequinum* Ransome (personal communication) first
advocated leaving the widest gap possible between the band ends without the

possibility of the band either falling off or trapping metacarpals. This method, using tough magnesium bands, has ensured total lack of injuries.

Many bats have a wide propatagium (antebrachial membrane) and bands applied over this immediately cut into the leading edge. Bonaccorso, Smythe and Humphrey (1976) and others have made small slits (up to 10 mm long) close to the anterior of the radius and inserted bands in the usual way. This appears to cause no inconvenience and few complications.

Variations to metal bands
Coloured bands. A number of authors have used colour-anodised bands (for example Cockrum, 1969; Ransome, 1971; Rybar, 1973) and these can be useful for marking the different sexes and aged bats and preventing the need to disturb them. Gaisler and Nevrly (1961) painted bands with nitroenamel paints using different colours and obtained 96 combinations of band when using the colours, two bands per bat and either left and/or right forearm. The main disadvantage is that bats gnaw the paint. However, I have found that if a very thin layer of paint is applied, particularly filling the band digits and inscription, this will remain for up to 8 years (Stebbings, unpublished).

Radioactive bands. It was known for many years that hibernating bats roused and moved periodically and often were likely to occupy crevices where they were invisible to the researcher. Punt and Nieuwenhoven (1957) modified the flanged ends of some bands making a tube in which a 2 x 1 mm rod of antimony-124 was glued. When attached to bats these bands were detectable up to 10 m away in humid air and rather less when in limestone crevices. Gifford and Griffin (1960) used iodine-131 in a similar way to detect homing bats up to 1 m through brick walls of a building.

Plastic bands
Gaisler and Nevrly (1961) used small, flanged, coloured celluloid bands and found them more successful than painted aluminium because the colour did not fade. Also, their elasticity allowed quick application. The main disadvantage was the lack of cipher. This problem can be overcome when marking large species. Bonaccorso *et al.* (1976) used coloured plastic bands with large embossed numbers to mark 1295 *Artibeus jamaicensis* (47 g). Of 180 recaptures, only 5.5 per cent were unreadable, while of 84 wing marked with aluminium bands 20 per cent were unreadable.

Bead chain necklace
Wilson (personal communication) has recently begun a bat marking programme in Panama using a metal bead necklace (a key chain) on which a bat band is placed. Captive bats have carried these for two years without problems. Although rather more difficult to apply than bands, this may provide safe marking, particularly for the larger species.

Discussion

Bats have been marked for over 50 years and a vast amount of information has been gained that otherwise would not have been obtained. We know, for example, that bats form discrete family groups, are faithful to particular roosts and may undertake migrations of 2347 km or more (Beron, 1963).

Bands have caused the deaths of some bats and much irritation to many others. Bopp (1954) suggests 25 per cent loss from populations should be allowed for mortality caused by bands but Sluiter and Heerdt (1957) and Dwyer (1965) thought bands were not a significant factor in their studies. Bat populations have declined as a result of banding, but this has been attributed more to the disturbance involved than to bands (Stebbings, 1969). It is well known that bats banded in hibernation often disappear immediately after handling. Only 6 of 78 bats banded in mid-winter on one visit were retaken on a subsequent inspection a few weeks later (Gilbert and Stebbings, 1958). Rybar (1973) found 36–66 per cent of bats leaving hibernacula immediately following banding. Dinale (1968) found the average weight of banded bats to be less than unbanded ones after one year.

Because of declining bat populations (Stebbings, 1971) in many parts of the world many workers have stopped casual bat marking. In the United States the U.S. Fish and Wildlife Service has introduced a moratorium on the issue of new bands except for important ongoing studies (Jones, 1976).

Marking bats is still an essential means of obtaining certain types of information which are essential for the conservation of bats, for example distribution, range, movement, population size and population dynamics. For these, permanent tagging is required and it is essential that the tags cause no irritation. Those now used in Britain do not cause injuries if applied carefully, and providing bats are not disturbed during critical periods in hibernation and during parturition, no harmful effects ensue. It would be useful if more countries produced comprehensive bat banding manuals similar to that of the United States (Greenhall and Paradiso, 1968).

Acknowledgments

I thank Mr T. J. Pickvance for his insistence on producing a perfect bat band and for his co-ordination of the development programme. This could not have been achieved without the willing co-operation of Mr G. C. Lambourne (Lambournes Ltd) over many years. Dr Don Wilson (U.S.F.W.S.) kindly provided information and specimens of U.S. bat bands and Mr H. Arnold produced the photographs. This work was supported by a contract from the Nature Conservancy Council.

References

Aellen V. (1961). Le Baguement des Chauves-Souris au Col de Brètolet (Valais). *Archs Sci., Genève,* **14**, 365–392.

Allen, A. A. (1921). Banding Bats. *J. Mammal.,* **2**, 53–57.

Anon (1976). Bat Banding. *A Report, Division of Wildlife Research, CSIRO* (Aust) 1974–76, 42.

Barbour, R. W. and Davis, W. H. (1969). *Bats of America.* University of Kentucky Press.

Bels, L. (1952). Fifteen years of bat banding in the Netherlands. *Publtiës natuurh. Genoot. Limburg.,* **5**, 1-99

Beron, P. (1963). Le baguage des Chauves-Souris en Bulgarie de 1940 à 1961. *Acta theriol.,* **7** (4), 33-49.

Bonaccorso, F. J. and Smythe, N. (1972). Punch-marking bats: an alternative to banding. *J. Mammal.,* **53** (2), 389-390.

Bonaccorso, F. J., Smythe, N. and Humphrey, S. R. (1976). Improved techniques for marking bats. *J. Mammal.,* **57**, 181-182.

Bopp, P. (1954). Fledermaüse in winterschlaf. *Schweiz Natursch,* **20**.

Buchler, E. R. (1976). A chemiluminescent tag for tracking bats and other small nocturnal animals. *J. Mammal.,* **57**, 173-176.

Cockrum, E. L. (1956). Homing, movements and longevity of bats. *J. Mammal.,* **37**, 48-57.

Cockrum, E. L. (1969). Migration of the guano bat, *Tadarida brasiliensis. University of Kansas Museum of Natural History Miscellaneous Publications,* No. 51, 303-336.

Coetzee, C. G. (1965). Bat banding in Southern Africa. *Bull. zool. Soc. Southern Afr.,* **7**, 8-10.

Daan, S. (1969). Frequency of displacements as a measure of activity of hibernating bats. *Lynx,* **10**, 13-18.

Davis, R. B., Herreid, C. F. and Short, H. L. (1962). Mexican free-tailed bats in Texas. *Ecol. Monogr.,* **32**, 311-346.

Davis, W. H. and Hitchcock, H. B. (1965). Biology and Migration of the bat, *Myotis lucifugus,* in New England. *J. Mammal.,* **46**, 296-313.

Dinale, G. (1968). Studi sui Chirotteri Italiani: IX. Statistica di una popolazione di *Rhinolophus euryale* rinvenuta alla grotta pila 71 LA. *Notiz. Circolo Speleolico Romano* **13** (15-16), 13-17.

Dinale, G. and Ghidini, G. M. (1966). Centro inanellamento Pipistrelli: otto anni di attività (1957-1964). *Atti Soc. ital. Sci. nat.,* **105**, 91-101.

Dwyer, P. D. (1965). Injuries due to bat banding. *Third and Fourth Annual Reports on Bat-Banding in Australia,* CSIRO (Aust) Division of Wildlife Research, Technical Paper No. 9, 19-24.

Egsbaek, W. and Jensen, B. (1963). Results of Bat Banding in Denmark. *Vidensk. Medd. dansk naturh. Foren.* **125**, 269-296.

Eisentraut, M. (1934). Markierungsversuche bie Fledermaüse. *Z. Morph. Ökol. Tiere.,* **28**, 553-560.

Eisentraut, M. (1943). Zehn Jahre Fledermausberingung. *Zool. Anz.,* **144**, 20-32.

Fairon, J. (1967). Vingt-cinq années de baguage des Cheiroptères en Belgique. *Inst. r. Sci. nat. Belg.,* **43**, (28), 1-37.

Gaisler, J. and Hanák, V. (1969). Ergebnisse der Zwanzigjährigen Beringung von Fledermäusen (Chiroptera) in der Tsechechoslowakei: 1948-1967. *Acta Sci. nat. Acad. Sci. Bohemoslovacae Brno* **3**, 1-33.

Gaisler, J. and Nevrly, M. (1961). Theuse of coloured bands in investigating bats. *Vest.csl. zool. Spol.,* **25** (2), 135-141.

Gifford, C. and Griffin, D. R. (1960). Notes on homing and migratory behaviour of bats. *Ecology*, **41**, 378-381.

Gilbert, O. and Stebbings, R. E. (1958). Winter roosts of bats in West Suffolk. *Proc. zool. Soc. Lond.*, **131**, 329-333.

Greenhall, A. M. and Paradiso, J. L. (1968). Bats and bat banding. *Resour. Pub. Bur. Sport Fish. Wildl.*, **72**, 1-48.

Griffin, D. R. (1934). Marking bats. *J. Mammal.*, **15**, 202-207.

Griffin, D. R. (1936). Bat banding. *J. Mammal.*, **17**, 235-239.

Griffin, D. R. (1945). Travels of banded cave bats. *J. Mammal.*, **26**, 15-23.

Griffin, D. R. (1970). Migrations and homing of bats. In *Biology of Bats* (ed. W. A. Wimsatt), Academic Press, New York and London.

Griffin, D. R. and Hitchcock, H. B. (1965). Probable 24-year longevity records for *Myotis lucifugus. J. Mammal.*, **46**, 332.

Harting, J. E. (1889). Natterer's Bat, *Vespertilio Nattereri. Zoologist Series 3*, **13** (151), 241-248.

Herreid, C. F., Davis, R. B. and Short, H. L. (1960). Injuries due to bat banding. *J. Mammal.*, **41**, 398-400.

Hitchcock, H. B. (1957). The use of bird bands on bats. *J. Mammal.*, **38**, 402-405.

Hitchcock, H. B. (1965). Twenty three years of bat banding in Ontario and Quebec. *Can. Fld Nat.*, **79**, 4-14.

Howell, A. B. and Little, L. (1924). Additional notes on Californian bats. *J. Mammal.*, **5**, 261-263.

Jones, C. (1976). Economics and Conservation. In *Biology of bats of the New World family, Phyllostomatidae Part 1,* Special publications, The Museum, Texas Technical University 10, 133-145.

Manville, R. H. (1962). A plea for bat conservation. *J. Mammal.*, **43**, 571.

Mohr, C. E. (1934). Marking bats for later recognition. *Proc. Pennsylvania Acad. Sci.*, **8**, 26-30.

Mohr, C. E. (1952). A survey of bat banding in North America 1932-1951. *Nat. Speleol. Soc. Bull.*, **14**, 3-13.

Paradiso, J. L. and Greenhall, A. M. (1967). Longevity records for American bats. *Am. Midl. Nat.*, **78**, 251-252.

Perry, A. E. and Beckett, G. (1966). Skeletal damage as a result of band injury in bats. *J. Mammal.*, **47**, 131-132.

Poole, E. L. (1932). The mammals of Berks County. *Bull. Reading publ. Mus.*, **13**, 15-19.

Punt, A. and Nieuwenhoven, P. J. van (1957). The use of radioactive bands in tracing hibernating bats. *Experientia,* **13**, 51-54.

Ransome, R. D. (1971). The effect of ambient temperature on the arousal frequency of the hibernating Greater Horseshoe bat, *Rhinolophus ferrumequinum,* in relation to site selection and the hibernation state. *J. Zool. Lond.*, **164**, 353-371.

Rybar, P. (1973). Remarks on banding and protection of bats. *Periodicum Biologorum,* **75** (1), 177-179.

Ryberg, O. (1947). *Studies on Bats and Bat Parasites.* Svensk Natur, Stockholm.

Saint-Girons, H. and Saint-Girons, M-C. (1968). Le baguage des Chauves-souris par les Speleologues. *Spelunca Bull.,* **1**, 19-21.

Sherman, H. B. (1937). Breeding habitats of the free-tailed bat. *J. Mammal.*,

18, 176-187.

Sluiter, J. W. and Heerdt, P. V. van (1957). Distribution and decline of bat populations in S. Limburg from 1942 till 1957. *Overdr. Natuurhist. Maandblad,* **46**, 134-143.

Stebbings, R. E. (1969). Observer influence on bat behaviour. *Lynx* (n.s.), **10**, 93-100.

Stebbings, R. E. (1971). Bat protection and the establishment of a new cave reserve in the Netherlands. *Stud. Speleol.,* **2**, 103-108.

Strelkov, P. P. (1969). Migratory and stationary bats (Chiroptera) of the European part of the Soviet Union. *Acta zool. cracov.,* **14**, 393-440.

Topàl, G. A. (1962). Some experience and results of bat banding in Hungary. *Symposium Theriologicum* (Proceedings of the International Symposium on Methods of Mammalogical Investigation held in Brno, Czechoslovakia, 1960) 339-344.

Trapido, H. and Crowe, P. E. (1946). The wing banding method in the study of the travels of bats. *J. Mammal.,* **27**, 224-226.

Williams, T. C. and Williams, J. M. (1967). Radio tracking of homing bats. *Science,* **155**, 1435-1436.

Williams, T. C., Williams, J. M. and Griffin, D. R. (1966). The homing ability of the Neotropical Bat, *Phyllostomus hastatus,* with evidence for visual orientation. *Anim. Behav.,* **14**, 468-473.

10 *Marking fish*

Lindsay M. Laird*

Fish, a major world food resource, are still largely obtained by hunting wild animals rather than by farming. In 1975, 70 000 000 tonnes of wild fish were caught world wide, and the total production of farmed fish was 4 000 000 t. In Britain, 1 000 000 t were captured and about 2000 t farmed.

It is important to plan efficient exploitation of wild fish stocks, both to aid efficient fishing and for conservation purposes. Direct observations of fish are seldom possible, and so sophisticated techniques have been developed in order to study migrations, population sizes, growth rates and behaviour. These include a wide range of marks and tags: for a more detailed account, and illustrations of their use see Laird and Stott (1978).

Although fish farming provides relatively small amounts of fish at present, it is a developing industry. Marks may be used to distinguish the offspring of different parents when many thousands of fish are being held in the same cages. Marks and tags are also used to distinguish fish in experimental aquaria.

Methods Used for Recognition

In some studies it has been possible to distinguish, by natural features, fish stocks which share feeding grounds but spawn at different times or on different spawning grounds. Frost (1963) showed that char, which spawn at different times in Lake Windermere, could be separated both by the numbers of gill rakers and by the growth rate as determined from their otoliths. Otolith shape has been used to distinguish different herring stocks (Messieh, 1972). Blood characters may vary between races, for example analysis of transferring polymorphism has shown that two races of Atlantic salmon exist in British waters (Payne *et al.*, 1971; Child *et al.*, 1976).

Parasites have also been used to distinguish some fish stocks. Kabata (1963) suggested parasites could be used as indicators where:

(1) High infestation rate occurs at some places but not others.
(2) The parasite is monogeneic (one host, simple life history).

*A graduate of Newnham College, Cambridge, Dr Lindsay Laird's research for PhD at Liverpool University was on the movements of salmon and trout in streams. She became interested in methods of handling and marking fish, and has worked at the Universities of Stirling and Aberdeen on salmonids in farms; she has also investigated the effects of freeze branding and anaesthetics on fish, and is currently investigating maturation problems in salmonids.

(3) Infection persists over a reasonably long period and does not fluctuate seasonally.

(4) The parasite has wide environmental tolerance.

The use of naturally occurring marks requires specialised detection and usually involves killing the fish. It is seldom applicable other than for distinguishing geographically isolated stocks.

Applied Marks

Tissue alteration

Fin punches
Petersen (1896) punched holes in the fins of plaice in order to follow their migrations. The method has subsequently been used successfully by a number of workers including LeCren and Kipling (1963) who used a 4 mm diameter leather punch to mark char.

Fin clipping
Stuart (1958) studied the effects of fin removal, which, together with clipping, may be used as a convenient batch mark. However, care must be taken when selecting which fin to clip, as some fins are obviously involved in locomotion or behaviour, for example the dorsal and anal fins of salmonids. It is generally agreed that removal of the adipose fin of salmonids has little effect on growth and movement.

Although fins usually regenerate after clipping and punching, it is often possible to distinguish new growth by the altered branching patterns of the fin rays. Regeneration occurs fastest in tropical warm waters.

Fin ray clips
Some types of fish such as perch and tilapia have protruding tips to the rays of the dorsal and anal fins. Rinne (1976) showed that it was possible to clip these tips. Using this, fish can be numbered individually up to $2^n - 1$ where n is the number of rays in the dorsal fin. In heavily exploited populations there may, however, be confusion caused by breakages of fin ray tips in nets. Similarly, naturally deformed fins may be mistaken for regenerating clipped fins particularly in fish of hatchery origin.

Chemicals

The use of dyes and other chemicals for marking fish has been comprehensively reviewed by Arnold (1966).

Dyes
These may be administered in several ways. Attempts to mark eggs and fry by immersion in solutions of dyes have met with little success for long-term study. Most dyes are toxic to fish when administered at concentrations high enough to

produce an identifiable mark. A more successful use of the immersion technique was devised by Eipper and Forney (1965) who applied a concentrated solution of Sudan Black to the cut edges of newly clipped fins. After regeneration a coloured line is clearly visible on the fins.

Small fish have been successfully marked by incorporating dyes into food (Loeb, 1966). Adding powdered Sudan Black to the food of maturing adult Brown trout has been shown to stain both the developing eggs, and the fry hatching from them, for six weeks after the fry have begun feeding (Bagenal, 1967).

Injected dyes, notably Alcia Blue, have been used in many studies. Injection may be by means of a syringe inserted subcutaneously, often at a fin base or mandible, or by the use of a dental jet inoculator (Hart and Pitcher, 1969). Coloured liquid latex can also be injected to mark fish (Davis, 1955). Needles operated by electric vibrators have been used successfully to tattoo pigments under the skin (Dunstan and Bostick, 1956).

Variation of injection sites and the number of marks applied can be used to identify individual fish.

Radioactivity
Either elements which can be activated when exposed to radioactivity (Trefethen and Novotny, 1963) or radioactive compounds, may be used to produce a lasting mark. Detection obviously requires sophisticated equipment.

Fluorescence
Fluorescent dyes may be introduced by tattooing or by using a compressed air gun. It has been found that mixing these substances with melamine sulphonamide formaldehyde resin improves retention time (Phinney and Matthews, 1973).

Branding

There are four main ways of applying this increasingly popular marking method to fish.

Hot branding
Brands heated electrically (Johnson and Fields, 1959) and by boiling water (Groves and Novotny, 1965) and wood burning pencils (Buss, 1953) have all been used with some degree of success.

Cold branding
Brands cooled by a mixture of ethanol and carbon dioxide ice have produced marks lasting for up to 6 weeks on Chinook salmon and Rainbow trout (Everest and Edmundson, 1967). Brands cooled by liquid nitrogen produce more consistent results (Mighell, 1969) and are readily identifiable for 18 months in Atlantic salmon (Piggins, 1972). The pathological effects of this method have been studied and tissue damage shown to be minimal (Laird *et al.,* 1975). Raymond (1974) xamined thermal branding and showed its success to be dependent on the type f fish, size and shape of the brand, temperature, and length of application time of the brand to the fish.

Chemical branding
An extremely convenient and inexpensive method has recently been developed for branding Channel catfish which uses a silver nitrate pencil (Thomas, 1975). The required number or symbol can simply be written on the side of the fish.

Laser branding
A ruby laser can be used to mark large numbers of fish individually without handling (Anon, 1971; Raymond, 1974). Equipment is expensive and slight variations in voltage may lead to illegible marks.

Tagging

The above methods are recommended for use primarily when batch marks are required. For individual numbering several kinds of tags have been developed. Tagging of fish has a long history; Walton in *The Compleat Angler* describes the use of coloured wool as a form of tag.

Internal tags

Many commercially important fish are not handled before processing. These fish may be marked by tags implanted internally, which are either magnetic themselves, or are detected by magnets in the processing plant. For anchovies a tag has been developed which can be inserted either intramuscularly or into the head cartilage. These fish reach a maximum size of 57 mm; a tag measuring 1×0.25 mm can be colour coded to give individual numbers up to 4096 (2^{12}) (Leary and Murphy, 1975). Char, which are difficult to mark using external tags, have been successfully tagged subcutaneously; the tags are detected by means of a metal detector (LeCren, 1954; Moore and Mortimer, 1954).

External tags

Strap tags
These are similar to those used commercially for marking chicken wings. They consist of a long flat piece of metal, bent over so that a point on one end locks in a hole on the other; pliers are used to close the tag, which may be fastened round the pre-opercular bone (Goldspink and Banks, 1971). Fastening these tags round the mandible appears to depress the growth, probably by interfering with feeding. These and other types of external tags may affect the recapture of fish where nets are being used, marked fish becoming entangled and caught in disproportionately large numbers.

Flag tags
These are usually small square or oblong plastic plates on which numbers or short instructions to the finder are printed. They may be attached by silver wire, Monel metal or monofilament. They are attached by passing one or two needles (depending on the number of attachment threads) through the dorsal musculature in front

of the dorsal fin on anaesthetised fish. Fish anaesthetics have been well document-
ed (Bell, 1967; Laird and Oswald, 1975). Enough thread is left to allow for growth
but not so much as to tangle in underwater vegetation. Tag colour may be important; brightly coloured tags are easily visible on recapture but may also be visible
to predators, although it must be remembered that some colours are less conspicuous underwater than in air (Lythgoe, 1975). Modifications of the wired-on
tag include the hydrostatic Lee tag (a transparent plastic cylinder of neutral buoy-
ancy with a message inside), and the double plate tag in which plates are attached
on either side of the body below the dorsal fin.

Spaghetti tags
These are strips of plastic tubing 0.25-2.5 mm in diameter, passed through the
dorsal musculature (as with flag tags) and with the ends sealed together. Information is printed on the tubing.

Anchor tags
These are modifications of the marks used to attach price tickets to clothing in
shops (Dell, 1968). They consist of a plastic 'flag' or tube, attached to a T-piece of
flexible plastic. The tube is inserted by means of a gun with a needle pushed into
the dorsal musculature. The gun shoots out the tag so that the T-piece lodges on
the other side of the interneurals from the side of insertion and opens out parallel
to the vertebral column forming a firm attachment.

There are many variations on these basic tag types. The obvious advantages of
tags are that fish can be numbered individually and that instructions can be given
to the finder. They are easy to detect by untrained personnel. Disadvantages are
that only fish above a certain size (with most methods 100 mm) can be tagged,
they are relatively expensive both in materials and manpower needed for application, and tagging is more time consuming than some of the other marking
methods.

For the study of movements, tracking tags which emit radio or ultrasonic signals detectable by remote aerials or hydrophones can be used to determine the
fishes' position (Monan *et al.*, 1975). Radio is only satisfactory if used in very non-
conductive shallow freshwaters; the signal radiates well vertically from the waters'
surface and detection from aircraft has proved particularly successful. Radio signals
are not affected by underwater turbulance and air bubbles, which can cut down
sonic signals, but in sea water or any conductive water radio is severely attenuated.
Sonic tags operating at 50-250 kHz are inaudible to animals and underwater
ranges of up to 1 km are possible depending on battery power.

Tags are inserted into the stomach for the study of non-feeding salmonids on
up-river runs; if feeding might be affected, external attachment is preferable. The
emitted signal can also be used to telemeter data such as temperature, pressure (as
a function of water depth) (Luke *et al.*, 1973), swimming movement (Young *et al.*,
1972), heart rate (Priede and Young, 1977) or feeding activity.

A useful source of information on electronic tagging devices for fish is the
Underwater Telemetry Newsletter, edited by A. B. Stasko and published by the
Fisheries and Marine Service, Biological Station, St Andrews, New Brunswick,
Canada.

References

Anon. (1971). Laser marks in fish. *Agric. Res.,* **19**, 5.

Arnold, D. E. (1966). Marking fish with dyes and other chemicals. *U. S. Fish. Wildl. Serv., Tech. Pap.* **10**; 44pp.

Bagenal, T. B. (1967). A method of marking fish eggs and larvae. *Nature,* **214** (5083), 113.

Bell, G. R. (1967). A guide to the properties, characteristics and uses of some general anaesthetics for fish. *Bull. Fish. Res. Bd Can.,* **148** 2nd edn.

Buss, K. (1953). A method of marking trout by branding. *Prog. Rep. Pa Fish Comm.,* September 1953.

Child, A. R., Burnell, A. M. and Wilkins, N. P. (1976). The existence of two races of Atlantic salmon (*Salmo salar* L.) in the British Isles. *J. Fish. Biol.,* **8**, 35-43.

Davis, C. S. (1955). The injection of latex solution as a fish marking technique. *Invest. Indiana Lakes Streams,* **4**, 111-116.

Dell, M. B. (1968). A new fish tag and rapid, cartridge-fed applicator. *Trans. Am. Fish. Soc.* **97**, 57-59.

Dunstan, W. A. and Bostick, W. E. (1956). New tattooing devices for marking juvenile salmon. *Res. Pap. Wash. Dept. Fish.,* **1** (4), 70-79.

Eipper, A. W. and Forney, J. L. (1965). Evaluation of partial fin-clips for marking largemouth bass, walleyes and rainbow trout. *N. Y. Fish Game J.,* **12**, 233-240.

Everest, F. H. and Edmundson, E. H. (1967). Cold branding for field use in marking juvenile salmonids. *Progve Fish Cult.,* **29**, 175-176.

Frost, W. E. (1963). The homing of char (*Salvelinus willughbii*) (Gunther) in Windermere. *Anim. Behav.,* **11**, 74-82.

Goldspink, C. R. and Banks, J. W. (1971). A readily recognisable tag for marking bream (*Abramis brama* L.) *J. Fish. Biol.,* **3**, 407-411.

Groves, A. B. and Novotny, A. J. (1965). A thermal marking technique for juvenile salmonids. *Trans. Am. Fish. Soc.,* **94**, 386-389.

Hart, P. J. B. and Pitcher (1969). Field trials of fish marking using a jet inoculator. *J. Fish. Biol.,* **1**, 383-385.

Johnson, E. E. and Fields, P. E. (1959). The effectiveness of an electric hot wire branding technique for marking fingerling steelhead trout. *Tech. Rep. Sch. Fish. Univ. Wash.,* No. 47, 5p.

Kabata, Z. (1963). Parasites as biological tags. *Spec. Publs int. Commn. NW. Atlant. Fish.,* **4**, 31-37.

Laird, L. M., Roberts, R. J., Shearer, W. M. and McArdle, J. F. (1975). Freeze branding of juvenile salmon. *J. Fish. Biol.,* **7**, 167-171.

Laird, L. M. and Oswald, R. L. (1975). A note on the use of Benzocaine (Ethyl P-Aminobenzoate) as a fish anaesthetic. *J. Inst. Fish. Mgmt.,* **6**, 92-94.

Laird, L.M. and Stott, B. (1978). Marking and tagging. In *Methods for Assessment of Fish Production in Freshwaters* (ed. T. B. Bagenal) Blackwells, Oxford.

Leary, D. F. and Murphy, G. I. (1975). A successful method for tagging the small fragile engraulid *Stolephorus purpureus. Trans. Am. Fish. Soc.,* **105**, 53-55.

LeCren, E. D. (1954). A subcutaneous tag for fish. *J. Cons. perm. int. Explor. Mer.,* **20**, 72-82.

LeCren, E. D. and Kipling, C. (1963). Some marking experiments on spawning populations of char. *Spec. Publs. int. Commn. NW. Atlant. Fish.,* **4**, 130-139.

Loeb, H. A. (1966). Marking brown trout fry with the dye Sudan Black B. *N. Y. Fish. Game J.* **13**, 232-233.

Luke, D.McG., Pincock, D. G. and Stasko, A. B. (1973). Pressure-sensing ultrasonic transmitter for tracking aquatic animals. *J. Fish. Res. Bd Can.,* **30**, 1402-1404.

Lythgoe, J. N. (1975). Problems of seeing colours under water. In *Vision in Fishes* (ed. M. A. Ali) Plenum press, New York and London.

Messieh, S. N. (1972). Use of otoliths in identifying herring stocks in the Southern Gulf of St. Lawrence and adjacent waters. *J. Fish. Res. Bd Can.,* **29**, 1113-1118.

Mighell, J. L. (1969). Rapid cold-branding of salmon and trout with liquid nitrogen. *J. Fish. Res. Bd Can.,* **26**, 2765-2769.

Monan, G. E., Johnson, J. H. and Esterberg G. F. (1975). Electronic tags and related tracking techniques aid in study of migrating salmon and steelhead trout in the Columbia river basin. *Mar. Fish. Rev.,* **37** (2), 9-15.

Moore, W. H. and Mortimer, C. H. (1954). A portable instrument for the location of subcutaneous fish tags. *J. Cons. perm. int. Explor. Mer.,* **20**, 83-86.

Payne, R. H., Child, A. R. and Forrest, A. (1971). Geographic variation in the Atlantic salmon. *Nature,* **231**, 250-252.

Petersen, C. G. J. (1896). The yearly immigration of young plaice into the Limfjord from the German Sea. *Rep. Dan. biol. Stn.,* **6**, 1-48.

Phinney, D. E. and Mathews, S. B. (1973). Retention of fluorescent pigment by coho salmon (*Oncorhynchus kisutch*) after two years. *Progve Fish Cult.* **35**, 161-163.

Piggins, D. J. (1972). Cold branding as a smolt marking technique. *J. Inst. Fish. Mgmt.,* **3**, 9-11.

Priede, I. G. and Young, A. H. (1977). The ultrasonic telemetry of cardiac rhythms of wild brown trout (*Salmo trutta* L) as an indicator of bio-energetics and behaviour. *J. Fish. Biol.,* **10**, 299-318.

Raymond, H. L. (1974). State of the art of fish branding. *Mar. Fish. Rev.,* **36**, 1-6.

Rinne, J. N. (1976). Coded spine clipping to identify individuals of the spiny-rayed fish Tilapia. *J. Fish. Res. Bd Can.,* **33**, 2626-2629.

Stuart, T. A. (1958). Marking and regeneration of fins. *Freshwat. Salm. Fish. Res.,* **22**, 1-14.

Thomas, A. E. (1975). Marking channel catfish with silver nitrate. *Progve Fish Cult.,* **37**, 250-252.

Trefethen, P. S. and Novotny A. J. (1963). Marking fingerling salmon with trace elements and non-radioactive isotopes. *Spec. Publs. Int. Commn NW. Atlant. Fish.,* **4**, 64-65.

Young, A. H., Tytler, P., Holliday, F. G. T. and MacFarlane, A. (1972). A small sonic tag for measurement of locomotory behaviour in fish. *J. Fish. Biol.,* **4**, 57-65.

11 *Marking invertebrates*

T. R. E. Southwood*

Invertebrates are marked for a variety of purposes: for studying their movement or the behaviour of individuals and particularly for estimating their population size by capture-recapture methods ('The Lincoln Index'). The requirements of all these experiments are the same, namely that:

(1) the marks should be recognisable and durable
(2) the animal's behaviour and survival is not affected

The second requirement does not always receive the attention that is due to it. This review is intended to outline the methods (further details of which are given in Southwood (1966, 1978)) and stress the techniques of handling and release.

Animals may be marked individually using a colour code of dots on various parts of the body. Examples of coding systems are Richards and Waloff's (1954) for grasshoppers (figure 11.1), Ehrlich and Davidson's (1960) for butterflies and Sheppard *et al.* (1969) for mosquitoes. It is important that the code should always contain the same number of marks (even for the 'early' numbers, that is 001 and not simply 1) because otherwise it is impossible to tell if no. 6 is really no. 6 or no. 86 with the '8' lost. However, the small size of most invertebrates poses considerable problems for individual marking, and this is not usually undertaken unless essential for the project.

Group marking methods are more widely used; that is, all the animals encountered or released on a particular day are given the same mark.

Group Marking Methods

Most marking methods have been developed for insects, although some have been applied to Crustacea and Mollusca.

Paints and solutions of dyes

Quick drying cellulose paints have been widely used. They may be applied with a pin ('head end') or a dried grass stem: care has to be exercised as they are so quick drying that they may not adhere properly. Felt pens and similar devices have been

*Professor T. R. E. Southwood, FRS, is Head of the Department of Zoology and Applied Entomology at Imperial College, London, and Director of the Imperial College Field Station at Silwood Park; he is the author of *Ecological Methods*, and has worked extensively on population studies of insects in the field. He is currently working on the relationship between habitat characteristics and the ecological strategies of their flora and fauna.

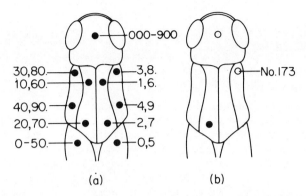

Figure 11.1 A system for marking grasshoppers individually
(developed by Richards and Waloff, 1954); (a) the full pattern, the
left hand number of each pair is represented by a white spot in the
position shown, and the right hand number by a red (or other
colour spot) in that position; (b) a marked grasshopper, number
173, showing the application of the pattern to an individual (after
Southwood, 1966).

found convenient and suitable 'dye dispensers' for larger insects. Dyes may be
dissolved in aqueous or alcoholic solutions as appropriate, and sprayed on to the
insect. The advantage of this method is that it reduces handling; its disadvantage
is that sense organs may be impaired unless the spray is carefully directed.

Dyes in powder form

Both fluorescent or non-fluorescent dyes have been used for marking hairy animals
and are applied from a 'puffer' or by agitating the dust by an air-stream. Fluorescent dyes [particularly Helecon] are usually to be preferred, as they may be detected under ultraviolet light while the insect is still alive, perhaps even in the field,
and after dark. Other dyes usually have to be detected by dropping acetone, or
some other solvent, on the insect; the dye in solution drips to form a coloured
spot on white blotting paper or filter paper placed below it.

Labels

Small labels giving limited information may be attached to the wings of butterflies,
locusts and other large insects. Care must be taken to ensure that the insects are
fully mature, otherwise the teneral wings may be distorted by the adhesive (Sello-
tape or a quick-drying glue).

Mutilation

Clearly such marks can only be made in non-living tissue, where they will not
affect behaviour. The teeth on the carapaces of crabs seem to provide one such
site, here notches may be made without detriment. The elytra of beetles are
another site.

Marking by injection

Crustacea have been marked by injecting non-toxic dyes (marking inks) into the
centre of the abdomen.

Self-marking with coloured materials

These techniques have noteworthy advantages in that the amount of handling is
considerably reduced; where the mark is internal, it provides a method of marking
immature stages that is carried into adult life and not lost at ecdysis. Calco Red
and related oil soluble dyes have been found very satisfactory for marking moth
larvae; the dye may be incorporated in a vegetable oil and included with the larval
diet (see also Daum *et al.*, 1969). When many flies (Diptera) emerge from their
puparia, they have an organ (the ptlinum) on the head which is extendable and
functions rather like a ram to force their way through the soil or other material.
Once the fly is 'free' the ptlinum retracts permanently, but its position is marked
by a U-shaped ptlinal suture on the face. It has been found that if a fluorescent
powder is incorporated in the media around the puparia, the adults of fruit-flies,
house-flies and probably several other types are 'self-marked' at emergence: their
ptlinal suture glows under ultraviolet light.

Self-marking with rare elements

This is a very recent technique and involves the use of elements such as rubidium
and dysprosium that are rare in the earth's crust. The element is included in the
insects' food and incorporated (unfortunately usually only briefly) in their tissues.
Its detection depends on killing the insect and placing it in the neutron beam of a
nuclear reactor: the gamma emission spectra are then analysed and the rare element
will give a characteristic and unusual peak in the spectrum (Berry, Stimman and
Wolf, 1972).

Radioactive isotopes

Radioactive isotopes may be utilised as external or internal labels, or incorporated
into the animal's tissues. Labels may be detected in the field, but tissue-incorporated
marks have to be detected in the laboratory, usually by X-ray film. Radioactive
cobalt (^{66}Co), iron (^{59}Fe) and tantalum (^{182}Ta) are common labels. Their attachment to the exterior of the insect's body presents some problems (Sanders and
Baldwin, 1969); if placed internally these labels need to be gold plated to protect
them from corrosion and the insect from toxic effects (Fredericksen and Lilly,
1955). It has been found that labels with high activity may cause malformations,
even labels of lower strength must undoubtedly affect behaviour. A reasonable
guideline seems to be that the initial dose in labels should not exceed 10 μCi and
should be as small as possible compatible with detection.

Radioactive phosphorus (^{32}P) and sulphur (^{35}S) are the isotopes most commonly incorporated into insects through feeding. They may be mixed with a sugar
solution and 'offered' on filter papers (Lewis and Waloff, 1964), or they may be
incorporated in the host plant (Wiegert and Lindeborg, 1964). One advantage of

this method is the very low levels of radioactivity that may be used [for example, 0.5 μCi/l for ^{32}P and 20 μCi/l for ^{35}S (Lewis and Waloff, 1964)].

On recapture the marked animals are identified by exposing them to X-ray film; different levels of masking enable phosphorus and sulphur-marked animals to be separated (Gillies, 1958).

Handling

Insects are commonly anaesthetised for marking, but many anaesthetics have been shown to prematurely age honey-bees, and they presumably have similar effects on other insects. Chilling to between 1 and 5 °C is probably the best method of rendering them inactive; if an anaesthetic is to be used carbon dioxide is preferable.

Murdoch (1963) designed a method for holding beetles under a net while they are marked, and more delicate types can be held by a suction tube (Muir, 1958).

Certainly handling should be kept to a minimum and care should be taken that the mark in no way impedes the animals movement or sense organs. After marking the insects should be kept in uncrowded conditions.

Release

The release of the animal after marking is an operation that is seldom given adequate consideration. A few methods, such as spraying a dye or 'painting' a coloured dot, may be done in the field, depending on the animals' size and activity. Field marking is usually to be preferred, for studies (for example Greenslade, 1964) have shown that marked insects can show abnormal movement soon after release.

If the animal has to be marked in the laboratory, two approaches can be used to minimise the effect of the handling disturbance (in addition to the precautions already outlined). For example, the many species which have a marked periodicity of activity should be released during the inactive period, preferably at its start. It is especially important to avoid the release of small flying insects in the middle of the day, when their escape flights may carry them beyond the shelter of the habitat into winds or thermals that can transport them for miles. Of course, only apparently healthy, unharmed individuals should be released.

Secondly, if the purposes of marking are for a mark and recapture experiment, the release sites should be chosen carefully and scattered throughout the habitat. It is essential that the marked animals mix with the rest of the population; this may be checked to some degree by a comparison of the ratio of marked to unmarked individuals in the samples from various parts of the habitat; the significance of the difference may be checked by a χ^2 test (Iwao *et al.*, 1963).

References

Berry, W. L., Stimman, M. W. and Wolf, W. W. (1972). Marking of native phytophagous insects with Rubidium: a proposed technique. *Annls. ent. Soc. Am.*, **65**, 236–238.

Daum, R. J., Gast, R. T. and Davich, T. B. (1969). Marking adult boll weevils with dyes fed in a cottonseed oil bait. *J. econ. Ent.,* **62**, 943-944.

Ehrlich, P. R. and Davidson, S. E. (1960). Techniques for capture-recapture studies of Lepidoptera populations. *J. Lep. Soc.,* **14**, 227-229.

Fredericksen, C. F. and Lilly, J. H. (1955). Measuring wireworms reactions to soil insecticides by tagging with radioactive cobalt. *J. econ. Ent.,* **48**, 438-442.

Gillies, M. T. (1958). A simple autoradiographic method for distinguishing insects labelled with phosphorus −32 and sulphur −35. *Nature,* **182**, 1683-4.

Greenslade, P. J. M. (1964). The distribution, dispersal and size of a population of *Nebria brevicollis* (F.) with comparative studies on three other Carabidae. *J. Anim. Ecol.,* **33**, 311-333.

Iwao, S., Mizuta, K., Nakamura, H., Oda, T. and Sato, Y. (1963). Studies on a natural population of the large 28-spotted lady beetle, *Epilachna viginioctoma-culata* Motshulsky. 1. Preliminary analysis of the overwintered adult population by means of the marking and recapture method. *Jap. J. Ecol.,* **13**, 108-117.

Lewis, C. T. and Waloff, N. (1964). The use of radioactive tracers in the study of dispersion of *Orthotylus virescens* (Douglas and Scott) (Miridae, Heteroptera). *Ent. exp. Appl.,* **7**, 15-24.

Muir, R. C. (1958). On the application of the capture-recapture method to an orchard population of *Blepharidopterus angulatus* [Fall.] [Hemiptera-Heteroptera, Miridae] . *Rep. E. Malling Res. Sta. 1957,* 140-147.

Murdoch, W. W. (1963). A method for marking Carabidae [Col.] . *Ent. mon. Mag.* **99**, 22-24.

Richards, O. W. and Waloff, N. (1954). Studies on the biology and population dynamics of British grasshoppers. *Anti-Locust Bull.,* **17**, 182pp.

Sanders, C. J. and Baldwin, W. F. (1969). Iridium-192 as a tag for carpenter ants of the genus Camponotus [Hymenoptera:Formicidae] . *Can. Ent.,* **101**, 416-418.

Sheppard, P. M., MacDonald, W. W., Tonn, R. J. and Grab, B. (1969). The dynamics of an adult population of *Aedes aegypti* in relation to dengue haemorrhagic fever in Bangkok. *J. anim. Ecol.* **38**, 661-702.

Southwood, T. R. E. (1966). *Ecological Methods.* 1st edn, Methuen, 391 pp.

Southwood, T. R. E. (1978). *Ecological Methods.* 2nd edn, Chapman and Hall (in press).

Wiegert, R. G. and Lindeborg, R. G. (1964). A 'stem well' method of introducing radioisotopes into plants to study food chains. *Ecology,* **45**, 406-410.

Section 3 *Marking by tissue removal and modification*

Ian F. Spellerberg

Marking animals by removal and modification of tissues attracts the attention and concern of many people, representing a wide range of scientific and humanitarian interests. But to judge from the four chapters in this section and comments received during the conference, there is general agreement on a number of important points concerning these kinds of marking. The first point is that, before undertaking a project, the research worker must consider carefully whether the animals in fact need to be marked—and if so, whether methods involving tissue mutilation are the appropriate ones. Other points of agreement can be summarised as guidelines for the investigator; they have been stated elsewhere, but I think it important in this context to summarise them again. The marking process should be as painless as possible, involving minimal stress for the animal and minimal opportunity for infection. It should interfere as little as possible with normal behaviour and with such natural processes as moulting, and it should result in a mark which provides valuable and reliable information in sufficient quantities to justify the hazards of marking.

The form and general characteristics of mammals make them relatively easy to mark without transgressing these guidelines. Dr Twigg's chapter shows that many specialised studies on mammals, both in the field and in the laboratory, have demanded special techniques for marking individuals; it is opportune that they be reviewed and evaluated carefully, in terms both of animal welfare and of the project objectives. Compared with mammals and birds, the form and structure of reptiles—especially snakes—make them more difficult to mark satisfactorily. Dr Swingland presents a wide review of methods of marking reptiles, while Mr Prestt and I deal in more detail with methods of handling and marking snakes, with particular reference to Mr Prestt's field studies of adders. Amphibians also are difficult animals to mark satisfactorily. Although not mentioned in the following chapters, there are a number of studies which should be noted. Breckenridge and Tester (1961) used radioactive materials, and Daugherty (1976) used freeze branding; Woodbury (1956) has published a good review of marking techniques for amphibians.

Rafinski (1977) has reported a valuable technique for marking amphibians in which skin autografts were used as tags on several hundred specimens of newts. The grafting was successful in more than 95 per cent of cases and individuals could be recognised in the field after three years.

Freeze branding is a new and specialised method of marking which has been used in a variety of studies, including work on molluscs (Anderson, 1973; Richter, 1973), fish, amphibians, reptiles and mammals. Mr Newton's review shows clearly that the freeze branding technique has very important applications, with many advantages which have yet to be explored fully.

Although there may be general agreement on guidelines for marking animals by mutilation, I am not sure that there is agreement on the training and supervision of research workers, especially those who are embarking on a marking programme for the first time. I suggest that training and supervision in these circumstances are essential, and I very much hope that these proceedings provide incentive for discussion on these lines.

References

Anderson, E. (1973). A method for marking Nudibranchs. *The Veliger*, **16** (i), 121-122.

Breckenridge, W. J. and Tester, J. R. (1961). Growth, local movements and hibernation of the Manitoba toad, *Bufo hemiophrys. Ecology*, **42**, 637-646.

Daugherty, C. H. (1976). Freeze-branding as a technique for marking anurans. *Copeia*, 1976 (4), 836-838.

Rafinski, J. N. (1977). Autotransplantation as a method for permanent marking of Urodele amphibians (Amphibia, Urodela). *J. Herpetol.*, **11** (2), 241-242.

Richter, K. O. (1973). Freeze-branding for individually marking the banana slug: *Ariolimax columbianus* G. *NW. Sci.*, **47** (2), 109-113.

Woodbury, A. M. (1956). Uses of marking animals in ecological studies: marking amphibians and reptiles. *Ecology,* **37** (4), 670-674.

12 *Marking mammals by tissue removal*

G. I. Twigg*

Many species of both wild and domestic mammal may be marked by the
removal of tissues, in such a manner that individuals may be recognised throughout the rest of their life. Some tissue removal techniques are less permanent and
at the same time less damaging to the animal. When selecting the most favourable
method, the research worker must choose the one which will do the job effectively
yet at the same time cause the least possible distress to the animal. As with most
marking methods the twin aims of the permanence of the mark and the ease
with which it can be seen have also to be taken into account, and the worker
has to balance these factors in making his final choice.

There is some prejudice against using tissue removal methods because of their
very nature; yet when carried out carefully and with the best interests of the
animal in mind, they may in fact occasion less distress in performing and less
trouble subsequently than the attachment of a variety of bands and tags. The
following methods are in common use in wildlife research as well as in the
veterinary and domestic sphere: ear, toe and fur clipping, tail docking, branding
and tattooing.

Ear Clipping

The ears of many mammals are convenient marking sites because they are often
relatively large and furthermore are situated at the topmost point of the animal,
enabling identification to be made at a distance without the need to recapture
the animal. One advantage of ear (and toe) clipping is that simple equipment
can be used, a point of some importance when carrying out field work in
remote areas.

Methods and equipment

The ears of small mammals such as rodents, hares and rabbits are either
punched (using the sort of punch sold by poultry food dealers as 'chicken
toe punches') or have small portions clipped out of the outer margin using fine
dissecting scissors. The latter should be sharp, and between individual animals

*Dr Graham Twigg is a Senior Lecturer in Zoology at Royal Holloway College, London.
His research has included studies of the Brown rat in British coalmines and rodent
infestations of sugar cane in the Caribbean; more recently he has worked on leptospirosis
and other diseases of wild mammals.

should be wiped clean and, preferably, sterilised in alcohol to reduce the transfer of blood parasites. A local anaesthetic is needed. Ethyl chloride is satisfactory and can be bought in 100 ml dropping bottles from Bengue and Co. Ltd, Mount Pleasant, Alperton, Wembley, Middlesex.

A good local anaesthetic is dichlorodifluoromethane (CCl_2F_2). This is bought as a pressurised refrigerant in handy aerosol cans. A fine plastic tube enables the jet to be directed to a very small area. The two brands we have used are 'POLAR SPRAY' produced by Medical Aerosols Ltd, London and 'ARCTON 12'.

Mice ears

The ears of wild mice, either the House mouse *Mus musculus* or the Wood mouse *Apodemus sylvaticus* are large enough and sufficiently lacking in hair to allow small punches or snips to be made so that individuals can be recognised. Blair (1941) used a punching technique in which 5 basic loci were utilised on the margin of each ear, one ear showing units and the other tens. Using ears alone 99 animals could be marked without repeating.

Berry (1970) working on the House mouse used three positions on each pinna, for making either a hole on the body of the pinna or a notch on its outer margin. With a code of hole, notch or double notch, nine combinations could be recognised on each ear (figure 12.1). Using the left ear for tens and the right ear for units, a series of 99 is possible or, by keeping the sexes separate, 2 x 99. Ears occasionally became torn, but unless this happened the number remained unequivocal for life. Short and Woodnott (1963) give a useful pictorial representation of ear clipping codes for mice.

The ears of voles and shrews are too small and hairy to allow this method of marking to be used.

Rabbit and cattle ears

Methods similar to the above have been in use for these species for many years. Today, however, light plastic markers in bright colours are used as ear tags. With rabbits they have the advantage that recapture is unnecessary for identification of individuals.

Web punching in beavers

Akin to ear punching is the method of punching holes in the foot webs of aquatic mammals such as the beaver (Aldous, 1940). The equipment is simple: a hand operated leather punch and some rubber tubing. The toes are spread and a hole is punched through the web with the cutting tube. A clean cut hole is ensured by placing a thin pad of rubber or leather on the heel of the punch, so that the cutter goes completely through the flesh.

When the toes are spread to open the web, care is necessary to make sure that the upper and lower parts of the skin are not pulled unevenly, because the dorsal and ventral parts of the web are separated by fasciae which allow some flexibility. Failure to do this results in the upper and lower holes not corres-

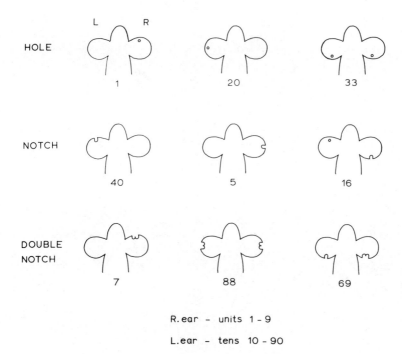

Figure 12.1 Ear clipping in mice.

ponding, and instead of a hole there appears a very small scar that is difficult to find.

The advantages claimed for this method are that it does not handicap the animal, and that while the tail often shows scars from fighting, the hind foot rarely does so. The marks are permanent and such a method can be used on muskrat and other web-footed species.

Toe Clipping

Technique

This is probably the most widely used method of individually marking small mammals, especially rodents. The technique consists of removing the nail and first joint of the toe with sharp dissecting scissors. It is no use merely cutting off the nail because this will grow again. A local anaesthetic is used, although in practice it is found that there is even less bleeding when no anaesthetic is used than the small amount which takes place when one is applied.

Suitable species for toe clipping

It is desirable that not more than two toes be treated on one animal and to

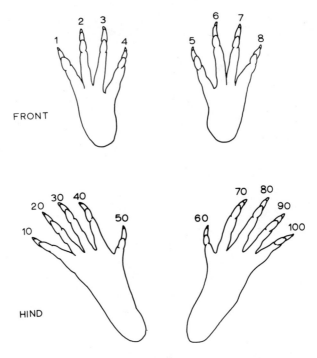

Figure 12.2 Toe clipping and numbering convention.

achieve this the toes of the animal are numbered. In a small rodent, holding the animal belly uppermost in the hand, the following numbering sequence is used. Reading from let to right the four toes of the right front foot are 1–4 and the four of the left front foot, again from left to right, are 5–8. The tens are counted on the hind feet which have five toes apiece. Starting with the right hind foot, left to right, the five toes are numbered 10–50 inclusive and the left hind foot is 60–100 inclusive (figure 12.2). In a sequence certain numbers must be omitted for example 9, 19, 29 . . . .

The shrews, which have five toes on each front foot, offer more combinations, but on rodents one series of 109 animals can be marked by toe clipping alone.

Most commonly the method is used on mice, voles and shrews but various other species have been marked in this way. Yerger (1953) clipped the toes of chipmunks. He used no anaesthetics and reported no infections. Golley (1961) toe clipped the Cotton rat *Sigmodon hispidus* and Reynolds (1945) used the method on a larger animal, the Opossum *Didelphis virginiana*. Sanderson (1961) clipped the toes of young opossums while they were still in the marsupial pouch but with this technique all members of a litter were marked the same way with no attempt to give an individual number to an animal.

It is possible to extend the number of marked animals using a method such as that adopted by Melchior and Iwen (1965) to mark Arctic ground squirrels *Citellus undulatus*. The authors claim that their system provides 899 numbers with the limitation of removing no more than one toe per foot. Many workers would be unhappy at the removal of as many as four toes and most small mammal research workers remove no more than two toes per animal.

'Footprinting' small mammals

To obtain a more natural view of small mammal movements, by avoiding repeated live trapping, some field workers have attempted to 'footprint' small mammals. After first catching and toe clipping the subsequent movements are identified by finding the individual footprints on specially prepared surfaces. Various workers have investigated this approach, including Mayer (1957), Justice (1961), Brown (1966, 1969) and Bailey (1968, 1969).

Fur Clipping

A less permanent but less damaging method of marking is to remove some of the fur in an identifiable pattern. The fur of mammals consists of two types of hair, the guard hairs and the underfur, the latter being of a different colour from the guard hair. Thus, when the brown dorsal guard hairs of, for example, a Wood mouse are clipped the grey underfur contrasts strongly with the surrounding brown. To make the mark the scissors are held flat, parallel to the body surface and gentle snipping of only a millimetre or two at a cut will remove the brown hair and reveal the dark underfur. As soon as a dark patch is evident the cutting has gone far enough and on no account must a bald patch be made. The diameter of each mark need not exceed five millimetres. Figure

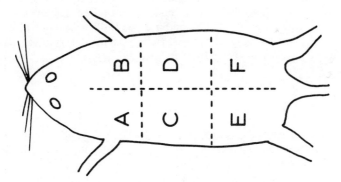

Figure 12.3 Fur clipping on the dorsal surface of a small mammal.

Marking code:
Animals 1–6 clipped A, B, C, D, E, F,
Animals 7–11 clipped AB, AC, AD, AE, AF
Animals 12–15 clipped BC, BD, BE, BF
(Note there is no BA as this would be the same as AB.)
As the series progresses, so more omissions are made to avoid duplication. Thus: CD, CE, CF.
By using 3 clips the series is extended viz. ABC, ABD, ABE, etc.
No more than 3 clips should be used.

12.3 shows the division of the dorsal surface of a small mammal into identification areas and it should be noted that *no more* than three sections should be clipped. This method is relatively short lived and at best the animals can only be identified until the next moult. There is, however, no element of pain, the process is very easy and it is a useful method of field identification.

The spines of hedgehogs may be clipped in patterns enabling the identification of individual animals.

Clipping hair tips—mice and voles

With such small animals the number of marks available is much less than with toe clipping. By dividing the dorsal surface into left and right shoulder, left and right flank and centre sections (figure 12.3) enough animals can be marked individually to be useful. When clipping, the best way to hold the animal is by the loose skin at the nape. The animal cannot turn to bite if sufficient skin is grasped. This operation can be carried out by one person but it is easier with two, one holding and one snipping.

Burning hair tips

This method is rarely used since clipping is equally satisfactory and safer.

Depilatories

There are various techniques for removing the hair. Mechanical clippers are available and in some cases chemical substances may be used. On large animals actual numbers may be marked with a depilatory and these can be viewed at distance without re-trapping. Chitty and Shorten (1946) working on wild Norway rats *Rattus norvegicus* employed a chemical depilatory paste, the numbers on the rats remaining visible for 2 or 3 weeks.

Tail Docking

Legislation in recent years has restricted tail docking. For identification purposes the removal of the terminal hairs on the tip of the tail is the nearest the wildlife biologist comes to tail docking, and this technique is clearly limited to only a few animals and does not have the scope of extensive individual identification of other methods.

Branding

This method consists of using either heat or low temperatures to make a permanent mark on the skin or horns. Especially in the case of heat branding there is removal of horn, fur and skin in making the mark.

Heat branding

Domesticated species
The horns of sheep and the tough, leathery skin of cattle are the main sites of
marking with owner's marks for identification. Heated branding irons of the
type which have been in use for many years are still widely used.

Wild mammals
Various wild species have been branded, especially the aquatic species for whom
other marking methods are rarely appropriate. The one exception that has come
to light is the attempt by Svihla (1934) who branded young Deermice *Peromyscus
maniculatus artemisiae* with a hot wire. The method was useful for the first four
weeks of life. By the fourth week hair growth made the brand indistinct and
then corresponding patches of hair were cut off with scissors.

Seals in particular have been most commonly marked by heat methods. As
early as the 1930s various workers were using brands in seal research. Lindsey
(1937) marked Weddell seals. When possible the brand was placed dorsally a foot
or two in front of the tail, the number first being clipped into the fur with shears.
Young animals were not branded until shortly before completion of the post-
natal moult. Using this system it was possible to follow 243 Weddell seals. The
permanence of such brands may be judged from the fact that Perkins (1945)
was able to read brands 5 to 7 years later in the Weddell seal and Scheffer (1950)
reported visible brands after 20 years in the Alaskan fur seal.

More recently, Rand (1950) used hot branding on seals in much the same way
as Lindsey. On adult seals the marks healed quickly, leaving a clear black outline
but they were progressively obliterated by growth and replacement of the coat.

The flat, thick tail of the beaver presents a suitable branding surface which
Bradt (1938) turned to after finding that tags on the tail were lost. On the beaver
tail the brand numbers were easily read when fresh, and could even be seen when
the animals were swimming under water. After one year only those numbers made
up of straight lines, for example 1 and 7, could be accurately deciphered. The
others were marred and obscure due to shedding or sloughing away of the scaly
surface adjacent to the curves and angles. As a result he became restricted to
combinations of 1 and 7 which were adequate for a limited number but could not
be used for large numbers. A code system was therefore adopted in which
straight lines were branded around the periphery of the tail with units on the
upper surface and tens on the undersurface.

It is clearly of value if the marks can be seen at a distance so that retrapping is
unnecessary. Aldous and Craighead (1958) branded Nelson bighorn sheep *Ovis
canadensis nelsoni* in southern Nevada with a horn brand similar to that used on
cattle. Each sheep had a different brand number and these could be read at 500
yards with a 30 × telescope. The method was further refined by outlining the
brand with paint so that the number could be more easily read.

Freeze branding

This is the most modern method and works by destroying the pigment-producing
process in the marked area and thus producing white fur. It was shown by

Farrel, Koger and Winwood (1966) to produce lasting identification marks on cattle, dogs and cats. The method must be carefully tested for each species so that the melanocytes are killed but not hair follicles in contact with the iron. For further discussion see chapter 15.

Hadow (1972) tested freeze branding on Fox squirrels *Sciurus niger*, Abert's squirrel *S. aberti*, male Hooded rats *Rattus norvegicus*, and adult and neonatal House mice *Mus musculus*. A copper branding iron which was cooled in a mixture of carbon dioxide ice and alcohol was applied to an area of shaved skin. Applications of 25–40 seconds produced clear white brands on squirrels, whereas 20–35 seconds was sufficient on rats and mice. The optimal application time on neonatal mice increased from 4–7 seconds at 1–3 days of age to 10–15 seconds at 9 days of age. Statistical tests on mortality and weight gain showed no differences between freeze-branded neonates and control littermates. Manatees *Trichechus manatus* have been freeze branded successfully in Guyana, using copper brands cooled in liquid nitrogen (Bertram, personal communication).

Freeze branding is the only technique available that produces permanent marks for identifying small mammals at a distance, and which can mark neonates for life. Hadow anaesthetised all adults except those of the Fox squirrels. He pointed out that if the cooled iron was held to the skin for less than the optimum time it would result in hairs with normal or intermediate pigmentation, whereas too long an application retarded hair regeneration and stressed the animal unnecessarily.

Taylor (1969) tried the method on *Rattus norvegicus*. He used methoxy-fluorane to anaesthetise animals. The copper branding irons of cross section 6 x 30 mm and 18 mm diameter were cooled in a solid carbon dioxide/alcohol mixture (about $-70°C$) and applied for from 2 to 15 seconds. After 8 weeks flecks of white fur were evident. However, the method went awry with one rat which slowly turned white all over.

Lazarus and Rowe (1975) attempted freeze marking of rodents with a pressurised refrigerant, dichlorodifluoromethane ($CC1_2F_2$). They found that application for 4 seconds or longer was equally effective in marking both shaven and unshaven laboratory mice *Mus musculus*. Two rat species, *Rattus norvegicus* and *R. rattus*, were marked by applying refrigerant to unshaven skin for 5–10 seconds. Attempts to mark Coypu *Myocastor coypus* were less successful. One benefit of using this method is that the local anaesthetic effect produced by the refrigerant makes general anaesthesia unnecessary. Using this spray with a narrow diameter directing device the use of stencils to obtain more specific markings is clearly possible.

Tattooing

Where an animal has large, relatively hairless ears, for example rabbits, this method may be used. The membranous skin of the bat wing may be tattooed but Griffin (1934) came to the conclusion that banding was of more use. The tattoo was laborious to apply and difficult to read. Furthermore, it had to be read by transmitted light so that marked bats were unlikely to be returned by those finding them. Keith *et al.* (1968) tattooed the ears of Snowshoe hares. A Franklin Rotary Tattoo was used because its large numbers are easily read and new numbers can be quickly turned into position. The tattoo ink in a roll-on plastic bottle greatly assists this operation. With such a tattoo set, three numbers or letters can be stamped on the ear of a 1-month-old Snowshoe hare.

Various tattooing forceps are available: on the one hand for tattooing the ears of mice (Lane-Petter, 1951) and at the other extreme for Polar bears. Lentfer (1968) tattooed the bears on the upper lip and in the right axilla and groin with identifying numbers applied with tattoo forceps (No. 6321, Jensen Salsbery Laboratories, Kansas City, Missouri). Craighead *et al.* (1960) tattooed Grizzly bear in the axilla.

Veterinarians widely practise ear tattooing, and it was this lead which prompted wildlife biologists to use the technique on wild mammals.

References

Aldous, S. E. (1940). A method of marking beavers. *J. Wildl. Mgmt*, **4**, 145–148.

Aldous, M. C. and Craighead, F. C. Jr, (1958). A marking technique for Bighorn sheep. *J. Wildl. Mgmt*, **22**, 445–446.

Bailey, G. N. A. (1968). Trap shyness in a woodland population of Bank voles (*Clethrionomys glareolus*). *J. Zool., Lond.* **156**, 517–521.

Bailey, G. N. A. (1969). A device for tracking small mammals. *J. Zool., Lond.*, **162**, 533–534.

Berry, R. J. (1970). The natural history of the House mouse. *Fld Stud.*, **3**, 219–262.

Blair, W. F. (1941). Techniques for the study of mammal populations. *J. Mammal.*, **22**, 148–157.

Brown, L. E. (1966). Home range and movement of small mammals. *Symp. zool. Soc. Lond.*, **18**, 111–142.

Brown, L. E. (1969). Field experiments on the movements of *Apodemus sylvaticus* L. using trapping and tracking techniques. *Oecologia* (Berl.), **2**, 198–222.

Bradt, G. W. (1938). A study of beaver colonies in Michigan. *J. Mammal.*, **19**, 139–162.

Chitty, D and Shorten, M. (1946). Techniques for the study of the Norway rat *Rattus norvegicus*. *J. Mammal.*, **27**, 63–78.

Craighead, J. J., Hornocker, M., Woodgerd, W. and Craighead, F. C. Jr (1960). Trapping, immobilizing and color-marking Grizzly bears. *Trans. 25th N. Am. Wildl. Nat. Res. Conf.*, 347–363.

Farrell, R. K., Koger, L. M. and Winward, L. D. (1966). Freeze-branding of cattle, dogs and cats for identification. *J. Am. vet. Med. Ass.*, **149**, 745–752.

Golley, F. B. (1961). Effect of trapping on adrenal activity in *Sigmodon*. *J. Wildl. Mgmt*, **25**, 331–333.

Griffin, D. R. (1934). Marking bats. *J. Mammal.*, **15**, 202–207.

Hadow, H. H. (1972). Freeze-branding: a permanent marking technique for pigmented mammals. *J. Wildl. Mgmt*, **36**, 645–649.

Justice, K. E. (1961). A new method for measuring home ranges of small mammals. *J. Mammal.*, **42**, 462–470.

Keith, L. B., Meslow, E. C. and Rongstad, O. J. (1968). Techniques for snowshoe hare population studies. *J. Wildl. Mgmt,* **32**, 801–812.

Lane-Petter, W. (1951). Mouse ear tattooing forceps. *J. Anim. Techns. Ass.,* **2**, 15.

Lazarus, A. B. and Rowe, F. P. (1975). Freeze-marking rodents with a pressurised refrigerant. *Mammal Rev.,* **5**, 31–34.

Lentfer, J. W. (1968). A technique for immobilizing and marking polar bears. *J. Wildl. Mgmt,* **32**, 317–321.

Lindsey, A. A. (1937). The Weddell seal in the Bay of Whales, Antarctica. *J. Mammal.,* **18**, 127–144.

Mayer, W. V. (1957). A method for determining the activity of burrowing mammals. *J. Mammal.,* **38**, 531.

Melchior, H. R. and Iwen, F. A. (1965). Trapping, restraining, and marking Arctic ground squirrels for behavioral observations. *J. Wildl Mgmt.,* **29**, 671–678.

Perkins, J. E. (1945). Biology at Little America III. *Proc. Am. phil. Soc.,* **89**, 270–284.

Rand, R. W. (1950). Branding in field-work on seals. *J. Wildl. Mgmt.,* **14**, 128–132.

Reynolds, H. C. (1945). Some aspects of the life history and ecology of the opossum in Central Missouri. *J. Mammal.,* **26**, 361–379.

Sanderson, G. C. (1961). Estimating opossum populations by marking young. *J. Wildl. Mgmt ,* **25**, 20–27.

Scheffer, V. B. (1950). Experiments in the marking of seals and sea-lions. *United States Dept. Int. (Fish & Wildl. Serv.) Special Science Report (Wildl.), No. 4, Washington.*

Short, D. J. and Woodnott, D. P. (1963). *The A.T.A. Manual of Laboratory Animal Practice and Techniques.* Crosby Lockwood and Son, Ltd, London.

Svihla, A. (1934). Development and growth of deermice (*Peromyscus maniculatus artemisiae*). *J. Mammal.,* **15**, 99–104.

Taylor, K. D. (1969). An anomalous freeze-branding result in a rat. *J. Zool., Lond.,* **158**, 214–215.

Yerger, R. W. (1953). Home range, territoriality, and populations of the chipmunk in Central New York. *J. Mammal.,* **34**, 448–458.

13 *Marking reptiles*

Ian R. Swingland*

This chapter reviews methods of marking reptiles (other than snakes; see
Spellerberg and Prestt, chapter 14) for ecological research. Marking methods or
systems mentioned are those used for future identification of an individual
in the hand or at a distance, and those used for identifying groups of individuals
with common characteristics, for example age cohorts or all individuals inhabit-
ing a region at a particular time.

Methods

The criteria for assessing suitability of a marking technique are that it should not
induce pain or stress, is unlikely to cause infection, will not inhibit movement,
and does not cause shedding of skin or scutes. It should where necessary be
permanent or long lasting, easily read, and adaptable to all size and age groups
of the animals. It should be easy to apply in field or laboratory, involving easily
made equipment and low-cost materials, and remain useful for identification
after death. The main methods of marking reptiles are scale-clipping, tattooing,
toe clipping, shell-notching, painting, tagging, branding and radiotelemetry, and
individuals may sometimes be recognised by natural marks.

Scale clipping

This is used almost exclusively for snakes (Blanchard and Finster, 1933; Conant,
1948; Spellerberg and Prestt, chapter 14). Fitch (personal communication)
used the method on Legless lizards *Ophisaurus*.

Tattooing

First used by Woodbury (1948), this method involves subdermal introduction of
a permanent dye to form readable marks. Dark skin cannot be marked in this
way, though ventral surfaces are usually pale enough to be tattooed successfully.
Modern dyes and inks are less liable to fade than the ones used by Woodbury.

*Dr Ian Swingland is a graduate of the Universities of London and Edinburgh, where he
worked on vertebrate memory and communal roosting. After a year in the Kafue National
Park, Zambia, setting up a monitoring programme to study large mammal ecology in
miombo woodland he joined the Animal Ecology Research Group, Oxford. He is currently
studying population regulation and the ecology of the giant tortoise of Aldabra Atoll,
Indian Ocean.

Toe clipping

In this most widely used method of marking lizards (Bellairs and Bryant, 1968) terminal phalanges of digits are amputated to a coded pattern (Stebbins and Robinson, 1946; Sexton, 1967; Bustard, 1968, 1969*a* and *b*, 1970, 1971; Pianka and Parker, 1972, 1975; Broadley 1974*a* and *b*; Ferner, 1974; Krekorian, 1976).

The coding system used by Broadley (1974*a*) on the Tree agama *Agama cyanogaster* involves using the left forefoot for a standard recognition mark, the middle digit being amputated. The right forefoot denotes the hundreds, the left hindfoot tens and the right hindfoot units. On each of these feet the first (inner) toe counts 1, the second toe 2, the third toe 4 and the fifth (outer) toe 7. The fourth toe is unsuitable for marking. By different combinations of toe clipping all identification numbers between 1 and 9 can be marked. Broadley (1974*a*) states that the amputations cause the lizard little inconvenience, the longest (fourth) toe on the hindfoot is never amputated, and at least two other toes always remain on each foot. When marking chameleons Broadley (1974*b*) followed approximately the same scheme but adapting it for the difference in foot structure. On the forefeet the toes are grouped together into an outer bundle of two and an inner bundle of three. All chameleons are given a standard mark by removing the front inner claw on the left forefoot, thus indicating a marked specimen. On the right forefoot the front outer claw is removed to indicate numbers in the '100' series. On the hindfeet the arrangement of toe bundles is reversed, three in the outer bundle and two in the inner. It is difficult to remove the middle claw of three, so this one is always left intact. On the hindfeet the front outer claw represents 1, rear outer 2, front inner 4 and rear inner 7, the remaining numerals being indicated by removing the two claws that add up to the required figure. The right hind foot is used for marking units and the left hind foot for marking tens. A major drawback is that hatchling chameleons (22–25 mm snout-vent length (SNV)) are too small to make it possible to remove selected toes with any accuracy under field conditions.

Bustard (1969*a*) found that initial markings (by toe clipping) had a disturbing effect on the gekkonid lizard (*Gehydra variegata*). Thirty-nine per cent of marked individuals were not seen again, and only 19 per cent were recaptured in the month following marking. Nevertheless subsequent recaptures of marked animals were high. Although Bustard (1969*b*) recorded no cases of natural loss of portions of the toes by the geckos *Diplodactylus williamsi* and *Gehydra australis*, he found three cases of natural loss of toes in the scincid lizard *Egernia striolata* (Bustard, 1970). However this loss was readily distinguished from the small portion removed in toe clipping. It is apparent that toe clipping is a very satisfactory technique for permanently marking lizards but its effects on the individuals' subsequent behaviour are unknown. Controlled experiments may be necessary to study this effect before any attempt is made at large scale marking for ecological research.

Shell notching

This method, first described by Cagle (1939) involves cutting notches in the marginals of the carapace with a hacksaw blade, file or sharp knife. The technique has been used successfully on freshwater turtles (for example Nichols, 1939; Emlen, 1969; Dolbeer, 1971; Ernst, 1971*a*; Ernst, Barbour and Hershey, 1974) a land tortoise (Rose and Judd, 1975) and marine turtles (for example Carr, 1967; Hirth, 1971; Hughes and Brent, 1972; Hughes, 1975).

Hughes (1975) used an ordinary leather punching tool on hatchlings of the Loggerhead turtle *Caretta caretta*. The site chosen for notching was the first marginal scute immediately left of the left supracaudal scale; or the first marginal immediately right of the right supracaudal. After notching, the wound was coated with gentian violet (1 per cent) and left to dry. The method proved to be quick, neat and although there was an initial reaction to the notching, the hatchling's behaviour returned to normal within a few minutes and no further signs of discomfort were observed. Notched hatchlings kept in captivity were harassed by other hatchlings biting the notched area but it is felt that this is unlikely to occur in the sea (Hughes and Brent, 1972). This method had limited applicability insofar as there are few individuals that can receive a unique mark unless a coding scheme is devised involving combinations of notches on different marginal scutes. Of 17 383 notched loggerhead hatchlings released over a 2 year period six were recovered (Hughes, 1975).

Rose and Judd (1975) marked the Texas tortoise *Gopherus berlandieri* by drilling small holes through the marginal scutes and underlying bone. Among freshwater turtles Ernst (1971*a*) used the notching technique with the Painted turtle *Chrysemys picta*. Notches were cut in the marginals of the carapace with a hacksaw blade or with a sharp penknife in the case of hatchlings or juveniles. He used the marking system code of Cagle (1939). Dolbeer (1971) working on the Eastern box turtle *Terrapene c. carolina*, used a file to mark the marginals. Some giant tortoises (*Geochelone gigantea*) on Aldabra Atoll were marked on the marginals by using a hacksaw blade in order to draw a few millilitres of blood for parasitological examination (Lowery 1971). Nine years later these individuals were still easily identifiable. This technique has also been used by Cloudsley-Thompson (1970) on *Testudo sulcata*. Scute carving and notching is used on the Galapagos giant tortoise *Geochelone elephantopus* (D. W. Snow, personal communication in Gaymer 1973; Viteri 1975).

Shell notching is a convenient and simple technique for marking chelonians. The mark is permanent (Moll and Legler, 1971) and in most cases, depending on body size, allows individual coding of many animals. Care must be exercised in notching to prevent bleeding and it is a good precaution to smear the notch with antiseptic, such as gentian violet, tetracycline or aureomycin. However, notching does not allow the individual to be recognised at a distance and may need to be used in conjunction with a more easily visible, but normally temporary method, such as painting or dyeing (Moll and Legler, 1971).

Painting or dyeing

An effective but temporary method, frequently used in association with more permanent but less easily read methods, is painting. It has been used on lizards (Noble, 1933) where paint or mercurochrome was used or by painting (white enamel) numbers on the back (*Uta mearnsi*: Hain, 1965). A lace monitor was painted with small orange spots of 'Lumigen' paint on each side of the head behind the eyes, which enabled it to be seen easily from 100 m through field glasses (Stebbins and Barwick, 1968). Pooley (1962) temporarily marked Nile crocodiles *Crocodylus niloticus* with paint.

As well as toe clipping, Jenssen (1970) used quick-drying paint and a coding scheme for his study of *Anolis nebulosus*. Individuals from outside his study area were painted with a blue spot on the body. Others, caught within his study area, were marked with yellow for males and orange for females. A spot on the neck counted 1, the back 2, the 'rump' 4 and the base of the tail 7, this giving, by combination, all digits between 1 and 9. The tail was painted white for 10s, green for 20s and blue for 30s. Fitch and Henderson (1976) have used a similar system on another anole.

Blanc and Carpenter (1969) used a red felt marking pen ('Onyx') on the iguana *Chalarodon madagascariensis*. Marks were made dorso-laterally on the shoulder, the middle of the back, and on the back legs. This system provided 60 combinations. Wilson (1968) painted numbers on Leopard tortoises *Testudo pardalis* as did Grub (1971) and Gaymer (1968) on Aldabran giant tortoises *Geochelone gigantea*; in both the latter studies the marks lasted for several years.

Tagging

Tags or discs bearing individual numbers have been used in several studies. They are easy to fix, clearly visible and usually outlast the wearer, though they may be lost through wear or cause infection. Bogert (1937) studied the growth rate of the Desert tortoise *Gopherus agassizi* and marked them with aluminium tags stamped with a number. Kaplan (1958) used commercially available aluminium bands with permanently embossed numbers (1–10 000). Two small holes were bored in the carapace margin, and the flange of the band was inserted into one of the holes and brought up through the other hole. This was then secured through the slot fastener. He found they were permanent and non-toxic. Hirth (1966) used stainless steel jaw tags on snakes and Pough (1970) and Pendlebury (1972) have used coloured plastic plugs also on snakes. Mohda (personal communication) tried using aluminium tags on the Nile crocodile *Crocodylus niloticus* but with little success.

Most of the tagging work has been done on marine chelonians. This involves the use of a stainless steel tag clamped on to the trailing edge of a front flipper. The tags are numbered on one face and on the other side are inscribed instructions for the finder in various languages. Adult females are usually the only ones tagged because they can be easily caught on a nesting beach. Hughes (1975) mentions using a small plastic tag on nestling turtles (see also McAllister *et al.*, 1965), large plastic 'Rototags' (Hughes *et al.*, 1967) and round yellow plastic tags normally used for sharks (Hughes and Mentis, 1967). However all plastic tags proved useless, and Hughes now uses Monel metal clinch tags supplied by the National Band and Tag Company (U.S.A.) with excellent results. Diamond (1976) used a metal tag on Hawksbill turtles *Eretomochelys imbricata* and Balasingam and Pong (1972) used both plastic and Monel metal tags on the Leathery turtle *Dermochelys coriacea*. They found the Monel metal tags difficult to apply as the flipper was too thick whereas the plastic tag (supplied by Dalton Supplies U.K.) was much easier to use. Nevertheless no longer-term trials were carried out.

Cloudsley-Thompson (personal communication) used coloured string bracelets tied around the limbs of geckoes *Tarentola annularis* but found that the animals always managed to get them off. However, by that time he had learned to recognise them individually. Spellerberg (personal communication) successfully used self-adhesive plastic tape as arm-bands on the Australian water skink *Sphenomorphus tympanum*.

A relatively new development, radioactive tagging (Griffin, 1952; Karlstrom, 1957; Harvey, 1965; Barbour and Harvey, 1968; Barbour *et al.*, 1969*a*, 1969*b*; Hirth *et al.*, 1969; Kramer, 1973), has only seldom been used on reptiles. Barbour *et al.* (1969*b*) used it on the Eastern worm snake *Carphophis a. amoenus*, Hirth *et al.* (1969) on the colubrids *C.c. mormon* and *Masticophis t. taeniatis* and the rattlesnake *Crotalus viridis lutosus*. The method of implanting the tag subcutaneously was described by Ashton (1975). Ward *et al.* (1976) drilled small holes 1 mm in diameter through the left 10/11 marginal scutes of the Spotted turtle *Clemmys guttata*. Waterproof acetate glue was used to anchor the radioactive pin (tantalum -182, 100 μCi, 1 x 5 mm, half-life 115 days). A portable beta-gamma survey meter and scintillation probe assembly was used to detect the individual. Apart from tantalum -182, cobalt -60 and iodine -131 have been used as tags; see also Linn (chapter 19).

This sytem does not allow recognition of individuals except by the position of the tag. It is useful for animals of secretive habit which burrow or use heavy cover. The half-life of the implant limits the time during which the mark is useful. The distance at which an individual can be sensed depends on (1) the sensitivity of the probe and meter, and (2) the strength of radiation from the tag.

Barbour and Harvey (1968) compared the behaviour and activity of radio-actively tagged and non-tagged rodents (*Microtus ochragaster, Baimomys taylori*) in the laboratory. They found no significant changes in the behaviour of the tagged individuals during a study period of 8 weeks. Harvey (1965) found that a 45 μCi ^{60}Co tag could be detected through 2 feet of soil, 3 feet of water or wood and 1.5 feet of limestone.

Branding

Branding with a hot iron was used by Woodbury and Hardy (1948) in their study of the Desert tortoise *Gopherus agassizi*. They found that if the brand was too light it would wear off after several years and if it was too deep regenerative changes would replace the burned portion. They also devised a coding scheme. Woodbury (1953) suggested 12-14 gauge wire to brand turtles and providing the brand was applied quickly a permanent mark was effected. Weary (1969) used the method on snakes whereas Clark (1971) applied brands to *Anolis carolinensis, Phrynosoma cornutum* and *Pseudemys scripta elegans*. He used 24 gauge (0.0201 inch) Hoskins chromal 'A' resistance wire (The Malin and Co., Cleveland, Ohio), which is 20 per cent chromium and 80 per cent nickel, for the brand. The heat source was a propane torch. Weary (1969) also tried an electric branding needle on two species of snake (Red-bellied *Storeria occipitomaculata*; Garter *Thamnophis sirtalis*). In the laboratory he used a mains-powered pyrographic needle whereas in the field he used a battery-powered soldering pencil.

Freeze branding (Lewke and Stroud, 1974) could be used on reptiles other than snakes. As a coolant they used Freon 12 (b.p. −21 °C) and Freon 14 (b.p. −41 °C) and shaped a brand from copper piping. They later improved on this by cutting a brand from synthetic foam and then styrofoam. In their opinion this method would be suitable for field use; disadvantages included a variable response by individuals to the brand, and the mark was not immediately obvious. For further information on freeze branding techniques see Newton, chapter 15.

Radiotelemetry

Radiotelemetry has been used in ecological studies of the larger reptiles such as the Lace monitor (Stebbins and Barwick, 1968) and the Aldabran giant tortoise (Frazier, 1971), in most cases to investigate thermoregulation. The technique has also been used with reptiles that are difficult to locate such as snakes (Fitch and Shirer 1971; Parker and Brown 1972; Brown and Parker 1976; Henderson *et al.*, 1976). With reduction in size of the transmitter and power source it is now possible to implant this electronic apparatus into smaller species without undue effects on behaviour (Fitch and Shirer, 1971).

Individual recognition by natural marks

Carlstrom and Edelstam (1946) first suggested the recording of skin patterns to identify individuals. They used the ventral scale pattern of snakes. Rand (1968), while studying the iguanas in Panama (*Iguana iguana*) recognised about 30 per cent of the population by the individual white markings on the shoulder region. Spellerberg (1977) has suggested that the neck scale pattern of lizards could be used for individual recognition; Harris (1964) used the gular pattern in his study on the Rainbow lizard *Agama agama*. In other instances abnormalities or scars can be used to identify an individual. Ernst (1971*b*), quoting Zangerl and Johnson (1957), mentions the use of shell abnormalities in 43 per cent of 118 species of turtle. Moulton (1963) used the scarring on the head of a Leatherback turtle *Dermochelys coriacea* to recognise the same individual again.

A Case History—the Aldabran Giant Tortoise

Gaymer (1973) used numbered titanium discs fixed into depressions cut into the scute of *Geochelone gigantea* using a metal–resin adhesive. Seven hundred tortoises were marked during field trials on Aldabra Atoll in 1969 and 1970. A further 6182 were marked during 1973/74 by Bourn (Bourn and Coe, 1978).

The aims in developing a marking technique for the Aldabran tortoise were to (1) take advantage of the large shell surface to attach a disc thus becoming an integral part of the skeleton, (2) avoid the problems of a protruding tag, (3) carry clear and ample information and (4) provide a safe and permanent mark at a reasonable cost (in both time and money) per animal.

Bourn (Bourn and Coe, 1978) used a modification of Gaymer's method by

Figure 13.1 An exploded view of the special bit used in cutting the depression for the disc.

cutting the round depression into the scute using an electric drill with a special bit (figure 13.1) and power provided by a portable generator. The bit was pushed against the third dorsal scute and a depression 1–2 mm deep was made. This was filled with freshly mixed 'Devcon F' aluminium-epoxy resin and a cleaned numbered titanium disc was placed in the depression, extruding resin around the edge. Self-adhesive tape was then placed over the disc temporarily holding it in place while the resin hardened (6 hours) and squashing the extruded resin flush with the carapace surface (figure 13.2). Each disc was numbered sequentially.

The disc (Imperial Metal Industries Ltd) was placed below the scute boss and slightly to the left or right (according to the year of marking). Bourn (1976) notes an annual disc-loss rate in the years following the 1969/70 markings of 0.5 per cent. He considers this to be acceptably low. However, if the discs had been made so that the stamped number protruded from the back surface of the metal then, if they had fallen out, the imprint of the number would have been left on the epoxy resin still remaining in the scute depression. This would have enabled animals which had lost their discs to be individually recognised.

Tortoises that were too small to be disced had numbers inscribed on the boss of their third dorsal scute using a rotary flexible drive shaft connected to an ordinary electric drill (figure 13.3). This method is quick and simple. Two years after being marked individuals were easily recognised in the field. No regeneration was noticed (figure 13.4). Recovery rate was 47 per cent of those marked, after a two-year period (Swingland, 1977; Swingland and Coe, 1978).

Both techniques (discing and etching) used on the Aldabran giant tortoise have proved highly effective. Nevertheless, the main disadvantage is that the equipment necessary to disc/etch large numbers of tortoises is heavy and cumbersome. However, Gaymer (1973) has described the use of a hand drill for cutting the disc depression if power is not available.

Figure 13.2 The marking disc in position.

Figure 13.3 The rotary bit in operation.

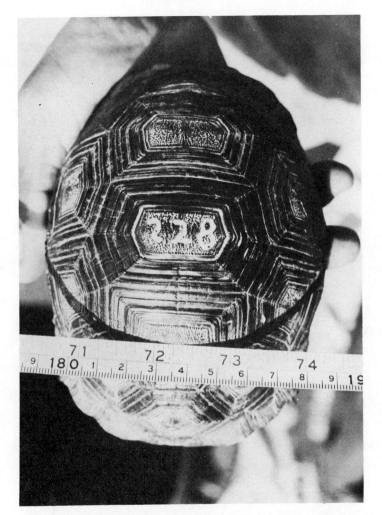

Figure 13.4 A marked tortoise two years after it had been etched.

Discussion and Conclusions

The wide range of reptilian body shapes and integumental structures, and their wide variety of habitats, make it difficult to devise standard methods of marking reptiles. To the proven methods of permanent marking, listed in this chapter, may be added such new and relatively untried methods as branding and radioactive tagging, which cannot be fully recommended without further field trials on a range of species. Individual recognition by natural marks remains the best method for species which show sufficient diversity between individuals.

In very few studies involving marking techniques has any attempt been made

to estimate the bias created by the marking process. All the methods described
in this chapter appear to cause mild adverse behaviour reactions (see, for example,
Bustard, 1969) which would affect certain categories of observations. The
Aldabran tortoise study was no exception to this generalisation. Once marked
with discs, giant tortoises quickly vacated the marking area. Though recovery
and recapture rates were high after seven or more months, the marking experience
upset the animals; marked animals were more wary of humans than unmarked
ones (Swingland, 1978). Scar tissue formed under the disc sites (figure 13.5).

Figure 13.5 The underside of a scute taken from a dead tortoise
showing the scar tissue formed under the disc site.

Though these effects had negligible influence on our long-term studies, short-
term observations of movement, distribution and estimates of home ranges
and population densities were likely to be biased. Small tortoises marked by
etching showed relatively little reaction to the marking process.

In all future studies attempts should be made to determine quantitatively
the degree and type of effect which handling and marking have on the subsequent
behaviour of study animals, and the length of time taken to revert to normal
behaviour (Swingland, 1978). With more attention paid to this point, and in
general to the health and welfare of the marked animals, many better
techniques for marking reptiles may still be developed.

Acknowledgement

I thank the Natural Environment Research Council for providing funds to work
on Aldabra Atoll, the Royal Society for providing the facilities and David Bourn
for some of the photographs used in this chapter.

References

Ashton, R. E. (1975). A study of movement, home range and winter behaviour of *Desmognathus fuscus* (Rafinesque). *J. Herpetol., 9,* 85–91.

Balasingam, E. and Pong, T. Y. (1972). Preliminary observation on nesting returns of the leathery turtle (*Dermochelys coriacea* Linn.) in Central Trengganu, Malaysia. *Malay. Nat. J., 25,* 6–9.

Barbour, R. W., Hardin, J. W., Shafer, J. P. and Harvey, M. J. (1969a). Home range, movements and activity of the dusky salamander *Desmognathus fuscus. Copeia,* 1969, 263–279.

Barbour, R. W., Harvey, M. J. and Hardin, J. W. (1969b). Home range, movements and activity of the eastern worm snake *Carthophis a. amoenus. Ecology, 50,* 471–476.

Barbour, R. W. and Harvey, M. H. (1968). The effect of radioactive tags on the activity of rodents. *Am. Midl. Nat., 79,* 519–522.

Bellairs, A. d'A, and Bryant, S. V. (1968). Effects of amputation of limbs and digits of lacertid lizards. *Anat. Rec., 161,* 489–496.

Blanc, C. P. and Carpenter, C. C. (1969). Studies on the Iguanidae of Madagascar. III. Social and reproductive behaviour of *Chalarodon madagascariensis. J. Herpetol., 3,* 125–134.

Blanchard, F. N. and Finster, E. B. (1933). A method of marking living snakes for future recognition, with a discussion of some problems and results. *Ecology , 14,* 334–347.

Bogert, C. M. (1937). Note on the growth rate of the desert tortoise *Gopherus agassizi. Copeia* 1937, 191–192.

Bourn, D. (1976). The giant tortoise population of Aldabra (Cryptodira: Testudinidae). *Zool. Afr., 11,* 275–284.

Bourn, D. and Coe, M. (1978). The size, structure and distribution of the giant tortoise population of Aldabra. *Phil. Trans. R. Soc. Lond. B., 282,* 139–175.

Broadley, D. G. (1974a). Marking/recapture studies on lizards at Umtali. *Rhodesia Sci. News, 8,* 307–309.

Broadley, D. G. (1974b). A preliminary report on a field study of Marshall's dwarf chameleon. *Rhodesia Sci. News, 8,* 310–311.

Brown, W. S. and Parker, W. S. (1976). Movement ecology of *Coluber constrictor* near communal hibernacula. *Copeia* (2), 225–242.

Bustard, H. R. (1968). The ecology of the Australian gecko *Heteronotia binoei* in northern New South Wales. *J. Zool., 156,* 483–497.

Bustard, H. R. (1969a). The population ecology of the gekkonid lizard (*Gehydra variegata* (Dumeril and Bibron)) in exploited forests in northern New South Wales. *J. Anim. Ecol., 38,* 35–51.

Bustard, H. R. (1969b). The ecology of the Australian geckos *Diplodactylus williamsi* and *Gehydra australis* in northern New South Wales. *Proc. Koninkl. Neder. Akademie van Wetenschappen* 72, 451–477.

Bustard, H. R. (1970). A population study of the scincid lizard *Egernia striolata* in northern New South Wales I. *Proc. Koninkl. Nederl. Adakemie van Wetenschappen* 73, 186–213.

Bustard, H. R. (1971). A population study of the eyed gecko, *Oedura ocellata* Boulenger, in northern New South Wales, Australia. *Copeia* 1971, 658–669.

Cagle, F. R. (1939). A system of marking turtles for future identification. *Copeia* 1939, 170-173.

Carlstrom, D. and Edelstam, C. (1946). Methods of marking reptiles for identification after recapture. *Nature,* **158**, 748-749.

Carr, A. (1967). *So Excellente a Fishe. A Natural History of Sea Turtles.* Natural History Press, New York, pp. 108-110.

Clark, D. R. (1971). Branding as a marking technique for amphibians and reptiles. *Copeia* 1971, 148-150.

Cloudsley-Thompson, J. L. (1970). On the biology of the desert tortoise *Testudo sulcata* in Sudan. *J. Zool. Lond.,* **160**, 17-33.

Conant, R. (1948). Regeneration of clipped subcaudal scales in a pilot black snake. *Chicago Acad. Sci. Nat. Hist. Miscellanea,* No. **13**, 1-2.

Diamond, A. W. (1976). Breeding biology and conservation of Hawksbill turtles, *Eretomochelys imbricata* L. on Cousin Island, Seychelles. *Biol. Conserv.,* **9**, 199-215.

Dolbeer, R. A. (1971). Winter behaviour of the eastern box turtle, *Terrapene c. carolina* L., in eastern Tennessee. *Copeia* 1971, 758-760.

Emlen, S. T. (1969). Homing ability and orientation in the painted turtle *Chrysemys picta* marginata. *Behaviour,* **33**, 58-76.

Ernst, C. H. (1971a). Population dynamics and activity cycles of *Chrysemys picta* in southeastern Pennsylvania. *J. Herpetol.,* **5**, 151-160.

Ernst, C. H. (1971b). Observations of the painted turtle *Chrysemys picta. J. Herpetol.,* **5**, 216-220.

Ernst, C. H., Barbour, R. W. and Hershey, J. (1974). A new coding system for hardshelled turtles. *Trans. Kentucky Acad. Sci.,* **35**, 27-28.

Ferner, J. W. (1974). Home-range size and overlap in *Scleoporus undulatus erythrocheilus* (Reptilia: Iguanidae). *Copeia* 1974, 332-337.

Fitch, H. S. and Henderson, R. W. (1976). A field study of the rock anoles (Reptilia, Lacertilia, Iguanidae) of Southern Mexico. *J. Herpetol.,* **10**, 303-311.

Fitch, H. S. and Shirer, H. W. (1971). Radiotelemetric study of spatial relationships in some common snakes. *Copeia* 1971, 118-128.

Frazier, J. F. (1971). Behavioural and ecological observations on giant tortoises on Aldabra Atoll. D. Phil. Thesis, Oxford.

Gaymer, R. (1968). The Indian Ocean giant tortoise *Testudo gigantea* on Aldabra. *J. Zool. Lond.,* **154**, 341-363.

Gaymer, R. (1973). A marking method for giant tortoises and field trials on Aldabra. *J. Zool. Lond.,* **169** (3), 393-402.

Griffin, D. R. (1952). Radioactive tagging of animals under natural conditions. *Ecology,* **33**, 329-335.

Grubb, P. (1971). The growth, ecology and population structure of giant tortoises on Aldabra. *Phil. Trans. R. Soc. Lond. B.,* **260**, 327-372.

Hain, M. L. (1965). Ecology of the lizard *Uta mearnsi* in a desert canyon. *Copeia* 1965, 78-81.

Hanks, J. (1969). Techniques for marking large African mammals. *Puku,* **5**, 65-86.

Harris, V. A. (1964). *The Life of the Rainbow Lizard.* Hutchinson Tropical Monographs, London.

Harvey, M. J. (1965). Detecting animals tagged with C^{60} through air, soil, water, wood and stone. *Trans. Kentucky Acad. Sci.,* **26**, 63–66.

Henderson, R. W., Nickerson, M. A. and Ketcham, S. (1976). Short term movements of the snakes *Chironius carinatus, Helicops angulatus* and *Bothrops atrax* in Amazonian Peru. *Herpetologica,* **32**, 304–310.

Hirth, H. F. (1971). Synopsis of biological data on the green turtle *Chelonia mydas* L. FAO Fisheries Synopsis 85.

Hirth, H. F., Pendleton R. C., King, A. C. and Downard, T. R. (1969). Dispersal of snakes from a hibernaculum in northwestern Utah. *Ecology,* **50**, 332–339.

Hirth, H. G. (1966). Weight changes and mortality of three species of snakes during hibernation. *Herpetologica,* **22**, 8–12.

Hughes, G. R., (1975). The marine turtles of Tongaland 8. *Lammergeyer,* **22**, 9-18.

Hughes, G. R., Bass, A. J. and Mentis, M. T. (1967). Further studies on marine turtles in Tongaland, I. *Lammergeyer,* **7**, 1–55.

Hughes, G. R. and Brent, B. (1972). The marine turtles of Tongaland 7. *Lammergeyer,* **17**, 40-62.

Hughes, G. R. and Mentis, M. T. (1967). Further studies on marine turtles, Tongaland, 2. *Lammergeyer,* **7**, 55–72.

Jenssen, T. A. (1970). The ethoecology of *Anolis nebulosus* (Sauria, Iguanidae). *J. Herpetol.,* **4**, 1–38.

Kaplan, H. M. (1958). Marking and banding frogs and turtles. *Herpetologica,* **14**, 131–132.

Karlstrom, E. L. (1957). The use of Co^{60} as a tag for recovering amphibians in the field. *Ecology,* **38**, 187–195.

Kramer, D. C. (1973). Movements of Western Chorus frogs *Pseudacris triseriata triseriata* tagged with Co^{60}. *J. Herpetol.,* **7**, 231–235.

Krekorian, C. O'N. (1976). Home range size and overlap and their relationship to food abundance in the desert iguana *Dipsosaurus dorsalis. Herpetologica,* **32**, 405–412.

Lewke, R. E. and Stroud, R. K. (1974). Freeze-branding as a method of marking snakes. *Copeia* 1974, 997–1000.

Lowery, R. A. (1971). Blood parasites of vertebrates on Aldabra. *Phil. Trans. R. Soc. Lond. B.,* **260**, 577–580.

McAllister, H. J., Bass, A. J. and Van Schoor, H. J. (1965). Marine turtles on the coast of Tongaland, Natal. *Lammergeyer,* **3**, 10–40.

Moll, E. O. and Legler, J. M. (1971). The life history of a neotropical slider turtle, *Pseudemys scripta* (Schoepft.), in Panama. *Bull. Los Angeles Mus. nat. Hist.,* **11**, 1–102.

Moulton, J. M. (1963). The recapture of marked leatherback turtles in Casco Bay, Maine. *Copeia* 1963, 434–435.

Nichols, J. T. (1939). Range and homing of individual box turtles. *Copeia* (1939), 125–127.

Noble, G. K. (1933). Experimenting with the courtship of lizards. *Nat. Hist.* **34**, 3–15.

Parker, W. S. and Brown, W. S. (1972). Telemetric study of movements and oviposition of two female *Masticophis e. taeniatus. Copeia* 1972, 892–895.

Pendlebury, G. B. (1972). Tagging and remote identification of rattlesnakes. *Herpetologica,* **28**, 349–350.

Pianka, E. R. and Parker, W. S. (1972). Ecology of the iguanid lizard *Caliisaurus draconoides*. *Copeia* 1972, 493-508.

Pianka, E. R. and Parker, W. S. (1975) Ecology of horned lizards: a review with special reference to *Phrynosoma platyrhinos*. *Copeia* 1975, 141-162.

Pooley, A. C. (1962). The Nile Crocodile (*Crocodylus niloticus*). *Lammergeyer*, 2, 1-55.

Pough, F. H. (1970). A quick method for permanently marking snakes and turtles. *Herpetologica*, 26, 428-430.

Prestt, I. (1971). An ecological study of the viper *Vipera berus* in Southern Britain. *J. Zool. Lond.*, 164, 373-418.

Rand, A. S. (1968). A nesting aggregation of iguanas. *Copeia* 1968, 552-561.

Rose, F. L. and Judd, F. W. (1975). Activity and home range size of the Texas tortoise, *Gopherus berlandieri*, in South Texas. *Herpetologica*, 31, 448-456.

Sexton, O. J. (1967). Population changes in a tropical lizard *Anolis limnifrons* on Barro Colorado Island, Panama Canal Zone. *Copeia* 1967, 219-222.

Spellerberg, I. F. (1977). Marking of live snakes for identification of individuals in population studies. *J. appl. Ecol.*, 14, 137-138.

Stebbins, R. C. and Barwick, R. E. (1968). Radiotelemetric study of thermoregulation in a lace monitor. *Copeia* 1968, 541-547.

Stebbins, R. C. and Robinson, H. B. (1946). A further analysis of a population of the lizard *Sceloporus graciosus gracilis*. *Univ. Calif. Publ. Zool.* 48, 149-168.

Swingland, I. R. (1977). Reproductive effort and life history strategy of the Aldabran giant tortoise. *Nature*, 269, 402-404.

Swingland, I. R. (1978). The natural regulation of giant tortoise populations on Aldabra Atoll: Movement. (in preparation)

Swingland, I. R. and Coe, M. (1978). The natural regulation of giant tortoise populations on Aldabra Atoll: Recruitment. *Phil. Trans. R. Soc. Lond. B*, (in press)

Viteri, L. H. A. (1975). Crecimiento Natural de los Galapagos de la raza *Geochelone elephantopus* penteri Isla Santa Cruz. *Revista de la Universidad Católica Ano III.* 8, 149-165.

Ward, F. P., Hohmann, C. J., Ulrich, J. F. and Hill, S. E. (1976). Seasonal microhabitat selections of spotted turtles (*Clemmys guttata*) in Maryland elucidated by radioisotope tracking. *Herpetologica*, 32, 60-64.

Weary, G. C. (1969). An improved method of marking snakes. *Copeia* 1969, 854-855.

Wilson, V. J. (1968). The leopard tortoise *Testudo pardalis babcocki*, in eastern Zambia. *Arnoldia*, 40, 1-11.

Woodbury, A. M. (1948). Marking reptiles with an electric tattooing outfit. *Copeia* 1948, 127-128.

Woodbury, A. M. (1953). Methods of field study in reptiles. *Herpetologica*, 9, 87-92.

Woodbury, A. M. (1956). Uses of marking animals in ecological studies: marking amphibians and reptiles. *Ecology*, 37, 670-676.

Woodbury, A. M. and Hardy, R. (1948). Studies of the desert tortoise *Gopherus agassizi*. *Ecol. Monogr.*, 18, 145-200.

Zangerl, R. and Johnson, R. G. (1957). The nature of shield abnormalitites in the turtle shell. *Fieldiana Geol.*, 10, 345-382.

14 *Marking snakes*

Ian F. Spellerberg and Ian Prestt*

Some groups of reptiles, for example chelonians, have been studied extensively in the field. By comparison the ecology of most ophidians is little known. This is perhaps not surprising because many kinds of snakes are difficult both to locate and to follow in their natural environment. Growing interest in ecosystems and concern for conservation have, however, stimulated research on this group, and several populations of snakes have recently been studied in the field. An important prerequisite has been the need to develop safe, reliable methods of capturing, handling and marking individuals. This chapter reviews recently developed methods of trapping and marking snakes, evaluating in detail the methods used in one particular study on the ecology of the Adder or Viper *Vipera berus* in southern England.

Capturing Snakes for Marking

Simple methods of capturing by hand are improved when the animal's ecology is known; knowledge of daily and seasonal behaviour helps in determining the best times for searching for animals (Spellerberg and Phelps, 1977), and information on population dispersion helps in planning routes for searching (Bauerle, 1972). In addition to capturing by hand, two further methods have been widely used for trapping snakes. The first takes advantage of the fact that many species, particularly those of temperate climates, winter inactively in communal dens. Dens provide excellent opportunities of capturing large numbers of snakes before they disperse in spring. Hirth *et al.*, (1969), Parker and Brown (1974) and Brown and Parker (1976*b*) describe techniques of placing fences or screens around wintering sites and catching emerging snakes.

The second method involves funnel traps, which have been used in many studies (Fitch, 1949; 1965; Fitch and Shirer, 1971; Prestt, 1971). Imler (1945)

*Dr Ian Spellerberg is a graduate of Canterbury University, New Zealand and La Trobe University, Australia. He worked on birds and mammals in Antarctica for three summers, studied reptile ecology in eastern Australia, then went on to study the temperature regulation of reptiles at the Max-Planck Institute for Behaviour and Physiology in West Germany. He is currently studying the ecology of European reptiles with particular emphasis on conservation methods.

Ian Prestt is a graduate of the University of Liverpool and a Fellow of the Institute of Biology. He held a number of posts in research and conservation in the Nature Conservancy, and was for a time Principal Scientific Officer in the Toxic Chemical and Wildlife Research Team at Monks Wood Experimental Station. In 1971 he became Deputy Director of the Central Unit on Environmental Pollution, and in 1974 Deputy Director of the Nature Conservancy. He is currently Director of the Royal Society for the Protection of Birds.

described and illustrated the typical funnel trap; Dargan and Stickel (1949), in an important early study, included suggestions as to how the traps should be spaced for population studies. Fitch (1951) illustrated and described in detail a simple funnel trap (a wire mesh cylinder with entrance cones at either end) used in conjunction with natural objects to guide snakes to the funnel mouths. In later accounts (Fitch 1960; 1963*b*) he evaluated the use of barriers, boards, screens and sheet metal drift fences as artificial guides. One effective arrangement (1963*b*) was to use a single barrier with a funnel trap at either end: usually the snake progressed along the barrier and into one of the traps.

For collecting smaller snakes, especially *Diadophis punctatus* and *Carphophis amoenus*, Clark (1966) used a simple funnel trap—basically a cone made from a sheet of metal mesh 45 × 60 cm inserted into a wide-mouth jar—with drift fences 2–5 m long. Later papers by Clark (1974) and Clark and Fleet (1976) compared numbers of snakes caught by hand with those caught in funnel traps, relative effectiveness varying with species and type of habitat. These papers also discussed fatalities arising from the use of different kinds of funnel traps. Bauerle (1972) also advocated use of funnel traps, noting that most deaths were due to small snakes (for example the Plains garter snake *Thamnophis radix*) becoming entangled in the wire mesh of the traps. This author also used pit traps in conjunction with short drift fences, but without success.

Marking and Identification of Individuals

Natural features

Regrettably, few attempts have been made to use natural markings for snake identification. Carlstrom and Edelstam (1946) reported a method of identifying individual Grass snakes *Natrix natrix natrix* based on variations in the patterns of black and white on the ventral surface. They showed by photography that patterns remained constant during the life of individuals and reported success in identification on recapture; in their view most other snakes are likely to have patterns suitable for individual identification. Carpenter (1952) and others have identified individuals with damaged tails and other natural marks, in conjunction with scale clipping and other marking schemes.

Radio markers and radioactive materials

Fitch and Shirer (1971) collected extensive and valuable data on movements and spatial relationships in large snakes (snout–vent length 50–151 cm) in Kansas, using radio markers similar to one developed by Shirer and Downhower (1968). Their paraffin-coated transmitters, self-pulsed, crystal-controlled transistor oscillators operating at 5 kHz intervals between 26.600 and 26.750 MHz, measured 50 × 21 × 14 mm; palped into the stomachs of the snakes, the emitted signals on distinctive carrier frequencies could be detected up to 130 m away. Fitch and Shirer noted that transmitters affected behaviour of large snakes only slightly; smaller Black racers *Coluber constrictor*, Garter snakes *Thamnophis sirtalis*, Copperheads *Agkistrodon contortrix* and King snakes *Lampropeltis calligaster*, in which the transmitters visibly distended the stomach, were more disturbed by their presence. Comparing rate and extent of movements of snakes marked by scale clipping with those carrying transmitters, they noted that most clipped snakes had empty stomachs when trapped, and seemed more vulnerable to trapping than their radio-carrying counterparts which behaved as though they had recently fed and were less inclined to travel. Similar radio-tracking techniques were used by Brown and Parker (1976*b*), Henderson, Nickerson and Ketcham (1976) and Parker and Brown (1972). Even in the dense vegetation of Peruvian rain forests Henderson *et al.* (1976) found this method successful with nocturnal and arboreal snakes.

Griffin (1952) has surveyed techniques of radioactive tagging in the field; see also recent population studies by Naulleau (1965) on Asp vipers *Vipera aspis*, and Barbour, Harvey and Hardin (1969) on the small worm snake *Carphophis amoenus*. In the latter, snakes 11–23 cm long were fitted subcutaneously with a 50–80 μCi tag of ^{60}Co alloy wire, implanted under the skin by hypodermic needle; the largest tags were 0.7 mm diameter and 5.00 mm long. Ten tagged snakes were each found on average 78.5 times, in home ranges of mean area 253 m^2. In earlier studies by these authors radiation from 45 μCi ^{60}Co tags was found to penetrate 0.61 m depth of soil, but not 0.76 m. Smith (1972) used 50 μCi ^{60}Co tags to label Eastern garter snakes *Thamnophis sirtalis sirtalis*, obtaining data on movements, habitat preference, individual activity ranges and hibernation sites. He noted that a young tagged snake, kept in the laboratory for ten months, showed no ill effects from this marking procedure.

Using methods similar to those of Barbour *et al.* (1969), Hirth, Pendleton, King and Downard (1969) tagged 196 snakes of three species; the tags were 400 μCi lengths of ^{182}Ta wire, 1 mm in diameter and 5 mm long. Most of the snakes were recovered at least once during one summer. Freshly tagged snakes could be detected at distances of 9 m on the surface, and 3 m when 30 cm below the surface in fine sand. After one half-life (115 days) range dropped to 6 m on the surface and 2 m in sand. Hirth and colleagues reported some necrosis due to radioactivity; after about one half-life a small, dark scab appeared over the implantation site. Damage was most noticeable in small Mormon racers *Coluber constrictor mormon* and in the thin tail of some Whip snakes *Masticophis taeniatus taeniatus*; Rattlesnakes *Crotalus viridis* were affected least. Clark and Fleet (1976) reported no gross evidence of injury, over a 35 months study period, in 27 Rough earth snakes *Virginia striatula*, using ^{182}Ta tags sited posteriorly in the body cavity.

Paints and surface tags

Quick-drying enamel paints and lacquers have been used for temporary markings, in particular for studies of moult (Dundee and Miller, 1968; Fitch, 1960; 1963*b*; Parker, 1976). Surface markers include small, bent aluminium plates sewn through the epidermis of the tails of Vipers *Vipera berus*, using aluminium thread (Viitanen, 1967); though easily seen, the markers caused local injury and were discarded. Pough (1970) inserted coloured plastic plugs through caudal scutes into the underlying muscles. In 23 snakes marked for periods exceeding one year only one plug was lost; there was no local inflammation, infection or necrosis, and the plugs did not interfere with ecdysis. Pendlebury (1972) attached coloured vinyl discs to the rattles of Rattlesnakes *Crotalis viridis*, threading monofilament nylon through the dorsal lobe of the second proximal segment. Ecdysis was not affected, and coded discs were successful in marking 27 snakes for at least ten months.

Tattooing and branding

Woodbury (1948, 1956) marked the dermal layer of snakes using a battery-operated tattooing needle, noting in his later study inaccuracies due to fading and misreading. Weary (1969) branded snakes with a 50 W pyrographic needle; brief contact was sufficient to burn a scale to the base without loss of blood, and there was no regeneration after two years. Clark (1971) branded amphibians and reptiles with chromium–nickel wire heated in a flame, achieving permanent marks on ventral and caudal scales. Lewke and Stroud (1974) freeze branded snakes, incorporating the angle system of coding developed by Farrell (1970). They reported varying success with different sizes, colours and species of snakes; the brands became clear only after the following moult, but caused no disruption of natural movement or moult, and no apparent pain or distress to the marked animal.

Scale clipping

Scale clipping or excision was first reported by Blanchard and Finster (1933) and has since achieved considerable popularity (Stickel and Cope, 1947; Fitch, 1949; Lang, 1969; Parker and Brown, 1974; Parker, 1976). Using a pair of fine scissors, the posterior edge of a ventral or caudal scute is clipped or nicked with a V-shaped incision, achieving a recognisable mark with minimal mutilation (figure 14.1).

Figure 14.1 Scale clipping in the snake *Coronella austriaca*. In this ventral view, the dark marks are where two pairs of scutes have been partly removed, exposing a darker coloured tissue beneath the overlapping scutes. If the anal scute is designated zero, then the code for the individual would be 7/8, 11/12.

Coding allows many snakes to be marked in one area. Blanchard and Finster (1933) counted caudal scutes from the anterior end of the tail; thus clipped second and fifth left, and fourth right, scale gave the number 254. An alternative code by Woodbury (1956) used the anal scute as a reference and numbered ventral scutes from the cloaca forward; clipping right or left sides of scutes provided many individual patterns of marking. Fitch (1960; 1963*a* and *b*) and Brown and Parker (1976*a*) describe other methods of coding suitable for snakes with single or double rows of caudal scales, and capable of accommodating almost 1000 animals with up to four clips. A simple code adopted by Prestt (1971) is described below.

Fraker (1970), working with Water snakes *Natrix sipedon sipedon*, reported that clips became unreadable after two years, and Conant (1948) found it hard to decypher clip marks on a large female Pilot black snake *Elaphe obsoleta obsoleta* after three years. Most other observers including Brown and Parker (1976*a*), Carpenter (1952), Spellerberg (1977), Spellerberg and Phelps (1977) and Tinkle (1957) have found clipping successful, with detectable scars present for the full length of their studies. Fitch (1963*a*) has advocated duplicate clipping on sub-caudals and ventrals, or at both anterior and posterior ends of the ventral scales, where regeneration is a problem. Great care is needed in clipping, to avoid damage to underlying tissues, infection, and interference with normal behaviour (Weary, 1969). Clipping is not recommended for snakes of less than one year old (Viitanen, 1967); mortality in this age group is already high, and handling should in any case be reduced as much as possible.

Handling and Marking Vipers: A Case Study

Prestt's study (1971) of the Viper or Adder *Vipera berus* in Dorset, England, depended much on successful marking and handling techniques, which are outlined below. In this study 166 individuals were marked and studied in the field for at least three summers. Further information was obtained from 194 post-mortem examinations and from studies of live individuals in an enclosure.

Handling

To overcome the problems and dangers of handling venomous snakes, five handling tubes of stiff but pliable transparent plastic were prepared. The tubes, of lengths and internal diameters 620×27 mm, 600×22 mm, 460×17 mm, 320×14 mm, 320×11 mm, were drilled at intervals for ventilation, and stoppered at both ends with corks attached to the tubes by threads. Snakes were held by the tail and introduced to the open end of the tube on the ground, usually moving in of their own accord.

Photography

A photographic record was made of the mid-dorsal pattern of juveniles, as a check against possible mistakes arising from incorrect clipping or rapid regrowth of cut scales; a fixed distance and lighting arrangement facilitated the photography, and the snake was held by enclosing it in the channel of an entomological setting board, and covered with a glass microscope slide.

Paint marking

Coloured spots of quick-drying enamel paint 1 cm in diameter were painted on the dorsal surface of the head and tail of each viper. Two colours were used, the anterior indicating the study area and the posterior the individual. For painting, the snakes were held in a gloved hand, and allowed to dry for three or four minutes in a botanical vasculum. A larger spot of brown paint, applied to the back of the neck, cracked and flaked when a snake swallowed food, and could therefore be used to detect when the animal had fed. Paint marks were lost when the skin was shed, but they served to identify shed skins and also to indicate frequency of shedding.

Scale clipping

The subcaudals of *Vipera berus* were considered to be too small for this purpose, so marking was carried out by clipping some of the large ventral scales using a fine pair of scissors. Once the anterior two-thirds of a viper had been contained within a snake-tube it could be laid on its dorsal surface and the ventral scales examined, counted and clipped with comparative ease (the ventral scale immediately anterior to the anal scale was designated number one). The clips were made at either edge of a scale, thus allowing a distinction of a left or right clip for each ventral. The clips on the right side of the body were referred to as the 'master' numbers, and these were associated with a series of different clips on the left side. In this way a large series of different combinations were provided.

As natural damage occasionally caused a tear resembling a clip mark on some of the ventrals, the clips were always made in pairs. The No. 1 and No. 2 ventrals were never clipped avoiding any possible damage to the cloaca. Clipping was never carried forward of ventral number forty, as this would have involved withdrawing too much of the snake's body from the snake-tube and there was increasing danger of miscounting once the larger numbers were reached. No single scale was clipped on both its right and left sides—a gap of at least one unclipped scale always being left between a right and left clipping. Both at the start and during the course of the work checks were made to assess whether or not the clipping of the scales produced any adverse effects. With only one exception, clipping proved to be harmless. The exception was an individual clipped a few days prior to sloughing. In this case the handling and clipping resulted in some slight malformation of parts of the new skin and some incomplete loss of the old. Following this incident, no further marking was attempted in individuals close to the time of sloughing—a condition readily distinguished by the dull opaque appearance of the snake.

During the course of the main study a total of 166 adult vipers were marked by clipping the ventral scales. Many of these were recaptured during the next three years and no ill effects of the clipping were found. For one population of 28 individuals during one season, their activities were followed almost daily and they were caught and examined weekly. No adverse effects were found and 18 were still alive and well at the end of the three years, 3 lived for two years, 6 for one year and 1 was killed by a farmer.

No difficulty was encountered in confirming marked individuals. Only slight regrowth of the cut scales occurred during the three years of the study and this regrowth was usually of a slightly coarser nature than normal growth and was often coloured orange and so contrasted with the black uncut scales. Natural damage equivalent to the cuts was common and healed readily as did the cut scales.

Conclusions and Recommendations

Having considered the range of techniques used for marking snakes, we conclude that—while paintmarking has useful short-term applications—carefully executed scale clipping is the most humane and reliable method of permanently marking individuals. Used in conjunction with photography (which takes into account the natural markings of individuals to be found in most species) scale clipping is of major value in studying such long-term aspects as population dynamics, and equally useful in short-term studies of moult and other short-term phenomena. Scale clipping is not, however, recommended for animals less than one year old.

References

Barbour, R. W., Harvey, M. J. and Hardin, J. W. (1969). Home range, movements and activity of the eastern worm snake *Carphophis amoenus amoenus*. *Ecology*, **50**, 470–476.

Bauerle, B. A. (1972). Biological productivity of snakes of the Pawnee site, 1970–71. *U.S.I.B.P. Grassland Biome Techn. Rep.*, No. 207, 1–72.

Blanchard, F. N. and Finster, E. B. (1933). A method of marking live snakes for future recognition, with a discussion of some problems and results. *Ecology*, **14**, 334–347.

Brown, W. S. and Parker, W. S. (1976a). A ventral scale clipping system for permanently marking snakes (Reptilia, Serpentes). *J. Herpetol.*, **10**, 247–249.

Brown, W. S. and Parker, W. S. (1976b). Movement ecology of *Coluber constrictor* near communal hibernacula. *Copeia* 1976, (2), 225–242.

Carlström, D. and Edelstam, C. (1946). Methods of marking reptiles for identification after recapture. *Nature*, **158** (4021), 748–749.

Carpenter, C. C. (1952). Comparative ecology of the Common garter snake (*Thamnophis s. sirtalis*), the Ribbon snake (*Thamnophis s. sauritus*), and Butler's garter snake (*Thamnophis butleri*) in mixed populations. *Ecol. Monogr.*, **22** (4), 235–258.

Clark, D. R. (1966). A funnel trap for small snakes. *Trans. Kansas Acad. Sci.*, **69** (1), 91–95.

Clark, D. R. (1971). Branding as a marking technique for amphibians and reptiles. *Copeia* 1971, (1), 148–151.

Clark, D. R. (1974). The Western ribbon snake (*Thamnophis proximus*): ecology of a Texas population. *Herpetologica*, **30** (4), 372–379.

Clark, D. R. and Fleet, R. R. (1976). The Rough earth snake (*Virginia striatula*): ecology of a Texas population. *Southwestern Nat.* **20** (4), 467–478.

Conant, R. (1948). Regeneration of clipped sub-caudal scales in a Pilot black snake. *Nat. Hist. Misc., Chicago Acad. Sci.*, **13**, 1–2.

Dargan, L. M. and Stickel, W. H. (1949). An experiment with snake trapping. *Copeia* 1949, (4), 264–268.

Dundee, H. A. and Miller, M. C. (1968). Aggregative behaviour and habitat conditioning by the Prairie ringneck snake, *Diadophis punctatus arnyi. Tulane Stud. Zool. Bot.,* **15** (2), 41–58.

Farrell, K. (1970). The angle numeration system. *Wash. State Univ., Math. Notes,* **14**, 3.

Fitch, H. S. (1949). Outline for ecological life history studies of reptiles. *Ecology,* **30** (4), 520–532.

Fitch, H. S. (1951). A simplified type of funnel trap for reptiles. *Herpetologica,* 7, 77–80.

Fitch, H. S. (1960). Autecology of the copperhead. *Univ. Kans. Publs Mus. nat. Hist.,* **13** (4), 85–288.

Fitch, H. S. (1963*a*). Natural history of the Black rat snake (*Elaphe o. obsoleta*) in Kansas. *Copeia* 1963, (4), 649–658.

Fitch, H. S. (1963*b*). Natural history of the Racer *Coluber constrictor. Univ. Kans. Publs Mus nat. Hist.,* **15** (8), 351–468.

Fitch, H. S. (1965). An ecological study of the Garter snake, *Thamnophis sirtalis. Univ. Kans. Publs Mus. nat. Hist.,* **15** (10), 493–564.

Fitch, H. S. and Shirer, H. W. (1971). A radiotelemetric study of spatial relationships in some common snakes. *Copeia* 1971, (1), 118–128.

Fraker, M. A. (1970). Home range and homing in the Watersnake *Natrix sipedon sipedon. Copeia* 1970, (4), 665–673.

Griffin, D. R. (1952). Radioactive tagging of animals under natural conditions. *Ecology,* **33** (3), 329–335.

Henderson, R. W., Nickerson, M. A. and Ketcham, S. (1976). Short term movements of the snakes *Chironius carinatus, Helicops angulatus* and *Bothrops atrox* in Amazonian Peru. *Herpetologica,* **32** (3), 304–310.

Hirth, H. F., Pendleton, R. C., King, A. C. and Downard, T. R. (1969). Dispersal of snakes from a hibernaculum in northwestern Utah. *Ecology,* **50** (2), 332–339.

Imler, R. H. (1945). Bullsnakes and their control on a Nebraska wildlife refuge. *J. Wildl. Mgmt,* **9** (4), 265–273.

Lang, J. W. (1969). Hibernation and movements of *Storeria occipitomaculata* in northern Minnesota. *J. Herpetol.,* **3**, 196–197.

Lewke, R. A. and Stroud, R. K. (1974). Freeze-branding as a method of marking snakes. *Copeia* 1974, (4), 997–1000.

Naulleau, G. (1965). Étude préliminaire de l'activité de *Vipera aspis* dans la nature. In *Distribution temporelle des activités animales et humaines* (ed. J. Medioni), Masson et Cie., Paris, pp 147–154.

Parker, W. S. (1976). Population estimates, age structure, and denning habits of Whipsnakes, *Masticophis t. taeniatus,* in a northern Utah *Atriplex-Sarcobatus* community. *Herpetologica,* **32** (1), 53–57.

Parker, W. S. and Brown, W. S. (1972). Telemetric study of movements and oviposition of two female *Masticophis taeniatus taeniatus. Copeia* 1972, (4), 892–895.

Parker, W. S. and Brown, W. S. (1974). Mortality and weight changes of Great Basin rattlesnakes (*Crotalus viridis*) at a hibernaculum in northern Utah. *Herpetologica* **30** (3), 234–239.

Pendlebury, G. B. (1972). Tagging and remote identification of Rattlesnakes.

Herpetologica, **28** (4), 349–350.

Pough, F. H. (1970). A quick method for permanently marking snakes and turtles. *Herpetologica,* **26** (4), 428–430.

Prestt, I. (1971). An ecological study of the Viper *Vipera berus* in southern Britain. *J. Zool. Lond.* **164**, 373–418.

Shirer, H. W. and Downhower, J. F. (1968). Radio tracking of dispersing Yellow-bellied marmots. *Trans. Kans. Acad. Sci.,* **71**, 463–479.

Smith, D. L. (1972). Movements of Eastern garter snakes (*Thamnophis sirtalis sirtalis*) tagged with radioactive cobalt. *Unpublished Ed. D. Thesis. Ball State University* Muncie, Indiana. 99 p.

Spellerberg, I. F. (1977). Marking live snakes for identification of individuals in population studies. *J. appl. Ecol.,* **14**, 137–138.

Spellerberg, I. F. and Phelps, T. E. (1977). Biology, general ecology and behaviour of the snake, *Coronella austriaca* Laurenti. *Biol. J. Linn. Soc.,* **9** (2), 133–164.

Stickel, W. H. and Cope, J. B. (1947). The home ranges and wanderings of snakes. *Copeia* 1947, (2), 127–136.

Tinkle, D. W. (1957). Ecology, maturation and reproduction of *Thamnophis sauritus proximus. Ecology,* **38** (1), 69–77.

Viitanen, P. (1967). Hibernation and seasonal movements of the Viper, *Vipera berus berus* (L.), in southern Finland. *Annls zool. Fenn.,* **4**, 472–546.

Weary, G. C. (1969). An improved method of marking snakes. *Copeia* 1969, (4), 854–855.

Woodbury, A. M. (1948). Marking reptiles with an electric tattooing outfit. *Copeia* 1948, (2), 127–128.

Woodbury, A. M. (1956). Uses of marking animals in ecological studies: marking amphibians and reptiles. *Ecology,* **37** (4), 670–674.

15 *Freeze branding*

D. Newton*

Freeze branding involves the depigmentation of hair by application of extreme cold. The cells known as melanophores which produce the skin pigment, are apparently killed by the freezing process.

The beginning of freeze branding can be traced to early work on rats by Taylor (1949), and Farrell *et al.* (1966). Commercial application of the technique to dairy cattle began in late 1967 in the United Kingdom. Among the early pioneers of the method was Mayday Agricultural Services. At this time many individual operators began branding and the Ministry of Agriculture took an active interest, initiating field trials.

Two distinct methods were available to farmers between 1968 and 1974, the difference being the coolant used. Liquid nitrogen had advantages in storage and constant temperature, whereas solid carbon dioxide was readily available, cheaper and produced better results. The work done by Day, McEwan Jenkinson and Walker-Love at the West of Scotland College of Agriculture was important in establishing the advantages of the carbon dioxide method in detail.

It would seem appropriate in this symposium to refer to levels of pain involved in the freeze branding of cattle. In doing so I make reference only to observations made by myself and colleagues. When a non-chilled iron is applied to an animal using similar pressure to that used when branding, the animal reacts in much the same way. It is of course dangerous to attribute human feelings to animal reactions; however, animals being branded on the rump seem to react as much to the fact that they cannot see what is being done, as to any sensation of cold.

One of my colleagues freeze branded himself on the forearm in the early days of the method, and reported a sharp tingling sensation followed by numbness. It is probably fair to point out that in cases of frostbite this anaesthetic effect is often the cause of damage occurring without the sufferer being aware, and to mention in passing that pain resulting from hot branding and caustic branding are thought to be extreme, and in the latter case frequently long lasting.

The Need for Freeze Branding

The need to identify individuals in different groups of animals varies, although the vast majority of our work is undertaken in the dairy herd, to enable management

*Derek Newton graduated in agriculture from Newcastle University in 1966 and has worked in the livestock industry, particularly in the marking and identification of pigs and cattle. He has been closely connected with freeze branding of cattle since 1968, firstly with West Cumberland Farmers Ltd, and latterly with Universal Livestock Services Ltd.

to select cows for extra feeding, medication, or mating, or to record yields. As freeze branding is one of the few permanent methods of identification it has an important function as a deterrent against theft. High cattle prices in the United Kingdom in recent years have accelerated the incidence of cattle rustling, and many police forces in remote districts now recommend freeze branding to farmers.

To be effective any form of identification must be clear, long lasting and easily read without handling the animals. Freeze branding is unique in its capability to fulfil these requirements. In recent years we have seen a further commercial use for freeze branding in identifying the products of specialist calf-rearing groups. Farrell has made spectacular use of his invention in the horse breeding world, and has freeze brand registration programmes under way in the United States, Australia and New Zealand.

Development in the U.K. Dairy Industry

The growth of freeze branding has been assisted in Britain by the increasing popularity of the black and white breeds, together with the swing to herring-bone milking parlours and increases in herd size. Rotation of milking staff, use of contract and relief milkers, and visits by artificial inseminators have all contributed to the need for bold, permanent and accurate identification as made possible by freeze branding.

While freeze branding is of value on red and light coloured breeds, it is never as spectacularly successful as on black and white or black animals. The best examples of the art of branding are found on animals branded while still growing, and it is significant that these animals retain minimum amounts of scar tissue on the brand. My estimate of current freeze branding levels is that 300 000 cattle per annum are branded in Britain. Our company is responsible for approximately 250 000, the rest being done by farmers themselves.

It may be appropriate to mention at this point that Universal Livestock Services are sole U.K. Licencees in respect of freeze branding, which is patented. The owners of the patent believe that this arrangement will promote a high standard of freeze branding as the men practising it are committed to its success for their living. This approach coincides with long-standing Ministry of Agriculture recommendations that branding be carried out by fully trained operators practising the technique regularly.

Comparison with Alternatives

Freeze branding has been criticised on the grounds of hide damage, and I therefore feel the need to remark on the accidental damage caused by other means of cattle identification. Tail-tape is frequently applied too tightly, causing the end of the tail to drop off when the blood supply fails. Ears may be mutilated by notching or by tearing out of tags. Having made these comments it is only fair to point out that severe over-branding can cause significant hide damage.

The Method—Growth of a Brand

Our current method has changed little since 1968. Minor improvements in equipment design and modifications to exposure and specific breed 'recipes' have been made. A mixture of high-grade alcohol and solid carbon dioxide is used to cool heavy brass irons, and the iron is applied to an area of the cow which has been prepared by clipping and washing. Some days after branding animals may produce a dry surface scale, which will rub off leaving pink skin below. Development of the brand proper will continue over subsequent months, white hair growing first at the margin of the brand and spreading towards the centre.

When totally white animals are presented deliberate over-branding may be used to produce a scar brand.

It is possible, although not always preferable to brand young animals with large 'adult-sized' brands, which grow with the animal. This gives even easier identification than normal. Conversely many breeders of show cattle require the branding of adult stock with small brands, which is both tidy and adequate where cattle are handled regularly and kept clean at all times.

Branding Sites

The majority of cattle are branded on the rump, but the introduction of rotary milking parlours has meant that hip and shoulder branding is now in demand. To reduce hide damage cattle have been branded on the jaw, although anyone who walks among cattle will at once realise the disadvantage of this site: they will turn to look at you! Mid-back branding has been used in rotary parlours and also on farms where visitors watch milking from a viewing gallery.

Branding other than Bovine Species

We have assisted with branding of deer, horses, donkeys and foxes, and are aware of the technique being used on whales, seals, trout, dogs and small mammals.

The Future

In conjunction with an electronic concern we are hoping to start work on the automatic recognition of freeze brands.

References

Farrell, R. K., Koger, L. M. and Winward, L. D. (1966). Freeze-branding of cattle, dogs and cats for identification. *J. Am. Vet. med. Ass.,* **149**, 745–752.

Taylor, A. C. (1949). Survival of rat skin following freezing. *J. exp. Zool.,* **110**, 77–112.

Section 4 Recognition without marking

Janet Kear

Up to this point the symposium has dealt largely with the capture of animals and the imposition of visible markings that enable the observer to tell individuals apart. Of course, no animals except identical twins are exactly alike. And wherever practical, training ourselves to recognise the natural differences that exist between individuals seems more humane than imposing foreign objects, brands, implants, rings etc, or removing tissue parts, in order to distinguish the animals that we are interested in. The major problem is that we use mainly our visual sense, and rely almost entirely on visible markings. Non-humans probably tell one another apart using other cues—odours in the case of mammals, for instance, and song in birds.

As we see from the following chapters by Miss Scott and Dr Ingham, it is undoubtedly possible to recognise individuals of particular kinds of animals, using naturally occurring features alone. The method is particularly useful for intensive studies involving relatively small populations and a few, thoroughly trained observers, but it breaks down when distinguishing characters are few or populations large. Dr Pennycuick's chapter explores the practical and theoretical limits of natural systems of identification, which cannot substitute for conventional marking when every individual of a sizeable population must be distinguishable with a high level of certainty. Nor is the method convenient when many observers are involved, as in zoos and in extensive schemes of marking and recovery.

Natural differences in body features should make possible controlled experiments which test the effects of capture and marking. Two populations could be treated in different ways—one caught, handled and ringed, while the other remained undisturbed. The marked animals could then be watched for evidence of changed behaviour patterns, breeding success, viability and other parameters, using the unmarked stock as controls. It is unfortunate that tests of this kind have not been accepted more often as standard checks, wherever conventional marking schemes are used.

An important aspect in the decision of what marks to use, and whether to use marks at all, is public opinion. To some extent our actions will be modified by public opinion, or by what we suppose the public outcry would be if we used a particularly conspicuous marking on a wild animal. What is a permissible technique on a laboratory animal, or even a wild rat or other nocturnal rodent, may be aesthetically inappropriate on garden birds or on a swan.

16 *Identification using natural markings*

C. J. Pennycuick*

Many animals show variable markings, or variations of size, shape or other attributes, that can be used to identify individuals. Identification systems based on natural attributes have obvious advantages in field studies of wild animals, where catching and marking individuals may be difficult or undesirable, but the reliability of such systems is difficult to assess. In this chapter the problem is presented in terms of the information content of a pattern. The amount of information required is first considered, and then methods of estimating the amount available from particular markings are suggested.

Limits to Reliability

It is important to realise from the outset that there is no way to be absolutely certain that an individual with particular markings is the only one so marked in the population. To be certain of this, artificial marks must be used, and the user must be able to ensure that no two are the same. Natural patterns do not come up in a regular sequence, and there is no guarantee that the same combination will not be repeated. The best one can do is to assess the likelihood of this happening. It is then a matter of judgment to decide whether the probability of a pattern being duplicated is low enough to be safely neglected.

Probability of Duplication

The probability that a pattern will be duplicated depends on two things:

(1) A complex pattern, containing a large amount of information, is less likely to be duplicated than a simple one with only a little information.

(2) There is more likely to be more than one 'copy' of a particular pattern in a large population than in a small one. Putting this another way, a more complex pattern is required to identify an individual in a large population than in a small one.

Measurement of information

In a general way it is obvious that a complex pattern should contain more infor-

*Dr C. J. Pennycuick is Reader in Zoology at the University of Bristol.

mation than a simple one. The information content of a pattern (or message) is determined by the number of possible patterns from which the particular one in question was selected. A very short written message, consisting of one letter, contains more information than one consisting of one digit, because the letter is selected from 26 possibilities, whereas the digit is one of only 10. In binary numbers, which consist only of the digits 0 and 1, there is even less information in each digit, because there are only two to choose from. The amount of information needed to choose between two equally likely possibilities, such as 0 and 1 in a binary number, is used as the unit of information. It was originally called the 'binary unit' but is now universally known as the 'bit'.

More generally, if N possible patterns are each equally likely to occur, then the information (in bits) obtained by unambiguously specifying one of them is I, where

$$I = \log_2 N \tag{16.1}$$

For instance, if the only possibilities are 'heads' or 'tails', the information needed

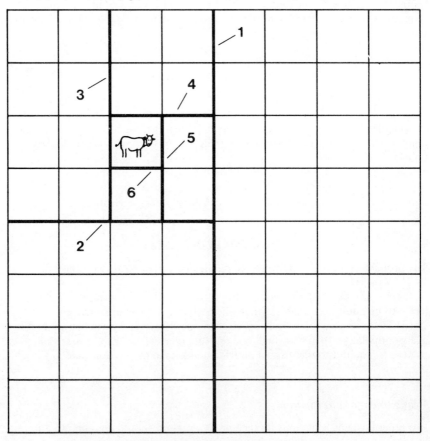

Figure 16.1 6 bits of information are required to identify 1 of 64 equally likely possibilities (after Goldman, 1953).

to specify one of them is 1 bit, since $\log_2 (2)$ is 1. Two bits are needed to select 1 of 4 equally likely possibilities, 3 bits to select 1 of 8, and so on.

Often specification of the pattern is imperfect, so that one unique pattern is not specified unambiguously. Instead, the possibilities are narrowed down to a small number n, out of the original set of N possibilities. In this more general case the information obtained is less than before, and is

$$I = \log_2 (N/n) \tag{16.2}$$

The point is illustrated by figure 16.1, which shows a cow in a chessboard-like field with 64 squares. A 6-bit message is needed to specify the exact square inhabited by the cow, since $64 = 2^6$. The heavy lines show one way in which the total area could be progressively narrowed down, by successive halving. The first bit rejects the right-hand half of the field. The second rejects the lower half of what remains, and so on. Six such halvings leave only one unrejected square.

Now suppose that the maximum length of message that can be handled is only 3 bits. Then the best we can do is to narrow down the cow's position to a group of 8 squares. More generally, if there were N equally likely possibilities before the message was transmitted, and a smaller number n afterwards, then the information content of the message is given by equation (16.2) above. In this example $N = 64$ and $n = 8$, so

$$I = \log_2 (64/8) = \log_2 (8) = 3 \text{ bits.}$$

Information needed for identification

To assess the reliability of an identification system we need to know the frequencies with which the different components of the pattern occur in the population. If the frequency (F) of some characteristic is 1, this means that all the individuals in the population have it. If only some of the individuals have the characteristic, F is a number less than 1, representing the proportion of individuals that have it. If the characteristic is a complex pattern, one of a large number of possible arrangements (as is necessary for an identification system), then F is a very small number, much less than 1. The minimum value of F is zero, for a characteristic that does not occur in the population at all.

For assessing the reliability of identification, we are concerned with the probability (q) that the given pattern will occur on more than one individual in the population. It was shown by Pennycuick and Rudnai (1970) that if the number of animals in the population is M, then q is related to F by the formula

$$q = 1 - (1 - F)^M - MF(1 - F)^{M-1} \tag{16.3}$$

The frequency of a pattern can be converted into its information content by Equation (16.2). Observing a pattern whose frequency is F is equivalent to selecting one of $1/F$ possibilities, so that

$$I = \log_2 (1/F) \tag{16.4}$$

If the observation is imperfect, and serves only to narrow down the possibilities to a group whose frequency is f, then from equation (16.2),

$$I = \log_2 (f/F) \tag{16.5}$$

The practical implications of Equation (16.3) are not intuitively obvious, but can be understood from figure 16.2, in which q has been plotted against information content, for various population sizes. Figure 16.2 shows that a small amount of information is completely useless for identification purposes, but there comes a 'break point', beyond which a modest increase in information produces a dramatic improvement in reliability. The bigger the population, the more information is needed to reach this break point.

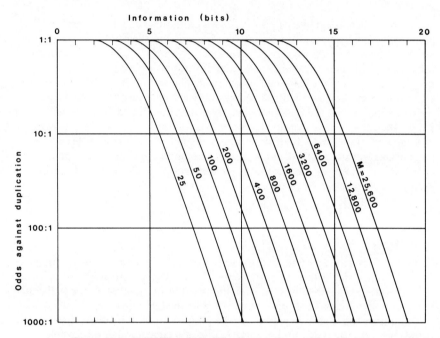

Figure 16.2 Reliability of identification can be considered in terms of the probability that a pattern will be duplicated. Each curve relates this probability to the information content of the pattern, for a particular population size (M).

For example, in a population of 100 individuals, 4 bits of information are needed before q drops perceptibly below 1. In other words, if an individual is identified by a pattern containing only this amount of information, there is virtually certain to be another with the same pattern in a population of that size. To lengthen the odds against duplication to 10:1 7.6 bits are required, and 9.4 bits for 100:1. Beyond this point the curve is almost straight, such that each additional 1.7 bits lengthens the odds against duplication by a further factor of 10. If the population number is greater, then more bits are required to reach the knee in the curve, or any specified value of q. For any given value of q, each doubling of the population number requires one additional bit of information. The effect is to move the entire curve to the right by 1 bit, without altering its shape.

How improbable does duplication need to be before identification can be considered 'reliable'? In most biological statistics one is concerned with the probability that a given result could have occurred by coincidence. In this case odds of 100:1 against are usually considered long enough for this explanation to be safely neglected. Often odds of 20:1 are accepted, because of the difficulty of getting anything better, but this is more risky. For identification in ethology it may be that odds longer than 100:1 are required, but this level is as good as any to choose as a starting point.

When the population size is given, the amount of information required to achieve odds of 100:1 can be read off from figure 16.2. Once this level has been achieved, a further 1.7 bits (which is not a great deal) will lengthen the odds to 1000:1, the next 1.7 bits to 10 000:1 and so on. No amount of information will ever achieve ∞:1 (that is certain identification), but odds of thousands to one are attainable, and that must surely be adequate for all practical purposes.

Information Content of a Pattern

Characters and values

Before the information content of a pattern can be estimated, it must first be divided up into 'characters', which should be independent of one another. Each character must be able to take at least two 'values'. For instance, Character 1 might be the animal's sex, which in most animals has two possible values, male and female. If the sex ratio is 1:1, then an observation of either sex yields 1 bit of information. If not, an observation of the rarer sex yields more information than one of the commoner sex.

For example, suppose we have a population in which the sex ratio is 1 male to 3 females. Then if an individual is seen to be male, this observation narrows the search for its identity down to a quarter of the population, so yielding 2 bits at one stroke (compare figure 16.1). This is more information than is obtained if the animal is female, since in the latter case we still have to search through three quarters of the population.

To put this more generally, let the frequency of value i be F_i. In the last example, if i is 1 for a male and 2 for a female, then $F_1 = 0.25$ and $F_2 = 0.75$. The information obtained from observing value i is I_i, where

$$I_i = \log_2 (1/F_i) \tag{16.6}$$

Thus for the above values, I_1 is 2.0 bits for a male, but I_2 for a female is only 0.42 bit.

Independence of characters

The need for independence of characters can be illustrated thus. Suppose the animal in question is one of those antelopes which have horns only in the male, and Character 1 is the animal's sex. Inadvisedly, we select Character 2 as the presence or absence of horns, with two values, (1) horns present, and (2) horns absent. If we have just observed that a particular individual is a male, then we know it will also have horns, so that (for males) $F_1 = 1$ and $F_2 = 0$. We now observe that the beast does indeed have horns, and proceed to calculate the information so obtained:

$$I_1 = \log_2 (1/F_1) = \log_2 (1) = 0$$

This result means that you get no information from observing something which you know already.

Each new character must be something whose value is not determined in advance by the values of other characters. In the above example 'horn shape' might be an acceptable character, if, say, two or three distinct types of horn shape could be distinguished. This character would not apply to females, but would provide extra information for identifying males.

Multiple character values

The number of possible values of a character is not necessarily, or usually limited to 2. Suppose, for instance, that the animal usually has a cluster of pigment spots on its nose, and that the number of spots is more commonly 3 or 4, but can vary from 0 to 5. 'Number of spots' could be a character, with six values, each with a frequency, and a corresponding information yield. Table 16.1 represents an imaginary set of values for this character.

Note from table 16.1 that:

Table 16.1 Frequencies for a character with discrete values

No. of spots		Frequency	Information (bits)
0		0.01	6.6
1		0.11	3.2
2		0.06	4.1
3		0.35	1.5
4		0.42	1.3
5		0.05	4.3
	Total	1.00	

(1) The frequencies have to add up to 1.00; in other words, every known variant must fit one or other of the values.

(2) Rare values yield more information than common ones.

(3) The fact of having many values in itself makes each one rarer, so that more information is obtained. Thus six equally common values would yield 2.6 bits each, as compared to 1 bit each for two equally common values.

How many values?

In spite of this, it does not follow that it is always advantageous to divide each character into as many values as possible, particularly where the values shade into one another. For instance, suppose the animal's coat colour is variable, and we use the colour of its face as a character. Rashly, we decide to recognise six values, whose frequencies, let us imagine, are the same as in the previous example (table 16.2).

Table 16.2 Frequencies for a character with
graded values

Colour	Frequency	
Black	0.01	
Dark grey	0.11 ⎫	
Medium grey	0.06 ⎬	0.52
Light grey	0.35 ⎭	
Very light grey	0.42	
White	0.05	

We now score an individual as 'medium grey'. This has been recorded with a
frequency of 0.06 in the population, and should therefore yield 4.1 bits (table
16.1). However, the boundaries between 'dark grey', 'medium grey' and 'light
grey' are not of the same all-or-nothing kind as those between 1, 2 or 3 spots.
Counting spots should yield the same result on different occasions, or when
done by different observers, but shades of grey cannot be identified with the
same lack of ambiguity. Medium grey can easily change to dark if the light is
poor, the animal wet or dirty, or the observer in a 'pessimistic' mood.

In practice, an observation of 'medium grey' might enable the observer to
say that the colour is definitely not completely black, and not very light grey,
therefore somewhere between dark grey and light grey. This is analogous to the
case of the cow in the chessboard field, whose position can be narrowed down
only to a group of squares, with correspondingly less information than if the exact
square were known. In the present example, the colour has been narrowed down
to a group of 3 categories, of which the total frequency is 0.11 + 0. 06 + 0.35 = 0.52.
The information obtained is then 0.94 bit, not 4.1 bits as originally hoped.

The grey scale illustrated is an example of 'spurious precision'. The imaginary
observer has tried to extract more information than is really present in his
observations. It is always dangerous to use characters whose values shade into one
another on a continuous scale. It is better to choose characters of a presence-or-
absence type, such as spots which are either present or absent, lines which are
either continuous or broken, and so on.

Setting up and Preliminary Assessment

The first step in devising an identification system is to search your animal from
end to end, and list all the characters you can find. It is, of course, essential to
use characters that are not likely to change in the course of the animal's life.
Structures like the horns and tusks of mammals, which continue to grow
throughout life in many species, must be treated with great caution; similarly with
marks caused by physical damage, since new wounds can be acquired while old
ones heal and disappear. Tusk shape and nicks in ears have been widely used for
identifying elephants, but such characters are only satisfactory in studies where
individuals are resighted frequently.

Genetically determined patterns of pigmentation are very stable, and have been
used to identify zebras (Petersen, 1972), eland (J. C. Hillman, unpublished), and

giraffes (Foster, 1966), among other animals. Patterns of wrinkles are also good, and have been used to identify black rhinos (snout: Mukinya, 1973) and ostriches (legs: L. Hurxthal, unpublished).

Number of characters needed

It is shown in books on information theory (for example Goldman, 1953) that the average amount of information obtained from a character is given by

$$\bar{I} = \Sigma F_i \log(1/F_i) \qquad (16.7)$$

where the summation is carried out over all values of the character.

   The total amount of information required to identify an individual reliably depends on the population size, and can be found from figure 16.2. Equation (16.7) can only be applied after the system has been set up, but as a general indication about 1 bit can be expected from each character, on average, using a mixture of characters with 2-5 values each. Thus if figure 16.2 shows that 10 bits of information are needed for reliable identification, a system with 10 characters may be expected to yield this amount *on average*, that is, about half the individuals will have more and half less.

   To get reliable identifications for nearly all individuals, the average must be well above the level required, to allow for combinations of common values. As a preliminary rule of thumb, 0.5 bit per character may be expected in the less favourable cases, so, to be somewhat conservative, find the number of bits required from figure 16.2 and look for twice that number of characters.

The trial sample

Once a suitable list of characters has been drawn up, this should be duplicated in the form of a coding sheet, and a trial sample of animals should be coded— preferably at least 100, unless the total number in the population is less than this. The frequencies of each value of each character can then be estimated. For instance, if Character 1 has two possible values, which occur in 39 and 61 of the first 100 animals, then their frequencies are estimated to be 0.39 and 0.61, respectively.

   Table 16.3 is a list of the frequencies of some of the character values in the Bewick's swan identification system, derived from a sample of 498 swans, for which this set of characters was coded by Mary Evans, using photographs. Alongside each frequency is given the corresponding amount of information [from Equation (16.4)]. To determine the information available about a particular swan, the information contributions from each character are simply added up.

   This can be illustrated by the swan 'Caldy', which is shown in figure 17.2a along with its coding sheet. The characters listed in table 16.3 are those for the right side only, and there is one additional character 'L', which is not shown on the coding sheet, but which refers to the shape of the feather line between the eyes. The two-digit characters on the coding sheet refer to rectangular arrays, as illustrated for T and G in figure 17.2b. These are treated as two separate

Table 16.3 Frequencies of Bewick's swan character values

Character	Value	Frequency	Information (bits)	Character	Value	Frequency	Information (bits)
L	0	0.396	1.34	Y2 (*cont.*)	6	0.0473	4.40
	1	0.0563	4.15		7	0.0545	4.20
	2	0.547	*0.87*		8	0.0218	5.52
D	*0*	0.759	*0.40*	FY1	0	0.200	2.32
	1	0.241	2.05		1	0.229	2.13
	2	0	—		2	0.0655	3.93
O	1	0.917	0.13		3	0.505	0.98
	2	0	—	FY2	0	0.207	2.27
	3	0.0714	3.81		1	0.458	1.13
	4	0	—		2	0.240	2.06
FD	1	0.0938	3.42		3	0.0727	3.78
	2	0.902	*0.15*		4	0.0291	5.10
E1	0	0.125	3.00	T1	*0*	0.317	*1.66*
	1	0.652	*0.62*		1	0.464	1.11
	2	0.0670	3.90		2	0.127	2.98
	3	0.156	2.68		3	0.0924	3.44
	4	0	—		4	0	—
E2	0	0.121	3.05	T2	*0*	0.110	*3.18*
	1	0.558	0.84		1	0.247	2.02
	2	0.268	1.90		2	0.514	0.96
	3	0.0446	4.49		3	0.129	2.96
	4	0.00893	*6.81*	Q	*0*	0.0743	*3.75*
Y1	1	0.273	1.87		1	0.478	1.07
	2	0.509	0.97		2	0.367	1.44
	3	0.215	2.22		3	0.0803	3.64
Y2	1	0.116	3.10	G1	0	0.904	*0.15*
	2	0.396	1.34		1	0.0964	3.38
	3	0.229	2.13	G2	0	0.131	2.94
	4	0.0618	4.02		*1*	0.639	*0.65*
	5	0.0691	3.86		2	0.231	2.11

characters in the table, one for the row and one for the column, for example
T1 = 0, T2 = 0, etc.

It can be seen from Scott's figure 17.2a that some characters have been left
blank because they do not apply. Thus D, O, and E are mutually exclusive categories, only one of which can apply. Also FY goes with Y and does not apply
to D or O swans. These omissions cause no difficulty in information assessment.
Characters which do not apply, or were not scored, are simply ignored, and the
information is added up for all those which do apply, and which were observed.

The values observed for Caldy are listed in *italic* type in table 16.3 together
with the corresponding information contributions, which add up to a total of

18.2 bits. It can be seen from figure 16.2 that this is sufficient to take the odds against duplication in a population of 5000 to well beyond the 1000:1 level. Identification of this particular swan is thus quite satisfactory and reliable. However, the following points may be noted:

(1) Out of the 10 characters listed, six yielded less than 1 bit each, and two yielded only 0.15 bit each. In each case one value of the character was much more common than the others, and Caldy had the common value. A swan which has the commonest values throughout cannot be reliably identified in a population of this size, without using a larger number of characters.

(2) More than a third of the total information (6.8 bits) came from one character, E2. The value 4 observed for this character has a frequency of 0.00893, that is it occurs only in 1 of every 112 swans to which the character applies. The occurrence of this highly distinctive value on the right-hand side of the face has rescued an otherwise undistinguished pattern. The left-hand side has the common value 1 for E2, which yields only 0.84 bit. If this had occurred on the right-hand side the total information would have been 12.3 bits. In a population of 5000 the probability of such a pattern being duplicated would be about 0.26 [Equation (16.3)] , which is totally unacceptable. This value is just about on the knee of the curve of figure 16.2. An additional 3 bits or so from further characters would have been required to bring the probability of duplication down below 1 in 100.

Variation of information content

The amount of information derived from the identification system varies from individual to individual, since combinations of common values yield less informa-

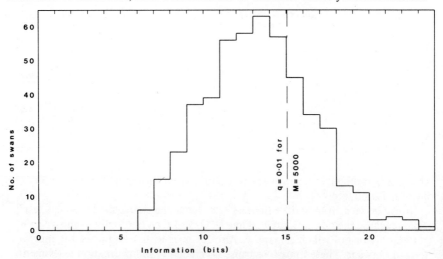

Figure 16.3 Distribution of information content in a sample of 498 Bewick's swans, coded by Mary Evans. The identification system is described by Scott in chapter 17. The information is derived from the characters listed in table 16.3, which refer to the right side of the face only, and are not the complete set.

tion than uncommon ones. Figure 16.3 is a histogram showing the distribution of estimated information content among the sample of 498 swans. A few can muster less than 7 bits, which would scarcely suffice to identify them in a population of 50, whereas one has 23 bits, sufficient to identify it in a population of over a million.

The 'population' in this case consists of all those swans which might turn up at Slimbridge. Assuming (perhaps optimistically) that 5000 swans are in a position to do this, about 15 bits of information are needed for 100:1 odds against a pattern being duplicated (figure 16.2). Figure 16.3 shows that only about 29 per cent of the swans in the sample exceed this level, with the characters so far considered, so evidently some more information is required.

Supplementing a Trial System

Adding more characters

The results for the swan system summarised in figure 16.3 shows that rather too few of the swans have sufficient information for reliable identification in a population of the size required. More information is needed to bring the bulk of them up to a useful level, and hence more characters must be found. This particular trial run was based on 15 characters, of which 14 refer to features on the right-hand side of the bill, and one applies to the face as a whole. A further four 'median' characters, based on features of the mandible, eyelids etc., could be added to increase the total information. In addition a further 14 characters could be obtained by simply repeating the 14 'right-side' observations on the left-hand side also.

Correlated characters

The latter procedure contains an element of risk in a bilaterally symmetrical animal, since there may be a tendency for the two sides to be similar. An extreme case of correlation between characters was given above (the antelope with horns in males only). It was seen that perfect correspondence between the values of two characters means that only one of them can be used. Such one-to-one correspondence is rare, however. More commonly two characters are correlated, without corresponding exactly. This means that once the value of Character 1 is known, certain values of Character 2 become more likely and others less likely than before. In other words the value of Character 1 contains some information about the value of Character 2, without specifying it exactly.

A simple statistical procedure can be used to determine whether two characters are in fact correlated, and if so how strongly, but no simple method has been devised as yet for determining the effect on the information content if they are. If enough data are available, the effect could be dealt with constructing a list of frequencies for the values of Character 2, and repeating this for *each* value of Character 1.

It is clear at any rate that if two characters are correlated less information can be obtained from them than if they are not, and that the stronger the correlation, the greater the reduction in information content will be. Probably a useful estimate of the information reduction can be obtained from the correlation coefficient, but no actual method of doing this is available at present.

Unwritten 'oddity' characters

A formal written identification system is generally supplemented in practice by further features, such as minor deformities or peculiarities of behaviour, which the observer is aware of, but which are not easily incorporated as formal characters. Subconsciously, the observer assumes that such characteristics are (1) stable, that is retained by the individual over a long period, and (2) very rare, or even unique to the individual. Such an oddity amounts to an additional character, with two values, (1) oddity present and (2) oddity absent. Provided the oddity is distinctive and easy to see, there is no reason why a character of this type, with one rare value, should not yield several bits of information about the few individuals that possess it.

There may be a temptation to identify an individual by an 'oddity' character alone, but this should be resisted. Such a character needs to be backed by further information, otherwise one cannot be confident that it really is restricted to one individual. It is easy to fall into a circular fallacy, whereby an individual is recognised by a single oddity, after which it is inevitably the only individual ever credited with that oddity.

Unwritten characters are generally not useful if more than one observer has to use the system. It is in any case usually worth the effort to write such characters down, and add them to the rest of the system.

General Limitations and Guidelines

Awkward individuals

The use of some additional characters would certainly raise many more of the Bewick's swans above the minimum useful level of 15 bits, but it can be seen from figure 16.3 that there is very little hope of raising the worst ones (with 6–7 bits so far) up to this level. This illustrates the general point that systems based on natural markings work better for some individuals (with rare patterns) than for others. It is best to accept the fact that some individuals can be identified reliably while others cannot, and to use the system only for purposes where this limitation is acceptable.

Population size

Although table 16.3 represents only a part of the swan identification system, it still contains 15 characters, and coding an individual from a photograph is quite a laborious operation. The system would give much better results if all the characters currently known were used, but the work needed in coding would then be approximately doubled. The heavy demand for information is due to the large population size involved. If the population were, say, 100, then the partial system illustrated by table 16.3 and figure 16.3 would be excellent as it stands, only about 12 per cent of the swans being below the 100:1 probability level in this case.

The general rule is that the larger the population size, the smaller the *proportion* of individuals that can be identified reliably. If the work of coding is to be kept within manageable bounds, then systems of this kind are best used where the population size is not too big. In the case of wild animals they work best in species where modest numbers of animals occupy a well-defined area, with a minimum of confusion due to immigration. This description unfortunately does not fit Bewick's swans, although this is not to say that the system is not useful for keeping track of the more distinctive individuals, especially as it is used in conjunction with rings which can be read from a distance.

References

Foster, J. B. (1966). The giraffe of Nairobi National Park: home range, sex ratios, the herd, and food. *E. Afr. Wildl. J.*, **4**, 139–148.

Goldman, S. (1953). *Information Theory*. Constable, London.

Petersen, J. C. B. (1972). An identification system for zebra (*Equus burchelli*, Gray). *E. Afr. Wildl. J.*, **10**, 59–63.

Mukinya, J. G. (1973). Density, distribution, population structure and social organisation of the black rhinoceros in Masai Mara Game Reserve. *E. Afr. Wildl. J.*, **11**, 385–400.

Pennycuick, C. J. and Rudnai, J. (1970). A method of identifying individual lions *Panthera leo* with an analysis of the reliability of identification. *J. Zool. Lond.*, **160**, 497–508.

17 Identification of individual Bewick's swans by bill patterns

Dafila K. Scott*

Though the number of animals that have to be recognised in a field study should depend on the questions being asked, the reverse is often true: the questions that can be asked depend on the number of animals that can be recognised. In this chapter I discuss the merits of individual recognition by natural variation in bill pattern in a population of wild Bewick's swans. This study population illustrates both the advantages and disadvantages of the method, and the extent to which it influences the questions that can be asked.

All identification systems depend on (1) detecting differences between individuals and recording them, and (2) storing records in such a way that they are available for reference. I will first describe the methods that have been used in the Bewick's swan study, and how they came to be used.

Historical Aspects

In 1923 it was first reported by the ornithologist Acland that in Bewick's swans there was individual variation in the pattern of black and yellow on the bill. This was noted again more recently by Geroudet (1962, 1963) and Sermet (1963) in Switzerland. In 1964 wild Bewick's swans first visited the pond in front of the director's house at the Wildfowl Trust, Slimbridge, and Peter Scott realised that all 24 individuals in the flock were individually recognisable. He drew the bill patterns of all the adults and named the birds in February 1964. The following year he was able to recognise 13 of the 18 adult birds that he had drawn the previous year.

Bill Pattern

The means by which he was able to recognise them is illustrated in figure 17.1: individuals vary both in the extent and pattern of black and yellow on the culmen, and also behind the nares on either side of the bill. Individuals were found to

*Dafila Scott is a graduate of Oxford University and is currently studying the social behaviour of Bewick's swans for the degree of PhD at Cambridge University. She has made several expeditions to study these birds on the continent as well as one to Alaska to study the conspecific Whistling swan on its natural breeding grounds.

Figure 17.1   Illustration of differences in bill pattern between
individuals.

vary in other aspects in addition to the pattern of black and yellow; for example,
the colour and pattern on the underside of the bill, the presence or absence of
pink in the gape and of yellow on the eyelids, and more complex characteristics
such as headshape and body shape could be used to identify individuals. All these
characteristics, except the last, are on the head. Since the differences are small, they
can be detected only with binoculars, unless the bird is within 5 m. The maximum
distance for identification by bill pattern in good conditions is about 200 m with
a telescope.

Recording Systems

The identity of individuals is first recorded by drawing the bill pattern on a sten-
cilled form (figure 17.2a). For each swan one copy of this drawing then goes into
a folder belonging to that particular swan while the other is put in a 'yearbook',
together with all the other individuals identified that winter. Although most
regular visitors can be recognised from memory, the yearbook serves as a reference
for observers, particularly in identification of individuals that are less well known.

The individual folders are filed in alphabetical order and serve as a reference
in cases where the swan's name can be remembered or guessed. They contain
(in addition to the identikit drawing and list of attributes) information on
arrival and departure dates, presence of consorts (for example mate, sibs),
number of offspring and a series of portrait photographs where available.

However, this system alone does not allow rapid access to data on particular
bill patterns as soon as numbers of recorded individuals exceed a few hundred.
When individuals returned that looked familiar to the observer or behaved as if
they had previous experience of Swan Lake, it was impossible to trace them
except by testing hunches, or searching systematically through the yearbooks or
folders. To overcome this it was necessary to find some way of coding the

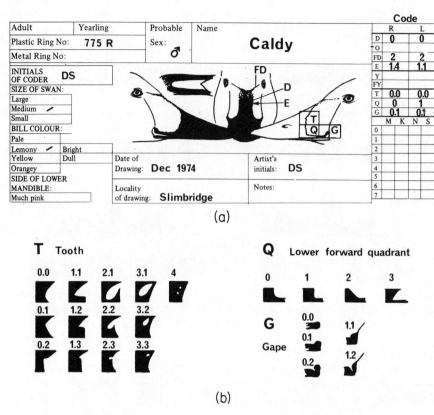

							Code	
							R	L
Adult	Yearling		Probable	Name		D	0	0
Plastic Ring No: 775 R			Sex: ♂	**Caldy**		O		
Metal Ring No:						FD	2	2
INITIALS OF CODER DS						E	1.4	1.1
						Y		
SIZE OF SWAN:						FY		
Large						T	0.0	0.0
Medium ✓						Q	0	1
Small						G	0.1	0.1

BILL COLOUR:					M	K	N	S
Pale				0				
Lemony ✓	Bright			1				
Yellow	Dull	Date of	Artist's	2				
Orangey		Drawing: **Dec 1974**	initials: **DS**	3				
SIDE OF LOWER				4				
MANDIBLE:		Locality	Notes:	5				
Much pink		of drawing: **Slimbridge**		6				
				7				

(a)

T Tooth

0.0	1.1	2.1	3.1	4

0.1	1.2	2.2	3.2

0.2	1.3	2.3	3.3

Q Lower forward quadrant

0	1	2	3

G

Gape

0.0 1.1

0.1

0.2 1.2

(b)

Figure 17.2 (a) Form on which details of a swan's characteristics are entered. (b) Examples of code categories within areas of the bill shown above.

pattern and other characteristics, as objectively as possible, and to combine this with an efficient data retrieval system.

Code

A code was devised (Scott, 1966) and later revised (unpublished) in which the bill is divided into areas and characters within each area are classified into relatively exclusive categories (figure 17.2b). At present every individual is drawn on a sheet which includes the swan's code numbers (figure 17.2a). A copy of this code sheet is then placed in one of three books holding the three main bill pattern types (darky, D; yellowneb, Y; pennyface, O). Within these books each individual is placed according to a specified order of characters (E, T, FD/FY, Q, G) based on an assumed order of significance. To find a swan it is necessary to code it and then to follow the procedure for placing it in the book.

This system provides one way in which apparently familiar but unremembered individuals of the kind described above may be found. It has the advantage that it is suitable for computerisation.

Possibilities for Study

The ability to recognise individuals provided access to many aspects of Bewick's swan biology which could not previously be investigated. It enabled us to examine basic questions about social structure, and daily and seasonal movement patterns. For example, it became apparent that, as in geese, individuals are highly traditional in their choice of wintering grounds, and that the flock is composed of the same kind of units: mated pairs with their offspring, unsuccessful or non-breeding pairs, and single birds (second winter or older). Information on life history characteristics can also amass: the oldest known wild bird (Lancelot) returned for his fourteenth winter in 1976/77 and 17 individuals had returned for 10 years or more. The average age at first breeding is 4 years ($n = 16$). And in 14 winters no case of divorce has been observed in a known breeding pair.

This method of identification has also allowed us to study relationships between individuals within the flock. For example in a recent study at Welney, Norfolk I have been able to investigate dominance relationships among 150 units in the flock, and to study the effects of parental dominance rank on that of their cygnets. In these studies, the advantages of bill pattern recognition are (a) that individuals can be recognised instantaneously from memory once they are regular visitors, and (b) that the most important part of the body involved in recognition is the head, and the observer is unlikely to miss incidents of behaviour during the process of recognition, which might be the case if it were necessary to look at different parts of the body or to read a numbered leg ring.

Another aspect which can be studied with quantifiable variation in bill pattern is kinship. One of the present aims is to determine criteria for relatedness in terms of similarity of bill patterns. Eventually this might allow an observer to ascertain kinship in large flocks during short-term studies. The advantage would be that past histories of individuals need not be known, nor the birds caught for blood samples to be taken for analysis. Preliminary analysis of the bill patterns of 14 families involving 64 individuals, coded on 29 characters, has shown quantitatively that relatives are more similar than non-relatives (P. Harvey, personal communication).

In addition to theoretical aspects of study, individual recognition by bill pattern has allowed us to examine practical questions; for example, recent work by Mary Evans has investigated the factors affecting how long different classes of individual stay on Swan Lake. These studies which are relatively short term and rely greatly on observer memory illustrate the possibilities which arise with individual recognition by bill pattern. However, there are a number of limitations which must be pointed out that affect the ease and accuracy of re-identification. These limitations inevitably diminish the number of questions that can be asked.

Limitations

The accuracy with which an animal can be recognised depends on the observer, the method of recording and storing the information, and the animal in question.

The observer

The present system of re-identification relies very largely on memory, and the advantages of this have been mentioned. But although the capacity of the human brain for storing faces is large (people have estimated that they can recognise and name around 900 faces), it is not infinite: its content of individual faces is continually changing as new ones are added and old ones suppressed. In the case of the swans, the human observer has several problems in remembering individuals: bill patterns are probably more difficult to remember than human faces; they take more familiarisation and are more easily suppressed, especially during the six month absence of the swans in the summer. Swans which are irregular visitors are hard to remember, partly because it is seldom possible to become familiar with subtle cues of body and head shape which are an essential aid to recognition by memory. Long-term absences, as when swans returned after missing several seasons, also make recognition difficult especially if the swan's bill pattern is not particularly distinctive and it has acquired a new mate. Even if the bird's behaviour suggests that it has had previous experience of the place, it may still be impossible to remember its name.

A final problem associated with relying on an observer's memory is that in long-term studies, when one observer leaves, it may bring the study to a close or it may take much time and loss of information to train another. However, observer continuity is extremely valuable since experience increases both speed and accuracy of detection of differences in bill pattern (Evans, 1977).

To minimise error, observers can be tested on their ability to recognise their study individuals. In one such test (Bateson, 1977) I was shown a series of slides, taken two weeks previously, of individuals from Welney and was able to identify correctly 29 of 30 of those where the bill pattern was clearly visible, and 23 of 30 where it was partly visible or blurred. However, such tests may not take into account fluctuations or lapses in memory and are time consuming to repeat.

The result of this reliance on memory is that individuals may return unrecognised and long-term data (for example on life-history characteristics) may suffer from inaccuracies. The inadequacy of the human memory requires the use of efficient recording and data retrieval systems. I will consider the limitations of the present systems.

Recording and data retrieval systems

As described, the practicalities of recording many hundreds of individual bill patterns over successive winters necessitated development of a coding system. The combination of portrait drawing, individual code and supporting portrait photographs, provided the most accurate system for recognition so far designed. But there are problems even with this. For example, portrait drawings vary in accuracy for many reasons, including differences in skill, practice and patience of the observer or in observing swans at close range and in good light, with the result that it is often difficult to recognise swans from drawings alone. Photographs overcome these problems but not all swans come within range for close-ups showing detail to be taken.

The code is also subject to problems of observer non-repeatability and bias.

Ideally the characters should be more exclusive. In addition, the swans have not been rigorously coded on all possible characters in the past, thus explaining in part the low levels of information on each swan (see Pennycuick, chapter 13). Another significant limitation is the method of filing—and thus of retrieving—the data, once coded.

The present system involves leafing through one of the three large code books to find a particular combination of values. For the present, therefore, this system works but inaccurately and inefficiently. Ideally it should be computerised: an on-line terminal would allow rapid access to a storage file, so that a newcomer's code could be typed in to see whether or not it was already on file.

The animal.

There are two additional sources of error in recognising individuals that are associated with the animal and its habits. First there are certain changes in bill pattern with age. These are most extensive between cygnet (first winter) and second winter birds' markings. Cygnets have grey, pink and black bills with no clearcut pattern, while by their second winter the pink has usually disappeared and the yellow and black pattern developed (figure 17.3). Some fast developing

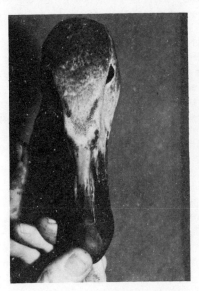

Figure 17.3 Changes in bill pattern from first to second winter in one individual (Caldy: January 1974 left, October 1974 right).

cygnets may show indications of real pattern towards the end of the winter in February or March and by drawing cygnets at this time it has been possible to identify a small proportion the next winter. Recognition of second winter birds in this way is usually backed up in 14.5 per cent of cases by observing them consorting with their parents. Then the drawings serve to indicate which of the previous years' cygnets (in a brood of more than one) has returned. But the method is inadequate for accurate recognition, especially as many cygnets leave before any definite indications of future bill pattern are apparent. It can be estimated from data on ringed birds that 34 per cent of cygnets would never be recognised on return. At Slimbridge, therefore, cygnets are not drawn or given names, and records of known age birds mostly begin in their second winter.

Changes are not restricted to the first year and may continue to a lesser extent into the second and third years, but these are seldom large enough to impair recognition. Of 23 ringed birds photographed in their second winter, and then again in a subsequent year, only two might not have been recognised on return but for the rings (Evans, 1977).

Similar portrait photographs of 20 adults (third winter or older), showed that no changes occurred in 15 birds. In the remaining 5, the changes were infinitesimal and would probably not have affected recognition. Once a bird is adult, therefore, the problems of instability of markings are trivial in Bewick's swans in comparison with other species. For example, mammals often show seasonal changes in coat colour or pattern or even hourly changes (for example seals, wet and dry) and many may change considerably with age after adulthood. But the loss of information on birds of known age in Bewick's swans is a serious drawback of the method. If it is impossible to recognise cygnets when they return the next winter (except when they consort with their parents) a whole series of potential questions is precluded.

The second source of error may be due to the animal's ecology. With Bewick's swans, accuracy can be maintained at Wildfowl Trust Refuges where individuals spend much time within 200 m of the observation hides. But in field conditions (for example on the fens in Norfolk) they are extremely wary and are usually more than 200 m away. Here, accuracy of recognition depends on a combination of weather conditions, familiarity with the swan and distinctiveness of its pattern. This illustrates a situation where the questions being asked will determine the time spent in gaining access to a flock within 200 m in order to recognise individuals.

Perhaps the final problem about the system of individual recognition by bill pattern is its plausibility. Many sceptics who have not watched Bewick's swans do not believe that it is possible to recognise a large number individually without the help of artificial marks. Fortunately, there is now quite a strong case to be made that observers may distinguish large numbers of this species. First there is evidence that people from different disciplines can detect differences and match similar patterns (Evans, 1977; Brown and Lewis, 1977). Secondly, recognition tests as described above (Bateson, 1977) provide evidence that observers can remember and re-identify individuals by name. Finally there is considerable anecdotal evidence of observers recognising and naming birds by bill pattern with witnesses present, and then subsequently reading a ring number that confirmed the identification.

Discussion

I have attempted to point out the advantages and disadvantages of identifying individual Bewick's swans by bill pattern and other body features and of the system in present use. It is clear that the major advantages of being able to recognise the birds in this way are that:

(1) It is unnecessary to catch or otherwise disturb the birds in order to mark them.
(2) Individuals can be recognised instantaneously once they are familiar to the observer.

However, if this method is used on its own it precludes certain questions of interest which can be answered relatively easily by using other methods of recognition (namely ringing and dyeing) as well. With a large proportion of ringed birds it is possible to study migration routes, and to investigate life history characteristics and return rates with accuracy. It also enables accurate studies of the social behaviour of individuals of known age and parentage and confirms their identification in field studies around Wildfowl Trust reserves. It thus allows more effective study of individuals in natural situations.

The greatest potential for recognition by bill pattern is in short-term studies, where observer memory can serve to a large extent as the data store and where inaccuracies due to memory lapse or changes in the swan's pattern are minimal. But ideally even here it is better to use other methods in conjunction with it. This illustrates how the method of identification may dictate the kinds of question which can be asked.

I have described some of the ways in which the current system of recording and of data retrieval might be improved. But all these details are solely relevant to this particular technique of recognition. Bewick's swans are not the only birds to show idiosyncratic markings. Of the other swans, Whooper and Whistling swans also show individual variation in bill patterns but to a lesser degree. Many waterfowl and other birds show variation in plumage, but these differences are less practical as means for identification. Apart from Bewick's swans the most striking cases of individual variation in markings are in mammals that show spots or stripes. These have been used for individual recognition in studies of, for example, wild dogs, hyenas, zebra, kudu, eland, giraffe. Other more subtle differences in markings, body shape and behaviour have been used in individual identification of mammals for example Black rhino (Mukinya, 1973) White rhino (N. Owen-Smith personal communication), African elephant (Douglas-Hamilton, 1975), lions (Schaller, 1972), Red deer (Clutton-Brock and Guiness, 1975), gorillas (Fossey, 1976), chimpanzees (Goodall, 1965), baboons (Hausfater, 1975) and macaques (for example Deag, 1974).

In all of these cases a compromise must be made between the benefits of not having to catch or mark the animals and the costs of making detailed, reliable records of individual differences, or of limitations in scope.

Clearly in some cases one or other cost is going to be too high and will be outweighed by the benefits of having accurately identifiable individuals. For example in a study population of 350 Red deer on the Isle of Rhum in Scotland, the differences between individuals in head shape, ear shape, inter-eye distance, rump pattern and coat colour are subtle and may change with age (and season in the case of coat colour), and require close and patient observation to detect them (Clutton-Brock and Guiness, 1975). So for more accurate, and efficient identification, individuals are marked as calves with eartags or expandable neck collars. Although one observer, who is continually present, can identify all individuals by natural characteristics, the present system of marking allows a team of workers to study the individuals, and ensures that, should the main observer leave, the study will not come to an end.

The same arguments apply to the Bewick's swan identification system. Ideally a combination of different techniques should be used in the proportions appropriate to the questions which can practically and efficiently be asked.

References

Acland, C. N. (1923). Notes on Bewick's swans in Glamorganshire. *British Birds*, **17**, 63-64.

Bateson, P. P. G. (1977). Testing an observer's ability to identify individual animals. *Anim. Behav.*, **25**, 247-248.

Brown, J. and Lewis, V. (1977). A laboratory study of individual recognition using Bewick's swan bill patterns. *Wildfowl*, **28**, 159-162.

Clutton-Brock, T. H. and Guiness F. (1975). Behaviour of red deer (*Cervus elaphus L.*) at calving time. *Behaviour*, **55**, 287-300.

Deag, J. M. (1974). A study of the social behaviour and ecology of the wild Barbary macaque *Macaca sylvanus*. Ph.D. thesis Bristol University.

Douglas-Hamilton, I. (1972). On the ecology and behaviour of the African elephant: the elephants at Lake Manyara. Ph.D. thesis Oxford University.

Evans, M. E. (1977). Recognising individual Bewick's swans by bill pattern. *Wildfowl*, **28** (in press).

Fossey, D. (1976). The behaviour of the mountain gorilla. Ph.D. thesis Cambridge University.

Geroudet, P. (1962). L'hivernage des *Cygnus bewickii* sur le Leman. *Nos Oiseaux*, **21**, 317-319.

Geroudet P. (1963). Retour des cygnes de Bewick sur le Leman. *Nos Oiseaux*, **27**, 181-182

Goodall, J. van-Lawick (1965). Behaviour of free-living Chimpanzees. Ph.D. thesis Cambridge University.

Hausfater, G. (1975). Dominance and reproduction in baboons *Papio cynocephalus*. *Contributions to Primatology*, Vol. 7, Karger, Basel.

Mukinya, D. (1973). Density, distribution, population structure and social organisation of the black rhinoceros in Masai Mara Game Reserve. *East Afr. Wildl. J.* **11**, 385-400.

Schaller, G. B. (1972). *The Serengeti Lion*. Chicago University Press, Chicago.

Scott, P. (1966). The Bewick's Swans at Slimbridge. *Wildfowl Trust Annual Report*, **17**, 20-26.

Sermet, E. (1963). Des cygnes de Bewick a Yverdon. *Nos Oiseaux*, **27**, 181.

18   *Primate markings*

Jennifer C. Ingram*

Individual recognition of primates in the field and laboratory often poses many problems for research workers, particularly those studying the behaviour of undisturbed populations.

Individual variations in facial and body characteristics are most obvious among the apes, and more difficult to detect in the smaller monkeys, such as squirrel monkeys and marmosets.

Natural Markers

Apes

In Schaller's (1963) long study of Mountain gorillas in the Virunga Volcanoes, on the borders of Rwanda, Uganda and Tanzania, he used the pattern of ridges and wrinkles on the animals' noses, combined with the shape and position of the nostrils to identify each individual. He made a collection of gorilla 'nose-print' diagrams for each group and over the past few years this has been extended by Fossey to aid the identification of individuals for subsequent research workers (see figure 18.1).

Goodall (1968) was able to identify the chimpanzees at Gombe Stream Reserve, Tanzania, mainly by differences in their facial structures. A library of face photographs was also compiled there.

Orang-utans have a great range of coat colours from dark chocolate brown to pale orange, as well as variations in body hair length. These variations, combined with the size, shape and colour of their faces, the shape of cheek flanges in the males and the amount of facial hair, enabled MacKinnon (1974) to identify individuals in his field study of orang-utan in Borneo.

Large monkeys

In most of the larger monkeys, such as baboons and macaques, there are differences in the sizes of males and females, as in the apes. Males are often easier to ident-

*Dr Jennifer Ingram graduated in Zoology from Southampton University in 1971. At present she holds a research appointment at the University of Bristol investigating the behaviour of Common marmoset monkeys living in family groups. Her PhD degree was awarded in 1975 on the basis of her work on parent–infant interactions and the development of young in the Common marmoset.

Figure 18.1 A gorilla family unit. Individuals are identified by the pattern of ridges and wrinkles on their noses, combined with the shape and position of the nostrils.

ify, being larger and usually fewer in number in each troop or group. Individual variations between females are less obvious.

After a few weeks of observation it is often possible to identify several animals easily within a group, which enables a field worker to decide which troop he or she is watching. Characteristics used for Gelada baboon harem groups of one male and several females included the presence of swellings on various parts of their bodies (Dunbar and Dunbar, 1975). These swellings are believed to be due to a parasite; eventually they burst, and in severe cases may lead to the death of the animal.

Kummer (1968) mainly relied on facial and anal scars to identify Hamadryas baboons. He also used the shapes of nostrils and supraorbital ridges, as well as the shape of hair tufts at the end of the tail. Useful cues for adult females were the relative lengths and position of their nipples, and infants belonging to identified mothers were characterised by size and sex only.

Other useful marks include torn ears, long blackened or broken teeth, stiff or broken fingers, bent and kinked tails and worn patches of fur. Such characteristics are often used in naming animals or groups as in Altmann and Altmann's (1970) study where male names included Shag, Whitetip, Kink and Humprump; and one group was named after a female with a twisty tail.

Coat coloration does not often vary enough to provide a useful method of identification, except perhaps in the Ruffed lemurs of Madagascar. Different individuals of this species have coats of all shades of brown, mixed with white, in conspicuous patterns, thus providing ideal individual markers. Occasionally unusual coat colours are seen in individuals of other species, such as the rare albino animals, or the occurrence of a brown and white Colobus monkey in a population of the normally black and white animals.

Figure 18.2 Individual facial variations in small monkeys, such as these common marmosets, are very difficult to detect, particularly in the wild. Animals are often identified by means of collars with coloured and numbered discs attached to them.

Small monkeys

Small monkeys, particularly those from South America, such as squirrel monkeys or the monogamous marmosets and tamarins, do not exhibit sexual dimorphism. Individual recognition becomes even more difficult and often impossible because of their small size and their tendency to live high in the tree canopy (figure 18.2).

The need for such recognition of individuals becomes most acute in long-term studies of primate populations where a series of research workers are involved, and need to be able to identify animals rapidly. These problems can be overcome to some extent if workers overlap in time with each other and can teach subsequent observers the important characteristics. Alternatively regular visits can be made by observers who know the monkeys well and thus any changes can be monitored over a period of years. However, in some cases it becomes necessary to mark animals in some way.

Artificial Marking

The main methods used in both field and laboratory studies are tattooing, ear tags, ear notches, collars with discs attached, and dyeing.

Tattoos and ear notches

The Cayo Santiago population of Rhesus macaques are tattooed with up to three letter or number combinations on their chests and inside left thighs when about 9 months old and these remain for life (Altmann, 1962; Berman, personal communication). They also have patterns of notches cut in their ears, which are easier to see at a distance, but several monkeys may have the same pattern and final identification is by means of the tattoo. New research workers can thus identify all animals in the population, but after a few months of observation, they no longer need to use these methods, since facial and body cues (described earlier) are sufficient.

Ear tags and dyes

Kummer used ear tags, made of coloured plastic strips, to identify Hamadryas baboons in Ethiopia. This method has also been used on troops of Vervet monkeys near Durban in South Africa (Basckin and Kriger, 1973) where a succession of research workers are involved in a long-term behavioural and ecological study. The tags have lasted for at least 3 years without being lost or pulled out and do not appear to affect the behaviour of the monkeys at all.

Kummer (1968) has also sprayed animals with marking dye. By this method, a few animals can be identified for several months, and also the colour is transferred to those animals with which the marked ones come into contact immediately after being marked and released. Again, neither the marked animals nor their partners paid any attention to the paint.

Collars and discs

Collars with discs attached are often used for the smallest monkeys, such as marmosets and tamarins, in field and laboratory situations (Ingram, 1975). The plastic discs can be coloured and numbered to aid rapid identification; this technique was recently used by Stevenson (personal communication) on Common marmosets in Brazil. These marmosets have white tufts of hair around their ears which can be dyed yellow in various combinations to identify the members of each family group.

Problems

There are obvious problems associated with both natural and artificial marking systems. New scars and injuries can be acquired in fights, which can completely change the appearance of an animal. Of the artificial markings, tattoos fade after several years, or can become obscured by the growth of hair, tags can be lost or pulled off, and dye marks fade with time.

Conclusions

Thus there is no simple answer to the problem of identifying individual primates. The large facial variations between the apes have enabled accurate and repeated recognition of many animals, but similar cues become more difficult to quantify and delineate for smaller primates, and thus difficult to describe to other workers. In long-term studies of these primates the continuous presence of one observer who can identify most individuals becomes necessary, or the use of one of the methods of artificial marking to facilitate recognition.

Acknowledgements

I am most grateful to Priscilla Barrett for the use of her diagram of a gorilla family group, and to *New Scientist,* London (the weekly review of Science and Technology) for allowing me to print it. I would also like to thank Robin Dunbar, Miranda Stevenson and Carol Berman for advice and information during the preparation of this manuscript.

References

Altmann, S. A. (1962). A field study of the sociobiology of rhesus monkeys, *Macaca mulatta. Ann. N.Y. Acad. Sci.,* **102** (2); 338-435.

Altmann, S. A. and Altmann, J. (1970). Baboon Ecology. *Biblthca Primatol.,* **12,** Karger, Basle.

Basckin, D. and Kriger, (1973). Some preliminary observations on the behaviour of an urban troop of vervets during the birth season. *J. behav. Sci.,* **1,** 287-296.

Dunbar, R. I. M. and Dunbar, P. (1975). Social dynamics of gelada baboons. *Contrib. Primatol.,* **6,** Karger, Basle.

Goodall, J. van Lawick (1968). The behaviour of free-living chimpanzees in the Gombe Stream Reserve. *Anim. Behav. Monogr.,* **1** (3).

Ingram, J. C. (1975). Parent–infant interactions in the common marmoset (*Callithrix jacchus*) and the development of young. Ph.D. Thesis. Bristol University.

Kummer, H. (1968). Social organisation of hamadryas baboons. *Biblthca Primatol.,* **6**, Karger, Basle.

MacKinnon, J. (1974). *In Search of the Red Ape.* Collins, London.

Schaller, G. B. (1963). *The Mountain Gorilla* (Ecology and Behaviour). University of Chicago Press, Chicago.

Section 5 Radioactive and radio-tracking techniques

S. K. Eltringham

The technique of attaching a radio transmitter to an animal in order to follow its movements has revolutionised the study of animal behaviour. The advantages of the method with small nocturnal creatures, and with the inhabitants of forest or thick bushland, are apparent from Macdonald's contribution, which also stresses some of the problems involved in radio-tracking. The warning is timely, because the undoubted advantages of the technique tend to obscure some of the very real difficulties. These are often technical; the biologist lacking expertise in radio technology should think very carefully before embarking on a radio-tracking programme, if expert advice is not readily available. The perfection of the apparatus is in the hands of the engineers, but the problems of catching the animal and attaching the transmitter remain with the biologist. Macdonald deals with the question of suitable harnesses and collars, as well as with the types of analyses that are or are not possible with the resulting data.

Radio-tracking may be said to be only a sophisticated form of visual marking, in which the mark is detected by radio transmission rather than visible light; indeed, the method does no more than locate the animal. Usually this is but the beginning, because the biologist will probably want to know what the animal is doing. Studies of activity have been greatly enhanced by radiotelemetry, which relies on the fact that the radio signal can be made to alter its characteristics with changes in temperature or movement of the transmitter. Implantation of sensors beneath the skin allows the body temperature, heart rate or other physiological variables to be monitored. These techniques are familiar in the medical field and were in the American space programme to record the health of astronauts. A serious problem in biological work has often been the short range of the transmitter, but this can be overcome by the use of a more powerful repeater elsewhere on the animal, to relay the signals. The advantages of telemetry are enormous, but there is a risk that the researcher will be overwhelmed by the mass of information that accumulates and selective treatment of the data is essential. Amlaner describes the recent developments in telemetry and discusses the type of information that can be derived. He also considers the effects of telemetry systems on the animal's welfare.

Although the miniaturisation of radio transmitters has enabled radio-tracking to be used with small animals, there is still a lower size limit. A good marking technique must not interfere in any way with the behaviour or activity of the animal, but with creatures the size of mice, no transmitter is so small that the animal is unaffected by it. However, marking with very small radioactive tabs solves the problem, and the variety of ways in which they can be used is described by Linn. As yet, there is no way of marking animals individually but Linn, in his review of the method, describes the sort of information that can be obtained.

19 Radioactive techniques for small mammal marking

Ian J. Linn*

The use of radioactive tracking of small vertebrates as an ecological tool dates from the early 1950s. The first published account of this technique is by Griffin (1952), who recorded nest visits of radioactively marked Semipalmated plover, using an automatic monitoring device. Griffin's paper is noteworthy also because it examines in a comprehensive and lucid manner the essential considerations which ought to be (but have not always been) observed by users of this and related techniques.

About the same time Godfrey (1953, 1954a, 1954b, 1955) was pioneering radioactive tracing methods for small mammals, and a number of other workers had entered the field, as witness a trickle of publications during the later 1950s. During the 1960s there was a flowering of work on small mammals, using radioactive marking methods, and there were many publications during this decade, continuing up to the present day. Some of these were of a review character, of variable quality and usefulness. Griffin (1952) has already been mentioned and despite the age of this paper it is still a valuable contribution, remarkable in having dealt so clearly with the subject at such an early stage in its evolution. Kulik's (1967) paper is particularly useful as in it he reviews in detail the interesting development by Russian scientists of the uses of radioactively marked metabolic substances, to tag both small mammals and their ectoparasites. Jenkins (1954) reviews insect work most helpfully, and mentions the idea of marking ectoparasites by allowing them to feed on hosts with radioactive isotopes circulating in their blood stream. Other reviews are by Pendleton (1956), Tester (1962), Sanderson (1966), Gerrard (1968-69), Gerrard (1969) and Bailey, Linn and Walker (1973).

The objective of most ecological work on small mammals using radioactive tracers is to identify a specific animal, and to acquire information about its behaviour in the field. Some special technique is necessary because the species under study is secretive, or nocturnal, or difficult to observe without disturbing it, or because it is desired to record activity without being present in person. It is now

*Ian Linn is a graduate of the University of Edinburgh, where he held a wartime post. After two years of research in the Department of Zoology, University of Bristol, he went to Exeter where he remains today as a Senior Lecturer. During 1970/71 he was seconded to Makerere University, Kampala, Uganda as Reader and Acting Head of the Department of Zoology. His main research interest over the years has been the ecology and behaviour of small mammals, but while in Africa he became interested in lions, and since returning to England has concentrated on carnivorous mammals, particularly the feral mink.

fairly clearly established that there are three different ways of using radioisotopes for these purposes viz. the isotope may be attached externally to the animal; the isotope, in a form which is inert as far as the animal's metabolism is concerned, can be introduced into the animal's body; the isotope can be introduced into the animal's body, but in a form which is incorporated into the animal's metabolism. The uses, advantages and disadvantages of these three methods will be discussed first. Some related techniques will then be considered, and finally there will be a discussion of the health hazards to both animals and investigators of these methods.

General Considerations

Griffin (1952) sets out admirably the basic factors to be considered when contemplating the use of this technique. Anyone who considers using the radioactive marking method should read his paper and heed his recommendations. Bailey *et al.* (1973) list 19 radioisotopes which have been used or suggested for use with small mammals, and provide a comprehensive table of the characteristics of the isotopes which is useful for reference.

The final selection of isotope will naturally depend on the nature of the proposed investigation, as will the selection of the detection method to be used. In field work on distribution and home ranges the possibility of accidental loss of the marker must always be considered, and an isotope with a short half-life will be advantageous from this point of view. It must be borne in mind that the Department of the Environment must be consulted if radioactive isotopes are to be used in the field in Britain, and that this Department has to take into consideration public opinion, so that hazards must be kept vanishingly small.

Radioactivity causes tissue damage, and the main problem in using radioactive markers is the need to strike a delicate balance between using sufficient strength of radiation to ensure ready detection, and keeping to a minimum the dose to which the marked animal is exposed. It should be emphasised that while humane considerations are of course of paramount importance, it is also good scientific practice to ensure that marked animals do not suffer radiation damage, as there is a strong possibility that the behaviour of such damaged animals would be abnormal, and data gathered from them of greatly reduced value compared with data from healthy animals. The reader is referred once again to Griffin (1952) for valuable thoughts on how to approach the choice of isotope.

As regards detection devices, the simplest is the familiar Geiger–Müller counter, readily available from many manufacturers in the form of a portable contamination monitor. For greater sensitivity a similar meter using the scintillation principle would be appropriate. It is worth noting that in the most sophisticated instruments it is possible to incorporate an electronic filter system which permits readier differentiation between, for example, low energy background radiation and high energy experimental radiation.

In its simplest form, the scanning is done by a human operator, but of course it is possible to attach various automatic recording devices, for example tape recorders (Barbour 1963) or chart recorders, to the detection instrument. Graham and Ambrose (1967) describe a versatile continuous recording system, and Frigerio and Eisler (1968) and Inglis *et al.* (1968) describe sophisticated monitoring devices.

The main problem with any kind of continuous recording is the power supply. Batteries have a limited life, and such installations are best located near a mains electricity supply.

When the radiation detection is of dead animals, animal fragments, faeces, or any comparable material which can be brought into the laboratory, the choice of detection instrument becomes much wider, and the advice of a competent physicist should be sought.

External Tags

External tags usually take the form of leg rings or, in the case of bats, wing tags, which either have been made radioactive or, more usually, have had radioactive material attached to them. Quite apart from the problem of radiation damage, there is the problem with this type of marking that the rings or tags themselves can cause serious damage to the animal, and must be used with circumspection. In fact, more than one author has now advised that leg rings should not be used at all for small mammals; see comments by Twigg (1975) and Fullagar and Jewell (1965).

The fact remains, however, that external tags have some distinct advantages, and may be the method of choice, when appropriate precautions are taken. The application of an external tag is relatively quick and easy, and is not accompanied by the hazard of possible infection which may accompany the use of an internal tag. Moreover, the radioactive material is usually spaced to some extent from the animal's tissues, and it is fairly easy to introduce some sort of screen, so that the animal is less likely to be damaged by β radiation.

Godfrey (1953, 1954a, 1954b, 1955) used Monel metal leg rings of the type then standard in the Bureau of Animal Population (now the Animal Ecology Research Group) at Oxford University for small rodent population work. A brass tube was soldered to the ring, and a length of ^{60}Co wire was fixed in the tube with plaster. The brass tube served to shield the animal from harmful β emissions. Activities of these rings for work on voles was 100–200 μCi. A similar ring was used for moles, with an activity of 80 μCi, but placed on the tail. This is possible because of the narrow-based club shape of the mole's tail. In more recent work on moles Meese and Cheeseman (1969) used rings essentially of the Godfrey design. Linn and Shillito (1960), for smaller mammals such as shrews and harvest mice, used a similar but lighter Monel metal ring in which the ^{60}Co was enclosed in a nickel tube, sealed and held in place with platinum solder. With all these rings care must be taken to place them tightly enough so that they will not slip off causing loss, or partly off causing damage, yet not so tightly that they will cause abrasion and swelling. The ring must not be used on juveniles which will grow and cause the ring to become too tight. Provided that these precautions are observed, and the animal is caught from time to time to check on the fit of the ring, the method can be used successfully.

Karulin (1970) used ^{60}Co wire with an activity equivalent to 1 mg of radium as a ring, but gives little detail. Cobalt-60 can be readily traced because of its high γ energies (1.17 and 1.33 MeV) but because of its long half-life of 5.26 years, lost rings would retain their radioactivity for many years, which could be a problem.

Punt (1955) and Punt and van Nieuwenhoven (1957) tagged bats with aluminium bands which had one end lengthened and folded back to form a small tube. In this tube was placed a small rod of antimony-124 with an activity of $250\,\mu$Ci. The high energy γ rays of this [124]Sb were able to penetrate the rock wall in the bats' habitat. An interesting point about [124]Sb is that it emits some β radiation, which could be harmful, but this β radiation is reduced if the isotope is allowed to stand for 3 weeks after activation, before use. There is little reduction in the γ activity in this time, as the half-life of [124]Sb is 60 days.

Iodine-131 is a cheap and convenient isotope, with a half-life of 8.04 days and adequate, if lowish, γ energies. Gifford and Griffin (1960) used it on standard bat tags, placing a small drop of solution containing about $5\,\mu$Ci of ^{131}I in the fold of the metal of the tag, allowing it to evaporate, then covering it with a quick-drying glue. The metal was then crimped over the isotope. Cope, Churchwell and Koontz (1961) used a similar method in which a colloidal suspension of gold-198 was pipetted on to the inner surface of a bat tag, dried for 10 minutes under an infrared lamp, then painted over with clear nail polish.

Michielsen (1966, and mentioned in Linn and Shillito, 1960) made leg rings of soft silver for shrews. Such rings would be useless for rodents, but the weak teeth of shrews cannot damage the metal. These rings cause little damage, and the fit can be easily adjusted. They can be irradiated so as to convert some of the silver to [110m]Ag. Michielsen gave them an activity of $200\,\mu$Ci which was adequate for tracking with the good γ radiation. She reported no ill effects from the considerable β emission. Using [198]Au rings containing 2 per cent copper, of 5 mCi activity (quoted in Bailey *et al.*, 1973), however, she reported some radiation damage, perhaps from β emissions. She now proposes to enclose the gold in a tube attached to a ring, after the style of Godfrey, and Linn and Shillito. Her experiments with chromium-nickel (quoted in Bailey *et al.*, 1973) were unsuccessful because of tracing difficulty, perhaps since the γ emissions from the chromium-51, on which tracing depended, were, at 0.323 MeV, of too low energy.

Bailey *et al.* (1973) described a method of using ^{131}I in the form of Ag[131]I, mixed with epoxy resin adhesive and placed in a thin-walled brass tube soldered to a standard Monel metal leg ring. This seems to be satisfactory. Their experiments with a paint containing Ag[131]I, applied to the fur on the dorsal surface of the necks of Wood mice and Bank voles, was not so successful, as the paint was quickly groomed off. They conclude that this is not a useful method.

For night viewing, the usual aid is reflective tape, which requires the use of a light. The recent development of the Betalight is a technique of promise with mammals large enough to carry them. They have been used successfully on rabbits, where they are glued to ear tags. These lights are available in several colours, and are visible up to 300 m with good binoculars. These lights are capsules filled with tritium which decays to emit β particles which cause a phosphor coating on the inside of the capusle to emit light. All the β radiation is absorbed by the phosphor, and none escapes to affect the bearer; see Twigg (1975) and chapter 12.

Inert Implants

The use of inert implants as tracer tags has found favour particularly in America, whereas the external tag has been the preferred method in Western Europe. The theoretical difficulties of the implant method are twofold. First, the method involves piercing the animal's skin, with the attendant hazard of infection. Secondly, the radioactive material, when in position, is in close proximity to, or even in direct contact with, the animal's tissues, and is therefore likely to cause radiation damage. In practice, these problems appear to be more theoretical than real, and inert implants, given reasonable care in their use, seem to be very well tolerated by the animals. This is important because, if there was any suspicion that toleration was poor, data collected from animals carrying inert implants would be highly suspect.

Kaye (1960) appears to be the first user of physiologically inert radioactive implants. He implanted ^{195}Au wires under the abdominal skin of Harvest mice. His implantation technique was similar to that used by many subsequent workers. The radioactive implant was placed inside the tip of a hypodermic needle, which was inserted under the skin of an anaesthetised mouse. The needle was then slowly withdrawn, while the implant was pushed out with a steel wire. Tags with activities up to 4.5 mCi were used. Gold–198 has lowish but adequate γ energies, and Kaye (1961) and Ambrose (1969) found it satisfactory in the field. Although there is considerable β emission, tissue damage has not been reported. The short half-life of the isotope (2.7 days) means that lost tags would rapidly lose most of their radioactivity.

Johanningsmeier and Goodnight (1962) used ^{131}I, the advantages of which have already been pointed out. The problem of the β emission was overcome to some extent by placing the isotope, dissolved in sodium sulphite solution, in a polyethylene capsule, thus placing some space between isotope and animal tissue. Insertion was achieved much as Kaye implanted his gold tags. Like Kaye's tags, the polyethylene capsules could be removed when no longer needed, with no apparent ill effect on the animals.

Barbour (1963) and Harvey and Barbour (1964, 1965) implanted pieces of cobalt alloy wire, containing about 55 μCi of ^{60}Co, subcutaneously in voles and Davis, Barbour and Hassell (1968) placed similar tags under the skin of the forearm of bats. Besides having high γ energies and a lot of β emission, cobalt is a very toxic metal, but these authors report no problems on either count. Cobalt-60 is readily traced, because of its high γ energies, even using low activity tags, but because of its long half-life (5.26 years) lost tags would retain most of their radioactivity for some considerable time, which might be a disadvantage. Hamar, Suteu and Sutova (1964) also used ^{60}Co in the form of needles, presumably of the type used in human radiotherapy, inserted under the dorsal skin of Mole rats. The needle would prevent the cobalt coming into direct contact with the animals' tissues.

Schnell (1968) placed ^{60}Co slugs with about 60 μCi activity in nylon tubes and sealed them with an epoxy glue. He also used a polyethylene pin filled with zinc-65 chloride with an activity of about 75 μCi. Karulin (1970) implanted ^{60}Co wire of an activity equivalent to 1 mg of radium subcutaneously. Cosgrove, Dunaway and Story (1969) used 3 mm ^{60}Co wires, encapsulated in nylon to absorb β-radiation, implanted subcutaneously in the interscapular region.

Graham and Ambrose (1967) used tantalum–182 wire with an activity of 50–75 μCi. Evans and Katznelson (1969) and Evans (1970) have also used similar implants. Tantalum–182 is a useful isotope for tagging purposes because of its high γ energies for easy tracing ($>$ 1 MeV), its low β emission and the physiologically inert nature of the metal. At 115 days its half-life is in the middle range. Inglis *et al.* (1968) implanted both [182]Ta and [195]Au.

Frigerio and Eisler (1968) suggest selenium-75 for small animals. It can easily be incorporated into epoxy resins which will adhere firmly to almost any surface, forming a hard, non-toxic coating. Such a coating is highly resistant to mechanical damage, and to leaching of the radionuclide. The γ energies of ^{75}Se are all less than 0.3 MeV, so are on the low side, and it might be necessary to use a tag of rather high activity to be readily discriminated from background counts. A particular advantage is that the isotope decays by electron capture, so that no charged particles are emitted, and a high local skin dose is avoided. At 121 days the half-life is in the middle range.

For larger animals, or when observation is to be continued for more than a year, Frigerio and Eisler suggest the use of sodium-22, which has a long half-life of 2.6 years, and high γ energies of 1.28 MeV. A difficulty with this isotope is that it emits β radiation in the form of positrons which could cause tissue damage, but a screen of 0.6 mm of aluminium between radionuclide and tissue will convert the positron into two less damaging γ rays of 0.51 MeV. The epoxy resin mixtures could, of course, be used equally well to make external tags.

Frigerio and Eisler also considered the effect on tracing efficiency of the tissue half values of the γ rays emitted by the isotopes they recommend. These could be important if any considerable portion of the animal's body came between the radioactive source and the detection device. This is unlikely to be the case in a dorsal implant being scanned from above, but could be a problem with a leg or wing tag, or where, as in Frigerio and Eisler's case, they were recording nest visits. The tissue half value of ^{75}Se is quoted by them as about 6 cm, that of the 0.51 MeV γ rays of [22]Na as 7.4 cm, and of the 1.28 MeV γ rays of [22]Na as 11.5 cm. Clearly these values are not negligible, and the [22]Na would be preferred for larger animals. Frigerio and Eisler, using a counting distance of less than 1 m, were in fact able to use quite weak tags of 50 μCi.

A relatively unusual method was tried by Bailey *et al.* (1973). The inert radioactive implant, in this case ^{131}I, was prepared in dispersed form, on the assumption that this would avoid any high local dose of radiation. Two forms of implant into the peritoneum of mice and voles were tried; first iodide bound to an ion-exchange resin, and second iodide precipitated as insoluble silver iodide. Unfortunately, the metabolic processes of the animals' bodies were able to deal with both these preparations, and their biological half-lives were only in the range of 1–4 days, making them useless except for the shortest-term investigations. This technique might, however, merit further development.

Introduction of Metabolisable Radionuclides

Radioactive material can be introduced into the animal's body in a form in which it can be incorporated into the animal's metabolism. This technique can be used, as can the two methods already described, for tracking animals. When used for this purpose, many metabolisable materials have the advantage that they are well dispersed throughout the body, avoiding the danger of high local doses of radiation.

This is not always so, however, and many elements are concentrated in specific localities within the body. Iodine, for example, becomes localised in the thyroid gland, while several elements are bone-seeking. Although this characteristic can be a disadvantage from the point of view of radiation damage, it can be made use of for some special purposes. Another snag with metabolisable substances is that their biological half-life may be quite short, and the traceable radiation may quickly reduce to an unacceptable level.

Metabolisable material can, however, be used for many purposes other than simple tracking. One valuable technique, first suggested by Jenkins (1954) permits ectoparasites to mark themselves by feeding on a host carrying a radioisotope in its blood. Developments of this method, which have mainly taken place in Russia, are reviewed in detail by Kulik (1967). Other techniques make use of the fact that materials incorporated into an animal's metabolic cycles may be deposited in specific locations in the body, voided with the faeces and urine, or passed on to the offspring. Metabolisable radioactive substances can be introduced into the animal's body by forced or natural feeding, by injection, or by implant.

Carrick (1956) tagged carrot bait with ^{131}I, and assessed the amount of bait eaten by measuring the radioactivity in the thyroid glands of wild rabbits.

Miller (1957) injected phosphorus-32 as H_3PO_4 solution into voles, and obtained information about their movements by detecting radioactivity at defaecation and urination stations (4 inch square aluminium sheets).

Rongstad (1965) implanted ^{45}Ca under the skin of several species of mammals, a technique pioneered by McCabe and LePage (1958) with pheasants. The calcium was in the form of calcium oxalate mixed with fat and enclosed in a gelatine capsule to delay release. An antibiotic was used during implantation to control infection. Implants were made into female rabbits, and the toe bones of young rabbits ashed and screened for radioactivity. An implant of 175 μCi into a Cottontail rabbit would ensure labelling of the fifth or sixth litters. A dose of 60 μCi would label one year's production of young (four litters) of a Snowshoe hare. The single annual litter of a 13-lined Ground squirrel could be marked with an implant of 20-40 μCi. Litter mates could be identified by level of radioactivity. In addition to identifying offspring, this technique yields data on movements and can help assess population levels. Meslow and Keith (1968) and Keith and Meslow (1968) used the method on wild Snowshoe hares.

Calcium-45 was also used by Twigg and Miller (1963) in a laboratory test on rats. The ^{45}Ca was fed in crushed wheat and screening of bones permitted identification of the isotope recipient after 113 days, and of offspring from a marked mother 10 weeks after she had received the isotope.

Constantine, Jensen and Tierkel (1959) did some preparation work for a study in which it was hoped to mark bats with ^{32}P and look for radioactivity in suspected predators. This seemed to be a reasonable possibility. Another laboratory study using ^{32}P was that of Shura-Bura, Tararin and Mel'nikov (1960). They fed the isotope to rats in bait, and carried out comprehensive studies involving autoradiography of bones and radioactivity of faeces.

Carbon-14 was used by Soldatkin *et al.* (1961) as ^{14}C-glycine or ^{14}C-acetic acid. The use of these rapidly metabolised biochemicals labelled serum proteins in gerbils (into the stomachs of which he had introduced the marked compounds) and made it possible to study the feeding activity of fleas in natural conditions.

Shura-Bura and Kharlamov (1961) used strontium-89, applied by injection or feeding, to study the movements of rats and mice and their fleas.

A number of workers have used ^{32}P to study the movements of mammals by locating radioactive droppings, viz. Rudenchik (1963) on the gerbil *Rhombomys opimus*; Stoddart (1970) on Water voles *Arvicola terrestris*; Birkenholz (1962) on muskrats *Neofiber alleni*; Litvin and Kareseva (1968) on voles *Microtus oeconomus*. Rudenchik also looked for 'radioactive' fleas as did Sviridov (1963) and Sviridov *et al.* (1963), also working on *Rhombomys opimus*. Bykovsky (1961) used ^{32}P to study the relative attractiveness of different baits, and the accidental mortality among other species during rodent poisoning campaigns.

Myllymäki (1969), Myllymäki *et al.* (1971) and Myllymäki, Paäsikallio and Häkkinen (1971) developed techniques for marking apple bait with ^{32}P, ^{131}I and ^{51}Cr, which they allowed the animals to take in the field. On recovering the animals they distinguished those marked with ^{32}P, which had whole body radio-activity, from those marked with ^{131}I where radioactivity was concentrated in the thyroid, and those marked with ^{51}Cr where radioactivity was concentrated in the spleen.

Kartman *et al.* (1958) and Hartwell *et al.* (1958) tagged fleas with cerium-144. The cerium forms a stable compound with the exoskeleton of the flea. Although the objective was mainly to trace fleas, radioactive vole and rat faeces were found, indicating that these mammals eat fleas.

Sulphur-35 was used as well as phosphorus-32 and carbon-14 to study the movements and ectoparasites of gerbils by Rudenchik *et al.* (1967) and by Korneyev (1967*a* and *b*). Iron-59 and zinc-65 were used as well as iodine-131 by Gentry, Smith and Beyers (1971) to study small mammal movements.

An interesting use of ^{65}Zn was made by Nellis, Jenkins and Marshall (1967) who fed and injected the isotope into a range of mammal species, and then identified radioactive faeces up to a year later, providing a useful marker for determining range and movements. Chromium-51 and scandium-47 can be used as faecal markers in man (Pearson, 1966) but have not so far been used in ecological work on animals for this purpose.

Special Techniques

Although they cannot be described strictly as small-mammal marking, three special techniques deserve a brief mention. The first concerns the marking of seeds of forest trees, with a view to gathering information on their fate. Lawrence and Rediske (1959), Radvanyi (1966) and Quink, Abbott and Mellen (1970) marked seeds with scandium-46 then exposed them to forest rodents, and afterwards searched for caches of seeds with a scintillation counter. Myllymäki and Paasikallio (1972) used the cheaper ^{32}P instead of ^{46}Sc to mark spruce seeds, and scanned forest mammals later to find out whether they had been eating the seeds.

The second technique uses radon-222 gas for studies on the burrows of digging animals, but the brief synopsis so far published by Ovchenkov and Nikoforov (1965) is not very informative.

In the third technique implanted lithium fluoride microdosimeters permitted estimates to be made of the time spent above ground by Pocket mice *Perognathus formosus* in an 8-ha circular area of the Mojave Desert irradiated by a ^{137}Cs source placed 15 m above the ground. The source was differentially shielded to give a more or less even dose over the experimental area, and the mice were largely shielded by earth from the radioactivity while in their burrows (French, Maza and Aschwanden, 1966).

Hazards

The only detailed assessment of the possible danger to field workers using the kind of methods described in this review seems to be that of Häkkinen, Myllymäki and Paasikallio (1970). They describe the precautions taken against accidental irradiation of workers using their techniques, and estimate the dose rates received by these workers. They come to the conclusion that dose rates are well within acceptable levels.

Not a lot is known about the effects of the kind of radiation received by animals which are the subject of the techniques described in this review. There is a certain amount of incidental data, but no full-scale investigation seems to have been made.

Häkkinen *et al.* (1970) measured dose rates received by small rodents eating their radioactive apple bait, and concluded that they were well below lethal. No behavioural disturbance was noted, and these authors conclude that dangers to experimental animals are more theoretical than real. They also consider that predators would have to consume unlikely quantities of radioactive prey to be at risk, and are not at serious hazard.

Lack of behaviour change was also accepted by Barbour and Harvey (1968) as an indication of no radiation damage from their ^{60}Co wire implants. They also noted that the animals suffered no weight loss, which they took to signify freedom from radiation damage.

Schnell (1968) also used weight as a criterion of the health of animals fitted with implants of 60-75 μCi, and found no weight loss. He made an attempt to determine actual dosage received by fitting three animals with glass rod dosimeters, and came to the conclusion that vital tissues got 39 R over 112 days, which he thought unlikely to produce adverse effects.

Frigerio and Eisler (1968) estimated a dose of only 20 rads/year from a 50 μCi tag on a 100 kg animal, but suggested as a precaution that tags should be placed in a relatively radio-resistant region of the body, such as the thorax. Hamar, Şuteu and Şutova (1963) carried out comprehensive dosage and radioactivity test on hamsters, mice and voles, and found that they could give 570 μCi of [32]P (1.5 μCi per g body weight) without apparent ill effects. Kaye (1965) mentions pilot experiments with miniature glass rod dosimeters to determine doses *in vivo*, but gives no details.

On the other hand, compared with these authors who noted no ill effects from radiation, some other workers report damage. Cosgrove *et al.* (1969) found that the ^{60}Co wire implants previously described caused carcinomata in 2 of 3 mice *Peromyscus maniculatus* in 10-20 months with contact doses of 2-15.7 R per day. Michielsen (quoted in Bailey *et al.* 1973) reported that [198]Au rings with 2 per cent copper, of 5 mCi activity, seemed to cause radiation damage. Litvin (1967) found that 0.5-2.0 mCi of ^{32}P killed voles *Microtus* sp., while 0.0625-0.25 mCi caused no apparent pathology.

In a series of papers (Koletsky and Christie, 1951; Hankins, 1954; Mewissen and Comar, 1959) reporting work on a variety of rodent species, the LD_{50} of ^{32}P is estimated to be 4.3–4.5 μCi per g body weight. Most experimenters are using 0.2–0.5 LD_{50}.

On the question of behaviour, Layne, Birkenholz and Carlson (1963) observed differences in the feeding and drinking behaviour of Cotton rats fed 0.5 LD_{50} of ^{32}P. Suter and Rawson (1968) noted disturbance of circadian rhythm in Deer mice given D_2O in their drinking water.

Kharlamov (1965) considered the modifying effects of radiation on flea behaviour.

It seems likely that, used with common sense and moderation, radioactive markers are quite safe for both researchers and animals, but it must be admitted that the evidence for this is sparse, fragmented, and usually based on small numbers of instances, so that a more comprehensive investigation of this problem would be welcomed.

Conclusion

In general, it may be concluded that radioactive marking, in all its variety, provides a valuable range of techniques which can enable researchers to gain access to information not readily available by any other methods. However, it must be borne in mind at all times that radiation is dangerous to both worker and animal, and the greatest care and circumspection must be observed in its use. Dose rates should be kept as low as practicable, and care taken to recover tags as often as possible. The environmental hazard must also be considered, and although this is usually vanishingly small, it should always be remembered that radiation hazards cause public alarm out of all proportion to the real danger, so that the greatest discretion should always be exercised.

References

Ambrose, H. W. (1969). A comparison of *Microtus pennsylvanicus* home ranges as determined by isotope and live trap methods. *Am. Midl. Nat., 81*, 535–555.

Bailey, G. N. A., Linn, I. J. and Walker, P. J. (1973). Radioactive marking of small mammals. *Mammal Rev., 3*, 11–23.

Barbour, R. W. (1963). *Microtus*: a simple method of recording time spent in the nest. *Science, 141*, 41.

Barbour, R. W. and Harvey, M. J. (1968). The effect of radioactive tags on the activity of rodents. *Am. Midl. Nat., 79*, 519–522.

Birkenholz, D. E. (1962). A study of the life history and ecology of the round-tailed muskrat (*Neofiber alleni* True) in north central Florida, Doctoral dissertation, University of Florida.

Bykovsky, V. A. (1961). Primenenie radioacktivnovo fosfora dlya samomarkirovki teplokrovnykh biotsenoza. *Materialy simpoziuma po primenenio biofiziki v oblasti zashchity rastenii* (Use of radioactive phosphorus for selflabelling warm-blooded animals. *Proceedings of a symposium on the applications of biophysics in the field of plant protection*). P. 32. Leningrad (In Russian).

Carrick, R. (1956). Radioiodine as an indicator of free-feeding activity of the rabbit, *Oryctolagus cuniculus* (L.). *C.S.I.R.O. Wildl. Res.,* **1**, 106–113.

Constantine, D. G., Jensen, J. A. and Tierkel, E. S. (1959). The use of radio-labeling in determining prey-predator relationships. *J. Mammal.,* **40**, 240–242.

Cope, J. B., Churchwell, E. and Koontz, K. (1961). A method of tagging bats with radioactive gold-198 in homing experiments, *Proc. Indiana Acad. Sci.,* **70** (1960), 267–269.

Cosgrove, G. E., Dunaway, P. B. and Story, J. D. (1969). Malignant tumors associated with cutaneously implanted ^{60}Co radioactive wires in *Peromyscus maniculatus. Bull. Wildl. Dis. Ass.,* **5**, 311–319.

Davis, W. H., Barbour, R. W. and Hassell, M. D. (1968). Colonial behaviour of *Eptesicus fuscus. J. Mammal.,* **49**, 44–50.

Evans, F. C. (1970). Seasonal effects of light, temperature and radiation on activity patterns of the meadow vole (*Microtus pennsylvanicus*). *Publs Mich. Univ. Dept. Zool.*

Evans, F. C. and Katznelson, M. (1969). Activity patterns in the meadow vole, *Microtus pennysylvanicus* Ord., under field conditions. *Bull. ecol. Soc. Am.,* **50**, 106.

French, N. R., Maza, B. G. and Aschwanden, A. P. (1966). Periodicity of desert rodent activity. *Science,* **154**, 1194–1195.

Frigerio, N. A. and Eisler, W. J. (1968). Low cost, automatic, nest and burrow monitor using radioactive tagging. *Ecology,* **49**, 788–791.

Fullagar, P. J. and Jewell, P. A. (1965). Marking small rodents and the difficulties of using leg rings. *J. Zool., Lond.,* **147**, 224–228.

Gentry, J. B., Smith, M. H. and Beyers, R. J. (1971). Use of radioactively tagged bait to study movement patterns in small mammal populations. *Annls Zool. Fenn.,* **8**, 17–21.

Gerrard, M. (1968–69). Tagging of small mammals with radioisotopes for tracking purposes. *Isotopes Radiat. Technol.,* **6**, 200–204.

Gerrard, M. (1969). Tagging of small mammals with radioisotopes for tracking purposes: a literature review. *Int. J. appl. Radiat. Isotopes,* **20**, 671–676.

Gifford, C. E. and Griffin, D. R. (1960). Notes on homing and migratory behaviour of bats. *Ecology,* **41**, 378–381.

Godfrey, G. K. (1953). A technique for finding *Microtus* nests. *J. Mammal.,* **34**, 503–505.

Godfrey, G. K. (1954*a*). Tracing field voles (*Microtus agrestis*) with a Geiger–Müller counter. *Ecology,* **35**, 5–10.

Godfrey, G. K. (1954*b*). Use of radioactive isotopes in small-mammal ecology. *Nature,* **174**, 951–952.

Godfrey, G. K. (1955). A field study of the activity of the mole (*Talpa europaea*). *Ecology,* **36**, 678–685.

Graham, W. J. and Ambrose, H. W. (1967). A technique for continuously locating small mammals in field enclosures. *J. Mammal.,* **48**, 639–642.

Griffin, D. R. (1952). Radioactive tagging of animals under natural conditions. *Ecology,* **33**, 329–335.

Häkkinen, U., Myllymäki, A. and Paasikallio, A. (1970). Radiation risks and avoidance of hazards in connection with mass marking of small rodents with radioisotopes. *EPPO Publications, Series A,* **58**, 237–248.

Hamar, M., Suteu, G. H. and Sutova, M. (1963). 'Home range' studies in rodents by marking with P^{32}. *Rev. biol. Acad. République Populaire Roum.*, **8**, 431-446.

Hamar, M., Suteu, G. H. and Sutova, M., (1964). Home range and activity studies of the mole rat (*Spalax leucodon* Nordm.) by Co^{60} marking. *Rev. Roum. Biol.* (*Serie Zool.*), **9**, 421-433.

Hankins, R. M. (1954). Effect of radioactive phosphorus (P^{32}) on the blood cells and other tissues of the cotton rat *Sigmodon hispidus. Kans. Univ. Sci. Bull.*, **36**, 1389-1421.

Hartwell, W. V., Quan, S. F., Scott, K. G. and Kartman, L. (1958). Observations on flea transfer between hosts; a mechanism in the spread of bubonic plague. *Science*, **127**, 814.

Harvey, M. J. and Barbour, R. W. (1964). An improved method for determining home range. *A.S.B. Bull.*, **11**, 47.

Harvey, M. J. and Barbour, R. W. (1965). Home range of *Microtus achrogaster* as determined by a modified minimum area method. *J. Mammal.*, **46**, 398-402.

Inglis, J. M., Post, L. J., Lahser, C. W. and Gibson, D. V. (1968). A device for automatically detecting the presence of small animals carrying radioactive tags. *Ecology*, **49**, 361-363.

Jenkins, D. W. (1954). Advances in medical entomology using radioisotopes. *Expl Parasit.*, **3**, 474-490.

Johanningsmeier, A. G. and Goodnight, C. J. (1962). Use of iodine-131 to measure movements of small mammals. *Science*, **138**, 147-148.

Kartman, L., Prince, F. M., Quan, S. F. and Stark, H. E. (1958). New knowledge on the ecology of sylvatic plague. *Ann. N.Y. Acad. Sci.*, **70**, 668-711.

Karulin, B. E. (1970). K metodike primeneniya izotopov dlya izucheniya podvizhnosti i aktivnosti melkikh mlekopitaioshchikh. (Technique for using isotopes for the study of mobility and activity of small mammals.) *Zool. Zh.*, **49**, 444-450. (In Russian).

Kaye, S. V. (1960). Gold-198 wires used to study movements of small mammals. *Science.*, **131**, 824.

Kaye, S. V. (1961). Movements of harvest mice tagged with gold-198. *J. Mammal.*, **42**, 323-337.

Kaye, S. V. (1965). Use of miniature glass rod dosimeters in radiation ecology. *Ecology*, **46**, 201-206.

Keith, L. B. and Meslow, E. C. (1968). Trap response by snowshoe hares. *J. Wildl. Mgmt*, **32**, 795-801.

Kharlamov, V. P. (1965). Izmeneniya aktivosti pitaniya i podvizhnosti blokh *Xenopsylla cheopis*, markirovannykh radioaktivnym fosforom P^{32}. (Changes in the feeding activity and mobility of the flea *Xenopsylla cheopis*, marked with radioactive phosphorus P^{32}.) *Zool. Zh.*, **44**, 547-552. (In Russian).

Koletsky, S. and Christie, J. H. (1951). Biologic effects of radioactive poisoning in rat. *Am. J. Path.*, **27**, 175-194.

Korneyev, G. A. (1967a). O kharaktere ispol'zovaniya poludennymi peschankami kolonii bol'shikh peschanok po resul'tatam radioaktivnovo mecheniya gryzunov. (On the nature of the utilisation of great gerbil (*Rhombomys opimus*) colonies by midday gerbils (*Meriones meridianus*) as revealed by radioactive labelling of the rodents). *Nauch Doklady Vȳssh. Shk. (Biol.)*, **1**, 26-30. (In Russian).

Korneyev, G. A. (1967*b*). K izuchenie mezhvidovykh ektoparazitarnykh kontaktov nekotorykh vidov mlekopitaioshchikh y poseleniyakh bol'shikh peschanok. (On interspecies ectoparasitic contacts of some species of mammals in colonies of great gerbils.) *Parazitologiya*, **1**, 233-237 (In Russian).

Kulik, J. L. (1967). Primenenie radioaktivnykh izotopov v ekologicheskikh i biotsenoticheskikh issledovaniyakh nazemnykh pozvonochnykh. (The use of radioactive isotopes in ecological and biocoenotic studies of terrestrial vertebrates.) *Zool. Zh.*, **46**, 1234-1246. (In Russian).

Lawrence, W. H. and Rediske, J. H. (1959). Radio-tracer technique for determining the fate of Douglas-fir seed. *Proc. Soc. Am. Forest.*, 1959, 99-101.

Layne, J. N., Birkenholz, D. E. and Carlson, L. (1963). Effects of phosphorus-32 on the cotton rat. *Q. Jl Fla Acad. Sci.* 26, 78-88.

Linn, I. and Shillito, J. (1960). Rings for marking very small mammals. *Proc. zool. Soc. Lond.*, **134**, 489-495.

Litvin, V. Yu. (1967). Ob optimal'nykh dozakh P^{32} dlya izotopnovo mecheniya v prirode serykh polevok. (On the optimal doses of P^{32} for isotope labelling of the common vole.) *Zool. Zh.*, **46**, 1088-1093 (In Russian).

Litvin, V. Yu. and Karaseva, E. V. (1968). Opyt izucheniya sutochnoi podvizhnosti polevok-ekonomok (*Microtus oeconomus* Pall.) metodom izotopnovo mecheniya. (A study of daily migrations of root voles by means of radioactive labelling.) *Zool. Zh.*, **47**, 1701-1706. (In Russian).

McCabe, R. A. and LePage, G. A. (1958). Identifying progeny from pheasant hens given radioactive calcium (Ca^{45}). *J. Wildl. Mgmt*, **22**, 134-141.

Meese, G. B. and Cheeseman, C. L. (1969). Radio-active tracking of the mole (*Talpa europaea*) over a 24-hour period. *J. Zool., Lond.*, **158**, 197-203.

Meslow, E. C. and Keith, L. B. (1968). Demographic parameters of a snowshoe hare population. *J. Wildl. Mgmt*, **32**, 812-834.

Mewissen, D. J. and Comar, C. L. (1959). The effect of cystamine on acute radiotoxicity of P^{32} in mice. *Nucl. Med.*, **1**, 47-53.

Michielsen, N. C. (1966). Intraspecific and interspecific competition in the shrews *Sorex araneus* L. and *S. minutus* L. *Archs néerl. Zool.*, **17**, 73-174.

Miller, L. S. (1957). Tracing vole movements by radioactive excretory products. *Ecology*, **38**, 132-136.

Myllymäki, A. (1969). Trapping experiments on the water vole, *Arvicola terrestris* (L.), with the aid of the isotope technique. In: *Energy Flow Through Small Mammal Populations*, (ed. K. Petrusewicz and L. Ryszkowski), pp. 39-55. Warsaw.

Myllymäki, A. and Pääsikallio, A. (1972). The detection of seed-eating small mammals by means of P^{32} treatement of spruce seed. *Aquilo: Seria Zool.*, **13**, 21-24.

Myllymäki, A., Pääsikallio, A. and Häkkinen, U. (1971). Analysis of a 'standard trapping' of *Microtus agrestis* (L.) with triple isotope marking outside the quadrat. *Annls Zool. Fenn.*, **8**, 22-34.

Myllymäki, A., Paasikallio, A., Pankakoski, E. and Kanervo, V. (1971). Removal experiments on small quadrats as a means of rapid assessment of the abundance of small mammals. *Annls Zool. Fenn.*, **8**, 177-185.

Nellis, D. W., Jenkins, J. H. and Marshall, A. D. (1967). Radioactive zinc as a feces tag in rabbits, foxes and bobcats. *Proc. 21 st Conf. Southeastern Ass. Game Fish Commissioners.* Columbia, S. Carolina, pp. 205-207.

Ovchenkov, V. Y. and Nikoforov, V. S. (1965). Vacuum method of determination of radon in the burrows of digging animals. *Materialy Komi Respublikanskoi Molodezhnoi nauchnoi, konferentsii, Tezisy dokladov. (Proceedings of a scientific conference of the Komi Republic Youth. Abstracts of Reports.)* Syktyvkar. (In Russian).

Pearson, J. D. (1966). Use of Cr^{51}-labelled haemoglobin and Sc^{47} as inert faecal markers. *Int. J. appl. Radiat. Isotopes,* **17**, 13–16.

Pendleton, R. C. (1956). Uses of marking animals in ecological studies: labeling animals with radioisotopes. *Ecology,* **37**, 686–689.

Punt, A. (1955). Radioactive banding of bats. *Acta physiol. pharmac. néerl.,* **4**, 439–440.

Punt, A. and Nieuwenhoven, P. J. van (1957). The use of radioactive bands in tracing hibernating bats. *Experientia,* **13**, 51–54.

Quink, T. F., Abbott, H. G. and Mellen, W. J. (1970). Locating tree seed caches of small mammals with a radioisotope. *Forest Sci.,* **16**, 147–148.

Radvanyi, A. (1966). Destruction of radio-tagged seeds of white spruce by small mammals during summer months. *Forest Sci.,* **12**, 307–15.

Rongstad, O. J. (1965). Calcium–45 labeling of mammals for use in population studies. *Hlth Phys.,* **11**, 1543–1556.

Rudenchik, Yu. V. (1963). Izuchenie podvizhnosti bol'shoi peschanki s pomosch 'io radioaktivnykh indikatorov. *Materialy nauchnoi konferentsii po prirodnoi ochagovosti i profilaktike chumy* (The study of mobility of great gerbils with the aid of radioactive indicators. *Proceedings of a scientific conference on the natural foci and prophylaxis of plague*) (ed. M. A. Aikimbaev), pp. 198–200. Alma-Ata. (In Russian).

Rudenchik, Yu, V., Soldatkin, I. S., Severova, E. A., Mokrievich, N. A. and Klimova, Z. I. (1967). Kolichestvennaya otsenka vozmozhnostei territorial 'novo peredvizheniya epizootii chumy v populyatsii bol'shikh peschanok (Severnye Kyzylkumy). (Quantitative evaluation of the possibilities of a territorial advance of plague epizooites in the population of *Rhombomys opimus* Licht. (North Kyzylkumy).) *Zool. Zh.,* **46**, 117–123. (In Russian).

Sanderson, G. C. (1966). The study of mammal movements—a review. *J. Wildl. Mgmt,* **30**, 215–235.

Schnell, J. H. (1968). The limiting effect of natural predation on experimental cotton rat populations. *J. Wildl. Mgmt,* **32**, 689–711.

Shura-Bura, B. L. Tararin, R. A., and Mel'nikov, B. K. (1960). K metodike radio-aktivnoi markirovki serykh krys s tsel'io izucheniya voprosov migratsii. (On the methods of radioactive labelling rats *Rattus norvegicus* with the aim of studying migration problems.) *Zool. Zh.,* **39**, 1700–1706. (In Russian).

Shura-Bura, B. L. and Kharlamov, V. P. (1961). Radioavtografiya kak metod vyyavleniya mechenykh gryzunov i ikh ektoparazitov pri izuchenii voprosov migratsii. (Autoradiography as a method to reveal labelled rodents and their ectoparasites when studying migration problems.) *Zool. Zh.,* **40**, 258–263. (In Russian).

Soldatkin, I. S., Novokreshchenova, N. S., Rudenchik, Yu. V., Ostrovsky, I. B. and Levoshina, A. I. (1961). Opyt izucheniya aktivnosti pitaniya blokh bol'shikh peschanok v prirodnykh usloviyakh s primeneniem radioaktivnykh indikatorov, (An experiment in studying activity of feeding of the fleas parasitizing Gerbillinae under natural conditions with the use of radioactive tracers.) *Zool. Zh.,* **40,** 1647-1650. (In Russian).

Stoddart, D. M. (1970). Individual range, dispersion and dispersal in a population of water voles (*Arvicola terrestris* (L.)). *J. Anim. Ecol.,* **39,** 403-425.

Suter, R. B. and Rawson, K. S. (1968). Circadian activity rhythm of the deer mouse, *Peromyscus*: effect of deuterium oxide. *Science,* **160,** 1011-1014.

Sviridov, G. G. (1963). Primenenie radioaktivnykh izotopov v izuchenii nekotorykh voprosov ekologii blokh. Soobshchenie 2. Kontakt zver'kov i.intensivnost' obmena ektoparazitami v populyatsii bol'shoi peschanki. (Application of radioactive isotopes for the study of some problems of flea ecology. Part 2. The contact of animals and intensity of the exchange of ectoparasites in the population of *Rhombomys opimus.*) *Zool. Zh.,* **42,** 947-949. (In Russian).

Sviridov, G. G., Morozova, I. V., Kaluzhenova, Z. P. and Il'inskaya, V. L. (1963). Primenenie radioaktivnykh izotopov pri izuchenii nekotorykh voprosov eko-logii blokh. Soobshchenie 1. Alimentarnye svyazi blokh roda *Xenopsylla* s bol 'shimi peschankami v estestvennykh usloviyakh. (Application of radioactive isotopes for the study of some problems of flea ecology. Part 1. Alimentary relations of fleas of the genus *Xenopsylla* with *Rhombomys opimus* Pall. under natural conditions.) *Zool. Zh.,* **42,** 546-550. (In Russian).

Tester, J. R. (1962). Techniques for studying movements of vertebrates in the field. In: *Proc. First natn. Symp. Radioecology,* (ed. V. Schultz and A. W. Klement) pp. 445-450.

Twigg, G. I. (1975). Techniques in mammalogy. Chapter 3. Marking mammals. *Mammal Rev.,* **5,** 101-116.

Twigg, G. I. and Miller, H. (1963). The use of calcium[45] as an agent for labeling rat populations. *J. Mammal.,* **44,** 335-337.

20 Radio-tracking: some applications and limitations

David W. Macdonald*

For centuries men have observed and interpreted tracks and signs left by animals. Fieldcraft has grown from a trapper's art into a biologists' science, which has been enhanced, rather than made obsolete by the advent of the most recent technology. Murie's (1936) meticulous 'Following fox trails' and Haglund's (1966) miles of skiing along lynx tracks are examples of the rewards of systematic tracking, a skill championed by Tinbergen (for example 1965). Ingenious deductions have been necessary because so many animals, in particular mammals, elude direct observation. Indeed because of hard ground, thick undergrowth and months without snow, insights gained from reading tracks are often limited to mere glimpses of the animal's lifestyle. For this reason the development of radio-tracking apparatus constitutes a revolution in the history of field biology. To answer the many biological questions for which glimpses of the animal's whereabouts and behaviour are insufficient, radio-tracking can provide continuous records not only of where an animal travelled, but also of when it was there. These attributes are marred by one shortcoming; while yielding information on *where* and *when* an animal moved, radio-tracking tells little of *what* it was doing. Nevertheless, radio-tracking techniques are useful additions to the skills and fieldcraft of biologists.

Equipment

In radio-tracking, radio signals are emitted continuously or at intervals by a small transmitter attached to the animal, and detected from a distance using one or more receivers with directional antennae. Though commercially produced apparatus is now available, much of the equipment used by field biologists is still laboratory made, using circuitry and design to suit the particular study.

Transmitter assemblies

For accounts of early transmitters see Cochran and Lord (1963), Verts (1963), Craighead, Craighead and Davies (1963). Transmitters consist of an oscillator

*David W. Macdonald is a Research Fellow of Balliol College, and member of the animal Behaviour Research Group, at Oxford University. His research interests include the adaptive significance of animal social systems and the relevance of this to sound wildlife management and conservation. He has worked in Britain and overseas on the behaviour of various carnivores, including foxes, wolves, jackals and hyaenas, and previously studied monkeys in Borneo and bird flocks in India. During the past 5 years he has worked extensively with radio-tracking.

which is normally, but not always, crystal controlled. The continuous pulsed signals can be adjusted to rates which vary from clicks to a buzz, so offering means of individual recognition when several are in use at the same time. Transmitter design and output are controlled by law, and also by practical considerations which make this a difficult field for the average biologist to enter without help. Zimmerman, Geraud and Charles-Dominique (1976) and Leuze (1977) provide up-to-date guidance for those who have no alternative but to make and test their own equipment, but biologists are advised to use commercially-made equipment wherever possible.

The signal generated by the transmitter is broadcast from an antenna, which may be a loose-ended length of wire (whip antenna), a circle or loop, or a dust-coil antenna—a cylinder of iron-impregnated resin wound with wire. Power is provided by batteries, which in many ways limit the performance of transmitters. Lithium sulphide cells maintain output longer than mercury batteries; lithium cells are more expensive, but provide twice the voltage per unit weight. In my experience, battery failure from shelf deterioration or moisture penetration is the commonest cause of transmitter dysfunction; batteries must be obtained as fresh as possible from the manufacturer or supplier, and sealed in the unit to ensure long life; see also Harding, Chute and Doell (1976). Recently, some use has been made of rechargeable solar cells (Aucouturier *et al.*, 1977).

Transmitter components may be waterproofed in beeswax and encapsulated in dental acrylic, epoxy resin or liquid plastic; with resins the catalyst should be used sparingly to prevent overheating during setting. Batteries are especially sensitive to heat; conducting epoxy glue is a safer alternative to solder. Complete, the transmitter with batteries should weigh less than 5 per cent of the animal for which it is designed—roughly the percentage weight of human clothing. Transmitter shape depends on the animal concerned. Collar transmitters are appropriate for most mammals (see, for example, Cochran and Hagen, 1963; Mech, Kuechle, Warner and Tester. 1965; Beal, 1967). For badgers *Meles meles,* Kruuk (in press) designed a backpack harness (figure 20.1), and Morris (1966) used a 'Wonderlastic' girdle on hedgehogs *Erinaceus europaeus.* Collars must be pliable, or hinged for flexibility if stiff, and carefully tailored to fit the individual. Machine belting and copper braiding (the latter bound in insulating tape to prevent fraying) make excellent collars which can be trimmed to length on the spot. Simple but foolproof fastenings are essential. A whip antenna may protrude above the harness or be built into it. A metal braid collar makes a serviceable loop antenna; care must be taken to seal the transmitter carefully at the point of emergence, to keep water out. Special structures on animals may be put to good use; transmitters have been embedded in the horns of Black rhinoceros *Diceros bicornis,* with a loop antenna set in a groove around the base of the horn (Anderson and Hitchins, 1971; see also Owen-Smith, 1971).

Transmitter packs for birds include a chest pack with loop antenna harness (Nicholls and Warner, 1968), and backpacks attached by loops under the wings, with a whip antenna trailing down the bird's tail (figure 20.2) (Hardy, 1977) or fixed to imped or natural feathers (Kenward, 1976, 1978; Dunstan, 1973). Swanson and Kuechle (1976) mounted a two-stage transmitter above a duck's bill, positioned so that different pulse rates were received as the head bobbed up and down during feeding.

Figure 20.1 An anaesthetised badger, wearing a radio harness with Betalight (embedded in the Perspex case of the transmitter) and diagonal strips of reflecting tape. Photograph: Dr C. Cheeseman, Crown Copyright Reserved—Reproduced by permission of H.M.S.O.

Figure 20.2 Tawny owl fitted with backpack, trailing antenna and visual marker tag. The radio transmitter is hidden beneath the dorsal feathers. Photograph: Dr A. R. Hardy.

Care is needed to determine whether the presence of the transmitter affects the wearer's behaviour. Boag (1972) found that Red grouse *Lagopus lagopus*

wearing transmitters fed less than those without (see also Boag, Watson and
Parr, 1973) and Sargeant, Swanson and Doty (1973) suggested that Teal *Anas
discors* carrying radio packs were more susceptible to predation by Mink
Mustela vison; see also Gilmer, Ball, Cowardin and Riechmann (1974). Signs of
collar abrasion (Beal, 1967) or weight loss indicate unsatisfactory design.
Hamilton (1976) found no significant differences in weight of leopards before
and after fitting them with transmitters, and Kenward (1977) found the weight
and behaviour of Goshawks *Accipiter gentilis* and a Sparrow hawk *A. nisus* little
affected by the presence of small transmitters. Trapping, rather than attachment
of transmitters, was believed to account for short-term changes in behaviour of
Water voles *Arvicola terrestris* (Leuze, 1976), in which feeding and activity
lessened after fitting. Cumming (1971) noted unusual excursions and activity in
Warthogs *Phacochoerus africanus* after capture.

Receivers and antennae

Designs for receivers have been published by Cochran and Nelson (1963) and
Seidensticker, Hornocker, Knight and Judd (1970); several models are
available commercially. Directional antennae are generally used, of simple H
shape (Adcock) or more complex (and usually more cumbersome) twin yagi
pattern. These work on the phase relationship between signals received by their
paired elements, giving maximum and minimum signal strength according to
their orientation in relation to the transmitter. Designs for directional antennae
are given in Cochran, Warner and Tester (1964) and Anderson and Hitchins
(1971). For portability, simple dipole antennae may be used directionally when
signal strength is good. Whatever the antenna, reception is better from a height;
Kolz and Johnson (1975) have described a device for elevating an antenna
above the roof of a car. A fully automated radio-tracking system has been
described by Cochran, Warner, Tester and Kuechle (1965).
    While a single directional antenna indicates the line along which a transmitter
is located, two or more situated some distance apart will, by cross-bearings,
indicate the actual position of the transmitter. Three kinds of error occur in
practice; (1) system error, inherent in the receiving equipment and its imprecise
operation, (Heezen and Tester, 1967), (2) movement error, due to the wanderings of the animal while it is being located, and (3) topographic error, due to
reflection and refraction of the radio signal (Tester, 1971). All three can be
reduced or eliminated with practice; the radio-tracker learns to accept and
operate within the limitations of his equipment and the landscape, and gradually
attains a subjective feel both for the movements of his study animals and for
the topographic problems of his study area (Verts, 1963).
    Data indicating successive positions and movement may be resolved into
x, y co-ordinates for analysis by use of an interactive co-ordinate plotter
(Partridge and Cullen, 1977).

Some Results from Radio-Tracking

Radio-tracking has proved especially useful in dealing with elusive animals,
notably carnivores (Mech, 1974) and nocturnal wanderers. My own studies of Red

foxes *Vulpes vulpes* illustrate the point. Several foxes, each with its own distinctive signal, were tracked over a variety of habitats. Some ranged very widely, while others remained in relatively small and clearly defined home ranges (Macdonald, 1976, 1977a). This supports evidence from ear-tagged foxes, killed at widely differing distances from their point of tagging (Jensen, 1968; Phillips, Andrews, Storm and Bishop, 1972), in indicating broad social categories of resident and itinerent animals (Sargeant, 1972; Storm, 1965; Niewold, 1974; Storm *et al.*, 1976). Radio-tracking has revealed similar categories in communities of other elusive carnivores, for example Wolves *Canis lupus* (Mech, 1970), Stoat *Mustela erminea* (Erlinge, 1977), Mountain lion *Felis concolor* (Hornocker, 1970), bobcat *Lynx rufus* (Provost, Nelson and Marshall, 1973), and Leopards *Panthera pardus* (Eisenberg and Lockhart, 1972). The significance of these two social categories in population regulation has already been established in more readily observable species, for example Red grouse *Lagopus lagopus* (Jenkins, Watson and Miller, 1963).

Radio-tracking studies have also confirmed that, as Murie (1936) and Burrows (1968) has suspected, resident social groups of one dog-fox and several vixens remain within family territories which are avoided by neighbouring groups (Ables, 1969; Macdonald, 1977a). The technique may now be used as a predictive tool to discover how individuals within these groups behave toward each other and to neighbours—a kind of study which would be practically impossible without a means of locating individuals. Indeed *predictive* tracking, which enables the biologist to find and observe his animal, is in general likely to prove far more instructive than *location* tracking, in which only the movements of the animal are recorded.

Though individual foxes were distinguishable by their radio signals, I found it helpful also to record details of their natural markings (colour patterns, injuries etc.) and to tag them with reflecting markers and Betalights (small phosphorescent light sources obtainable from Saunders Roe Developments, Hayes, Middlesex). These helped me to identify animals positively once they had been located, and to follow their behaviour at close quarters: reflecting markers could be seen at a distance of 350 m with a 34 watt infrared search lamp and infrared binoculars, and Betalights were visible at 200 m through standard 10 × 15 binoculars. Individua᾿ animals were also identifiable by combinations of small nicks cut from the ears under anaesthetic, in case other markers fell off.

Other studies of social organisation

Radio-tracking has been used in the study of social organisation and behavioural ecology in many mammalian orders. Among Primates, for instance, Charles-Dominique (1977a) radio-tracked prosimians; De Moor and Steffens (1971) studied Vervet monkeys *Cercopithecus aethiops*, and found differences in spatial organisation of neighbouring troops in different habitats—for example a troop in gallery forest defended 9.4 ha while one in acacia woodland ranged over 55.8 ha, (see also Anderson and De Moor, 1971; De Moor, 1970). As Vervet monkeys move in an integrated troop, these authors needed to radio-tag only one animal in order to locate each troop. In contrast Charles-Dominique (1977a and b) marked many small nocturnal Bushbabies *Galego alleni* in their extensive solitary ranges. By an ingenious circuit modification he determined the frequency with which individuals urinated to mark their territories.

Differences in the radio-tracking problems presented by different species are exemplified by Kruuk's studies (1972, 1976) of Spotted and Striped Hyaenas *Crocuta crocuta* and *Hyaena vulgaris*. A third member of the Hyaenidae, the Brown hyaena *Hyaena brunnea* of the Kalahari desert, proved extremely difficult to observe without radio-tracking. With radios, Mills (1976) was able to locate them in their 150–544 km² ranges and mark them with Betalights, then accustom them to his presence in a jeep; their social life bore little resemblance to hearsay, and the study provided useful material for conservation planning (figure 20.3).

Figure 20.3 Brown hyaena fitted with transmitter collar, Betalight and individual code number. Photograph: G. Mills.

Predation studies

Mech (1967) attached transmitters to Snowshoe hares *Lepus americanus* and Cottontail rabbits *Sylvilagus floridanus*, within range of the Cedar Creek automated station described by Cochran *et al.* (1965) from which foxes were also being tracked. He was able to follow the hunting of a radio-tagged hare by a radio-tagged fox, later recovering the remains of hare and still-functioning transmitter from the fox's cache. Stoddart (1970) described a transmitter which, monitoring temperature of a rabbit's skin, showed by changing pulse-rate the time of the rabbit's death; see also Brand, Vowles and Keith (1975). Sargeant (1972) studied the predation of foxes on waterfowl by radio-tagging, and the method has also been used to examine wolf predation on White-tailed deer *Odocoileus virginianus* by Hoskinson and Mech (1976); see also Peters and Mech's (1975) study of marking wolves by radio.

Animal marking

Home range studies

Apart from studies on foxes mentioned above, many other elusive animals have
been tracked over long distances by radio-tagging techniques. Long excursions
have been recorded for Leopards *Panthera pardus* (Eisenberg and Lockhart,
1972), Mountain lions *Felis concolor* (Seidensticker *et al.*, 1970), and even Brown
rats *Rattus norvegicus*, which have been shown to travel over 3 km in a night
(Taylor and Quy, 1977). Leuthold and Sale (1973) tracked African elephants
Loxodonta africana over home ranges measuring up to 4000 km^2; Wyatt and
Eltringham (1974) and Douglas-Hamilton (1976) have used radios predictively
to locate and watch the same species. Inglis (1976) followed radio-collared
Wildebeest *Connochaetes taurinus* on annual migrations across the Serengeti.
Studies of less conspicuous animals have also benefited; Bertram (personal com-
munication) was able to watch daily a four-year old leopard located by collar
transmitter, where previously he had seen the un-tagged animal only four times
in $2\frac{1}{2}$ years.

General wildlife studies

Among the more general studies enhanced by radio-tracking techniques are the
long-term research of Mech (1966, 1970, 1974) on wolves and other carnivores;
see also Kolenosky and Johnston 1967. Radio-tracking of foxes has implications
for studies of the epizoology of rabies (Storm *et al.*, 1976; Macdonald 1977*b*);
Cumming (1971) has studied movements of warthog in relation to its role as
host of the Tsetse fly *Glossina morsitans*, a vector of trypanosomiasis (sleeping
sickness). McFarland (1977) has used radio-tracking as an aid to studying the
adaptive significance of moment-to-moment behaviour of Herring gulls *Larus
argentatus*. Harthoorn and McGinnis (1971) stress the need for studies of large
herbivores to improve exploitation of tropical habitats which are currently
being degraded by subsistence farming; McGinnis, Finch and Harthoorn (1971)
to this end have used a two-stage transmitting system to compare movements
and physiological responses of Boran cattle and wild ungulates in extreme local
climatic conditions; Brown (1971) has made similar comparisons between sheep
and kangaroos *Macropus* sp., with a view to the more effective use of land grazed
by both. For further discussion of biotelemetry methods see Amlaner (chapter
21).

Satellite tracking

The possibilities of recording movements of animals in remote areas, and
collecting physiological data from them, have been enhanced by the development
of satellite radio-tracking programmes (Buechner, Craighead, Craighead and
Cote, 1971). Craighead, Craighead, Varney and Cote (1971) have reported a
pilot study of the winter denning of a Black bear *Ursus americanus*, using the
Interrogation, Recording and Location System (IRLS) of the Nimbus III satellite.
The bear was tracked to its winter lair using a Craighead–Varney transmitter
(Craighead and Craighead, 1965); the IRLS equipment was then hidden in and
around the lair, and under the bear's bed. Satellite location of the lair was rather

inaccurate, with an average error of 3.77 km. More recent work with Polar bears *Thalarctos maritimus* from the Nimbus VI satellite is giving a location accuracy of better than 1 km (Anon., 1976). Similar equipment has been used to follow the migration of Elk *Cervus canadensis* (Craighead, Craighead, Cote and Beucher, 1972), using transmitter collars weighing 11.3 kg; air and skin temperatures were also monitored.

Interpreting radio-tracking data

Radio-tracking leads to the accumulation of large quantities of data on the movement of animals; subsequent analysis presents many problems. Sanderson (1966) has pointed out the inadequacy of techniques for interpreting location data, which are often interwoven with the concept of home range. Most of the problems centre on doubts about the true relationship between the animal's actual use of space, and the fragmentary glimpses of that usage afforded by sporadic radio-fixes, sightings or re-trappings. Theoretical and practical problems arising from radio-tracking data have been considered by Tester and Siniff (1965), Heezen and Tester (1967), Tester (1971), Storm (1965), Siniff and Tester (1965) and Siniff and Jesson (1969). Possible methods of reducing uncertainty in field data have been reviewed by Jennrich and Turner (1969), van Winkle (1975), Mazurkiewicz (1971) and Dunn and Gipson (1977).

Conclusions

Radio-tracking is a relatively new but already invaluable tool for the field biologist, enabling him to locate his study animals in situations where visual detection is difficult or impossible. However, when used solely to plot the locations and movements of animals, the method is under-exploited; the resulting data may be voluminous, but are often weak and difficult to interpret. More valuable results are gained when radio-tracking is used in a *predictive* sense, to facilitate *direct observation* and hence lead to a sound knowledge of the animal's behaviour and general biology. We may look forward to refinements of transmitters and receivers which will allow more accurate detection of position and movement, and at the same time monitor behaviour and both physiological and environmental variables—telling us even more about the biology of elusive species in their natural habitats.

Acknowledgements

I thank Charles Amlaner and Dr William Morris for valuable discussion of an early draft of this chapter; I thank also the colleagues who kindly allowed me to use their photographs to illustrate the text, and the R.S.P.C.A. for providing a pair of infrared binoculars which were an invaluable aid to predictive tracking throughout my research.

References

Ables, E. D. (1969). Home-range studies of red foxes (*Vulpes vulpes*). *J. Mammal.,* **50** (1), 108–119.

Anderson, F. and De Moor, P. P. (1971). A system for radio-tracking monkeys in dense bush and forest. *J. Wildl. Mgmt.,* **35** (4), 636–643.

Anderson, F. and Hitchings, P. (1971). A radio-tracking system for the black rhinoceros. *J. S. Afr. J. Wildl. Mgmt Ass.,* **1**, 26–35.

Anon. (1976). Biologists track a bear by satellite. *Microwaves,* **15** (9), 14.

Aucouturier, J. L., Chaillou, A., Nicholas, G., Canivenc, R., Marques, M., Govaerts, R., Mertens, R., Lauwers, F. and Van Overstraeten, R. J. (1977). Biotelemetry and radio tracking of wild birds–portable device using solar cells power supply. *Report of the IHSM European Hybrid Microelectronics Conference.* Bad Homburg, 1976, 7 pp.

Beal, R. O. (1967). Radio transmitter collars for squirrels. *J. Wildl. Mgmt.,* **31**, 373–374.

Beuchner, H. K., Craighead, F. C. Jr, Craighead, J. J. and Cote, C. E. (1971). Satellites for research on free roaming animals. *Bioscience,* **21**, 1201–1205.

Boag, D. A. (1972). Effect of radio-packages on behaviour of captive red grouse. *J. Wildl. Mgmt.,* **36**, 511–518.

Boag, D. A., Watson, A. and Parr, R. (1973). Radio-marking versus back-tabbing red grouse. *J. Wildl. Mgmt.,* **37**, 410–412.

Brand, C. J., Vowles, R. H. and Keith, L. B. (1975). Snowshoe hare mortality monitored by telemetry. *J. Wild. Mgmt.,* **39**, 741–747.

Brown, G. D. (1971). The responses of sheep and kangaroos to climate in a natural environment using multichannel telemetry. *Proc. Symp. Biotelemetry, Pretoria, 1971,* Council for Scientific and Educational Research, Pretoria, 8pp.

Burrows, R. (1968). *Wild Fox.* David and Charles, Newton Abbott, 202 pp.

Charles-Dominique, P. (1977a). Urine-marking and territoriality in *Galago alleni* (Waterhouse 1837–Lorisoidea, Primates)–a field study by radio telemetry. *Z. Tierpsychol.,* **43**, 113–138.

Charles-Dominique, P. (1977b). *Ecology and Behaviour of Nocturnal Primates.* Duckworths, London, 277 pp.

Cochran, W. W. and Hagen, T. E. (1963). Construction of collar transmitters for deer. *Minnesota Mus. nat. Hist. Tech. Rep.* No. 4.

Cochran, W. W. and Lord, R. D. Jr. (1963). A radio-tracking system for wild animals. *J. Wildl. Mgmt.,* **27**, 9–24.

Cochran W. W. and Nelson, E. M. (1963). The model D-11 direction finding receiver. *Minnesota Mus. nat. Hist. Tech. Rep.* No. 2, 14 pp.

Cochran, W. W., Warner, D. W. and Tester, J. R. (1964). The Cedar Creek automatic radio-tracking system. *Minnesota Mus. nat. Hist. Tech. Rep.* No. 7, 9 pp.

Cochran, W. W., Warner, D. W., Tester, J. R. and Kuechle, V. B. (1965). Automatic radio-tracking system for monitoring animal movements. *BioScience,* **15**, 98–100.

Craighead, F. C. Jr, and Craighead, J. J. (1965). Tracking grizzly bears. *BioScience,* **15**, 88–92.

Craighead, F. C. Jr, Craighead, J. J. and Davies, R. S. (1963). Radio-tracking of grizzly bears. In *Biotelemetry. the Use of Telemetry in Animal Behaviour and*

Physiology in Relation to Ecological Problems (ed. L. E. Slater), Macmillan, New York. pp. 133–148.

Craighead, F. C. Jr, Craighead, J. J., Cote, C. E. and Beuchner, H. K. (1972). Satellite and ground radio tracking of elk. *NASA Sci. Publ.,* **262**, 99–111.

Craighead, J. J., Craighead, F. C. Jr, Varney, J. R. and Cote, C. E. (1971). Satellite monitoring of black bear. *Proc. Symp. Biotelemetry, Pretoria, 1971,* Council for Scientific and Educational Research, Pretoria, 20 pp.

Cumming, D. M. H. (1971). Radio tracking of warthog; some results and their bearing on studies of game–tsetse fly relationships. *Proc. Symp. Biotelemetry, Pretoria, 1971,* Council for Scientific and Educational Research, Pretoria, 20 pp.

De Moor, P. P. (1970). Tracking vervet monkeys by radio. *Afr. Wildl.,* **24**, 1–8.

De Moor, P. P. and Steffens, F. E. (1972). The movements of vervet monkeys, *Cercopithecus aethiops,* within their ranges as revealed by radio tracking. *J. Anim. Ecol.,* **41**, 677–687.

Douglas-Hamilton, I. and Douglas-Hamilton, O. (1975). *Among the Elephants.* Collins and Harvill Press, London, 285 pp.

Dunn, J. E. and Gipson, P. S. (1977). Analysis of radio telemetry data in studies of home range. *Biometrics,* **33**, 85–101.

Dunston, T. C. (1973). A tail feather package for radio-tagging raptorial birds. *Inland Bird Banding News,* **45**, pp. 3–6.

Eisenberg, J. F. and Lockhard, M. (1972). An ecological reconnaissance of the Wilpattu National Park, Ceylon. *Smithson. Contr. Zool.,* **101**, pp. 1–118

Erlinge, S. (1977). Spacing strategy in stoat (*Mustela erminea*). *Oikos,* **28**, 32–42.

Gilmer, D. S., Ball, I. J., Cowardin, L. M. and Rechmann, J. H. (1974). Effects of radio packages on wild ducks. *J. Wildl. Mgmt,* **38**, 243–252.

Haglund, B. (1966). Winter habits of the lynx (*Lynx lynx,* L.) and wolverine (*Gulo gulo* L.) as revealed by tracking in the snow. *Viltrevy,* **4**, p. 299.

Hamilton, P. H. (1976). Movements of leopards in Tsavo National Park, Kenya, as determined by radio-tracking. MSc thesis, University of Nairobi.

Harding, P. J. R., Chute, F. S. and Doell, A. C. (1976). Increasing battery reliability for radio transmitters, *J. Wildl. Mgmt,* **40**, 357–358.

Hardy, A. R. (1977). Hunting ranges and feeding ecology of owls in farmland. Ph. D. thesis, University of Aberdeen.

Harthoorn, A. M. and McGinnis, S. M. (1971). The use of biotelemetric methods to monitor changes in deep and superficial body temperatures in four undomesticted African ungulates during forced exercise. *Proc. Symp. Biotelemetry, Pretoria, 1971,* Council for Scientific and Educational Research, Pretoria, 11 pp.

Heezen, K. L. and Tester, J. R. (1967). Evaluation of radio tracking by triangulation with special reference to deer movements. *J. Wildl. Mgmt,* **31**, 124–141.

Hornocker, M. G. (1970). An analysis of mountain lion predation upon mule, deer and elk in the Idaho Primitive Area. *Wildl. Monogr.,* **21**, 1–39.

Hoskinson, R. L. and Mech, D. L. (1976). White-tailed deer migration and its role in wolf predation. *J. Wildl. Mgmt,* **40**, 429–441.

Inglis, J. M. (1976). Wet season movements of individual wildebeeste of the Serengeti migratory herd. *E. Afr. Wildl. J.,* **14**, 17–34.

Jenkins, D., Watson, A., and Miller, G. R. (1963). Population studies of red grouse,

Lagopus scoticus, (Lathum) in north east Scotland. *J. Anim. Ecol.* **32** 317-76.

Jennrich, R. I. and Turner, F. B. (1969). Measurement of non-circular home range. *J. theor. Biol.,* **22**, 227-237.

Jensen, B. (1968). Preliminary results from the marking of foxes (*Vulpes vulpes*) in Denmark. *Dan. Rev. Game Biol.,* **5**, 1-8.

Kenward, R. E. (1976). The effect of predation by goshawks *Accipter gentilis* on woodpigeon, *Columba palumbus,* populations. D. Phil. thesis, Oxford University.

Kenward, R. E. (1977), Predation on released pheasants by goshawks in Central Sweden. *Viltrevy* (in press).

Kenward, R. E. (1978). Hawk studies using tail-mounted transmitters. *Om. Scand.* **9**, (in press).

Kolenosky, M. B. and Johnston, D. H. (1967). Radio-tracking timber wolves in Ontario. *Am. Zool.,* **7**, 289-303.

Kolz, A. L. and Johnson, R. E. (1975). An elevating mechanism for mobile receiving antennae. *J. Wildl. Mgmt,* **39**, 819-820.

Kruuk, H. (1972). *The spotted hyena: a study of predation and social behaviour.* Chicago, University of Chicago Press, 335 pp.

Kruuk, H. (1975). Functional aspects of social hunting in carnivores. In: *Function and evolution in Behaviour* (ed. G. Baerends, C. Beer and A. Manning) Clarendon Press, Oxford, pp. 119-141.

Kruuk, H. (1976). Social behaviour and foraging of the striped hyaena (*Hyaena vulgaris*) *E. Afr. Wildl. J.,* **14**, 91-111.

Leuthold, W. and Sale, J. B. (1973). Movements and patterns of habitat utilisation of elephants in Tsavo National Park. *E. Afr. Wildl. J.,* **11**, 369-384.

Leuze, C. (1976). Social behaviour and dispersion in the water vole, *Arvicola terrestris.* Ph. D. thesis, University of Aberdeen.

Leuze, C. (1977). A manual for the construction of the water vole transmitter collar unit. (Obtainable on request from Culterty Field Station, Newburgh, Aberdeenshire, Scotland).

Macdonald, D. W. (1976). Food caching by red foxes and some other carnivores. *Z. f. Tierpsychol.,* **42**, 170-185.

Macdonald, D. W. (1977a). The behavioural ecology of the Red fox: a study of social organisation and resource exploitation. D. Phil. thesis, Oxford.

Macdonald, D. W. (1977b). The behavioural ecology of the red fox. In: *Rabies, the Facts* (ed. C. Kaplan) Oxford University Press, pp. 70-90.

Mazurkiewicz, M. (1971). Shape, size and distribution of home ranges of *Clethrionomys glaroelus* (Schreber 1780). *Acta Theriol.,* **16**, 23-60.

McFarland, D. J. (1977). Decision making in animals. *Nature,* **269**, 15-21.

McGinnis, S. M., Finch, V. and Harthoorn, H. N. (1970). A radio-telemetric technique for monitoring temperatures from unrestrained ungulates. *J. Wildl. Mgmt.,* **34**, 921-925.

Mech, L. D. (1966). The wolves of Isle Royale. *U.S. Natn. Park Serv. Fauna Series,* **7**, 1-210.

Mech, L. D. (1967). Telemetry as a technique in the study of predation. *J. Wildl. Mgmt* **31**, 492-496.

Mech, D. L. (1970). *The Wolf.* New York, Natural History Press, 385 pp.

Mech, L. D. (1974). *Current techniques in the study of elusive wilderness carnivores.* Proc. XIth Int. Cong. Game Biol. Stockholm, 315-322.

Mech. L. D., Kuechle, V. B., Warner, D. W. and Tester, J. R. (1965). A collar for attaching radio transmitters on rabbits, hares and racoons. *J. Wildl. Mgmt,* **29,** 898-902.

Mills, M. G. L. (1976). Ecology and behaviour of the brown hyaena in the Kalahari with some suggestions for management. Proc. Symp. Endangered Wildlife in South Africa. University of Pretoria.

Morris, P. A. (1966). Hedgehogs in London. *Lond. Nat., 45,* 43-49.

Murie, A. (1936). Following fox trails. *Univ. Mich. Mus. Zool. Misc. Publ.,* **32,** 1-45.

Nicholls, T. H. and Warner, D. W. (1968). A harness for attaching radio transmitters to large owls. *Bird-Banding, 39,* 209-214.

Niewold, F. J. J. (1974). Irregular movements of the red fox (*Vulpes vulpes*) determined by radio-tracking. *Proc. Int. Cong. Game Biol. Stockholm,* 331-337.

Owen-Smith, R. N. (1971). The contribution of radio telemetry to a study of the white rhinoceros. *Proc. Symp. Biotelemetry, Pretoria, 1971,* Council for Scientific and Educational Research, Pretoria, 7 pp.

Partridge, B. L. and Cullen, J. M. (1977). A low cost interactive coordinate plotter. *Behav. Res. Meth. Instrument.* (in press).

Peters, R. P. and Mech, L. D. (1975). Scent marking in wolves. *Am. Sci., 63,* 628-637.

Phillips, R. L., Andrews, R. D., Storm, G. L. and Bishop, R. A. (1972). Dispersal and mortality of red foxes. *J. Wildl. Mgmt, 36,* 237-248.

Provost, E. E., Nelson, C. A. and Marshall, A. D. (1973). Population dynamics and behaviour in the bobcat. *Proc. 1st. Int. Symp. Ecol. Behav. Conserv. World's Cats* (ed. R. Eaton) 42-67. World Wildlife Safari, Winston, Oregon.

Sanderson, G. C. (1966). The study of mammal movements—a review. *J. Wildl. Mgmt, 30,* 215-235.

Sargeant, A. B. (1972). Red fox spatial characteristics in relation to waterfowl predation. *J. Wildl. Mgmt, 36,* 225-236.

Sargeant, A. B., Swanson, G. A. and Doty, H. A. (1973). Selective predation by mink *Mustela vison* on waterfowl. *Amer. Midl. Nat., 89,* 208-214.

Seidensticker, J. C., Hornocker, M. G., Knight, R. R. and Judd, S. L. (1970). Equipment and techniques for radio tracking mountain lions and elk. *Univ. Idaho, Forest Wildl. Range exp. Stat. Bull.,* **6.**

Siniff, D. B. and Jessen, C. R. (1969). A simulation model of animal movement patterns. In *Advances in Ecological Research* (ed. J. B. Cragg) **6,** Academic Press, London and New York, pp. 185-219.

Siniff, D. B. and Tester, J. R. (1965). Computer analysis of animal movement data obtained by telemetry. *BioScience, 15,* 104-108.

Stoddart, C. L. (1970). A telemetric method for detecting jack-rabbit mortality. *J. Wildl. Mgmt, 34,* 501-508.

Storm, G. L. (1965). Movements and activities of foxes as determined by radio tracking. *J. Wildl. Mgmt, 29,* 1-13.

Storm, G. L., Andrew, R. D., Phillips, R. L., Bishop, R. A., Siniff, D. B. and

Tester, J. A. (1976). Morphology, reproduction, dispersal and mortality of midwestern red fox populations. *Wildlife Monogr.,* **49**, 81 pp.

Swanson, G. A. and Kuechle, V. B. (1976). A telemetry technique for monitoring water fowl activity. *J. Wildl. Mgmt,* **40**, 187–189.

Taylor, K. D. and Quy, R. J. (1977). Long distance movements of a common rat (*Rattus norvegicus*) revealed by radio tracking. *J. Mammal.* (in press).

Tester, J. R. (1971). Interpretation of ecological and behavioural data on wild animals obtained by telemetry with special reference to errors and uncertainty. *Proc. Symp. Biotelemetry, Pretoria, 1971.* Council for Scientific and Educational Research, Pretoria, pp. 385–407.

Tester, J. R. and Siniff, D. B. (1965). Aspects of animal movement and home range data obtained by telemetry. *Trans XXXth N. Am. Wildl. Nat. Res. Conf.,* pp. 379–392.

Tinbergen, N. (1965). Von den Vorratskammern des Rotfuchses (*Vulpes vulpes* L.) *Z. Tierpsychol.,* **22**, 119–149.

Verts, B. J. (1963). Equipment and techniques for radio-tracking striped skunks. *J. Wildl. Mgmt,* **27**, 325–339.

van Winkle, W. (1975). Comparison of several probabilistic home range models. *J. Wildl. Mgmt,* **39**, 118–123.

Wyatt, J. R. and Eltringham, S. K. (1974) The daily activity of the elephant in Rwanzori National Park, Uganda. *E. Afr. Wildl. J.,* **12**, 273–289.

Zimmermann, F., Geraud, H. and Charles-Dominique, P. (1975). Le radio-tracking des vertebrates: conseils et techniques d'utilisation. *La Terre et la Vie,* **30**, 309–346.

21 Biotelemetry from free-ranging animals

Charles J. Amlaner, Jr*

During the past 25 years, interest has gradually focused on research which allows study animals to live in their normal environment. Initially it was thought that if animals were undisturbed and were allowed to become familiar with unnatural conditions, then subsequent changes in behaviour might be insignificant or non-existent. However, both laboratory and caged field conditions were later found to alter observable behaviour patterns. The more subtle, but equally important physiological changes were suspected but remained unmeasurable because of technological limitations. The concerned scientist then looked for techniques which would permit animals to remain in their natural habitat and which would also minimise behavioural and physiological changes. Biotelemetry (that is data transmission of biological information without direct connection between transmitter and receiver; see figure 21.1) was suggested as a possible solution to these problems. Different modalities including light, ultrasonics and radio have been used in various situations, but radiotelemetry has so far provided the most generally useful and adaptable approach (Mackay, 1974).

One of the pioneer workers in biotelemetry was Einar Eliassen (1960, 1963a and b) who used telemetry to try to evaluate the influence of free flight on energy metabolism, heart regulation and blood circulation of seagulls. His initial attempts at designing a transmitter capable of sending heart rate and stroke pressure were successful, and even though the state of electronic technology imposed several limitations, his study provided impetus for further research using telemetric devices on free ranging animals.

Over the past decade significant achievements in electronics have also advanced biotelemetry. Accomplishments in miniaturisation (for example transistors) and hybrid circuitry (that is integrated circuits containing resistors, capacitors, transistors, etc. in one small 'chip') have provided the means to resolve previously unanswerable questions. Radio signals from telemeters can now be utilised for three general purposes: (1) location of a subject by radio-tracking (using tracking telemeters); (2) the transmission of details on both physiological and/or environmental

*Charles Amlaner is a graduate of Andrews University, Michigan, U.S.A., where he received degrees in Biophysics and Zoology. He has been involved in experimentally evaluating the communication schemes of several gull species using remote controlled models of his own design and construction. Two years were also spent working under a US Air Force and Smithsonian Institute sponsorship assessing the most humane methods to rid aerodromes of gulls. As a member of Oxford's Animal Behaviour Research Group, he is currently using biotelemetry as an aid to study sleep patterns in free-ranging Herring gulls.

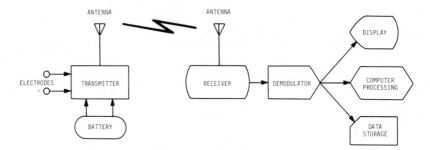

Figure 21.1 The basic components included within a biotelemetry system.

parameters (using biotelemeters); (3) monitoring activity patterns (using tracking or biotelemetry) (Mackay, 1974). Theoretically all three may be accomplished using a single transmitter but in practice they have been studied separately.

Several exhaustive accounts review the two major areas of telemetry research, namely medical telemetry (Slater, 1963; Caceres, 1965; Mackay, 1970, 1974; Fryer and Sandler, 1974) and radio-tracking (Schladweiler and Ball, 1968; Varney, 1971; Will and Patric, 1972; Zimmermann and Charles-Dominique, 1976; Macdonald, chapter 20). These review papers also cover general considerations such as size, weight and location of transmitter; transmitter and receiver design; battery size and weight in relation to transmission time and/or signal strength; encapsulation and hermetic sealing techniques; antenna design; harnessing methods (internal or external); signal retrieval, storage and data processing. I would refer the interested reader especially to Mackay (1970) and Slater (1963) for excellent treatises on general and theoretical considerations.

The object of this chapter is to present a review of techniques involving physiological biotelemetry. I will attempt to show, with several examples, how simple telemetry techniques enable the measurement of physiological parameters providing a good indication of an animal's response to its environment. Categories of questions that I believe are crucial in ascertaining an animal's welfare in the wild and in the laboratory will be described. Finally, I will discuss the impact of biotelemeters themselves on certain species, particularly emphasising activity patterns and individual welfare.

Physiological Telemetry Methods

Conveniently measurable and potentially important physiological parameters are temperature, respiration, electrocardiograms (ECG) including heart rate, electroencephalograms (EEG), electromyograms (EMG), heat flow and blood flow. Transmitters exist that are capable of sending any one (single-channel) or combination (multi-channel) of these parameters. I shall focus on measurements of temperature, respiration and ECG, primarily since careful design of transmitters, transducers (that is thermisters used in measuring temperature changes, pressure sensors to measure respiration etc.) and subsequent signal analysis for these parameters can produce simple and, in most cases, inexpensive results. The principal components of a simple biotelemetry system are displayed in figure 21.1.

Single-channel telemetry systems

As a general rule, earlier single-channel physiological systems were formed by modulation of single or multi-transistor radio-tracking devices (for example pulsed or
continuous signal output). They have the advantage of being smaller compared with
multi-channel transmitters except when several bits of information are being
retrieved and transmitted over a single frequency (multiplexing).

As an example of a simply designed single channel biotelemeter, Lord, Belrose
and Cochran (1962) described a transmitter originally used for tracking free ranging
rabbits. Later the same circuit was attached to a wild mallard *Anas platyrhynchos*.
As it breathed, the shape of a wire antenna that passed around the duck changed,
causing a modulation of signal in the transmitter. This modulation could be monitored in resting ducks (14 resp/min) and during 40 mph flights (96 resp/min). A
further discovery was made: a ratio of approximately two wing beats for every
respiration was noted while the birds were in flight.

As this approach reveals, a simple circuit was quite capable of transmitting important information about the biology of a free ranging animal. The only drawback was ambiguity in interpretation. Since the reported wing beat data were not
retrieved as a function of some designed transmitter/transducer arrangement but
rather were inferred by an interruption and small frequency shift between each
respiration curve, only an inferred relationship between frequency shift and wing
beat could be made.

Today we can improve on these results by defining relationships between
physiological parameters in unambiguous ways. The techniques require the transducers to be wired in such a way that their outputs mimic the desired physiological parameters. In spite of the limitations experienced in these early studies, the
idea of transmitting respiration rate of a free-flying duck clearly paved the way
for a new understanding of relationships between physiology and behaviour.

Not only are some behaviours simply not seen in caged animals, but even when
the subject appears to behave in an apparently 'normal' way, one can never be
confident that the effects of captivity have not affected its physiological state. For
instance Skutt, Bock, Haugstad, Holter, Hayes and Silver (1973) showed that even
after repeated exposure and training, certain species, such as the White-tailed deer
Odocoileus virginianus, assume abnormal physiological traits when in contact with
humans. Therefore in order to study the effects, for example, of varying ambient
temperatures on the body temperature, without modifying the animal's condition,
physiological telemetry must be used.

A temperature transmitter (figure 21.2) capable of transmitting on the FM
broadcast band was described by Skutt *et al.* (1973) as being an up-to-date pulsed-
carrier device utilising low power integrated circuits. Its designed lifetime was
approximately 1 year using three small mercury batteries. The receiver signal was
a series of audible 'clicks' which have a frequency dependent on temperature. Using
a calibration curve for that particular transmitter a determination can be made of
the physiological temperature to a sensitivity of 0.1 °C. Some applications of this
will be described later under the section 'temperature as an indicator of behavioural
state'.

Several simple temperature-sensitive telemeters have resulted from modified
tracking transmitters. They are more than adequate for most purposes and also
perform the useful dual function of giving the animal's position. But there are two

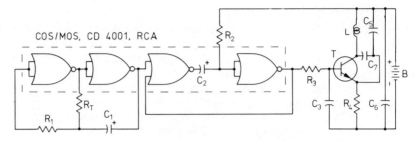

Figure 21.2 A temperature-sensitive transmitter using low power integrated circuitry and operating on the FM band. Component values are: R_1 4.7 MΩ, R_2 0.51 MΩ, R_3 47 kΩ, R_4 490 Ω, R_T 1.5 MΩ, C_1 0.1 μfd, C_2 1000 pfd, C_3 100 pfd, C_5 47 μfd, C_6 100 pfd, C_7 10 pfd, T D26G1, B 4.5 V d.c., L 5 turns of 36 gauge enamelled wire. (Redrawn after Skutt *et al.*, 1973).

particular dangers in using these single-transistor circuits for physiological measurements if they are not properly designed. First, frequency stability and pulse rate of the transmitter may be affected merely by changes in body posture. Secondly, as battery power decreases, the pulse repetition rate tends to drift making the initial calibration useless. Of course, these are pitfalls for any biotelemeter but especially of pulsed systems.

Smith and Crowder (1974) described an ECG transmitter used on aestivating sirens *Siren intermedia*. The system shown in figure 21.3 employs a magnetic switch allowing the unit to be turned off when data are not required, such as during the period of activity before aestivation. The switch activates when a strong magnetic field is passed near it, limiting needless current drain from the transmitter batteries and allowing over 2000 two-minute ECG measurements on one battery supply. A switch of this type may be used on any biotelemetry transmitter where

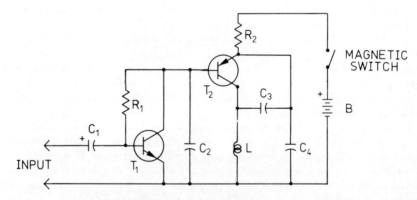

Figure 21.3 Schematic diagram of a subminiature ECG transmitter using a magnetic switch and operating on the FM band. Component values are: R_1 4.7 MΩ, R_2 1.0 kΩ, C_1 0.1 μfd (tantalum), C_2 470 pfd, C_3 15 pfd, C_4 47 pfd, T_1 D26E-5, T_2 2N3325, L 4 turns of 36 gauge enamelled wire, B 1.5 V d.c., S Hamlin MMRR-2-185 micromagnetic reed switch. (Redrawn after Smith and Crowder, 1974).

prolonged usage is expected and where switching is easily carried out. Another useful feature of this circuit is that transmission occurs on the standard FM broadcast
band (88–108 MHz), allowing the use of inexpensive, readily available receivers.

Multi-channel telemetry systems

For most physiological experiments it is desirable to obtain simultaneous recordings of multiple signals, especially when relationships are expected to exist between several behavioural and physiological variables. Each of the transmitted
signals may be designated as a discrete channel of information. An obvious method
of obtaining multiple channels of data would be to use several single-channel transmitters, but this usually necessitates redundant receivers and recording systems
which require extra maintenance and may be extremely costly. So when a number
of signals are required, a multi-channel system (frequently called a multiplexed
system) is usually the least costly and most efficient method to choose.

Two major subdivisions of multiplexing are common, namely time-division
multiplexing and frequency-division multiplexing. Time-division multiplexing
requires sequential sampling of each individual transducer (electrode) input. For
example, if five signals are needed, one might sample the first signal for 1 second,
then the second signal for 1 second etc. When all five signals have been sampled, a
cycle is completed after which the cycle may then repeat or turn off and cycle at
a later time (thus conserving power). Frequency-division multiplexing is characterised by multiple frequencies, each related to a particular channel. Again by
example, if five signals are needed, each channel may be separated by 5 kHz, that
is the first channel is 5 kHz, the second is 10 kHz, and so on. Subcarriers are used
to modulate (vary or turn on and off) a main carrier frequency which commonly
is the transmission frequency.

At the receiving end, special demodulators (figure 21.1) are required to sort out
the individual signals and to dispatch them to recording devices. This process is
usually accomplished by reversing the original encoding scheme used in the transmitter. In the case of time-division multiplexing, each part of the signal is sorted
according to a particular time relationship with a starting pulse signifying the beginning of each cycle. For frequency-division multiplexing each channel is recognised by a special filter which responds to its set frequency. That frequency will
be equal to the corresponding subcarrier frequency of a particular channel; in our
example each filter would be respectively tuned at 5 kHz increments. Both of the
techniques described above have been utilised in physiological telemetry.

An excellent example of an inexpensive multi-channel subcarrier biotelemetry
system of simple design was described by Smith and Salb (1975). Their system
incorporates three channels containing ECG, respiration and temperature and can
be used with conventional FM broadcast receivers. The authors also described a
demodulator which incorporated standard integrated circuits. The biological parameters (that is ECG, respiration and temperature) were displayed separately for
unambiguous recognition and analysis. The transmitter circuit was temperature
compensated so that it could be located away from the temperature sensor; a
feature that most single-channel transmitters do not possess. The over-all size of
the transmitter was 1 cm × 3 cm and could operate for several weeks on a single
set of batteries. Range varies with operating condition, (battery power, receiver

sensitivity and terrain) but 10–100 m is generally attainable. This range would be ideal for many studies involving assessment of animal welfare if the home range were not too large. The transmitter was small enough for use with vertebrates of the size of pigeons or rats and, using bigger and more powerful batteries to lengthen transmitter operation time and range, was suitable for use on larger animals. Studies of rabbits when influenced by predation, and the welfare of caged domestic hens, are applications possible with this transmitter.

An attractive feature of this system (Smith and Salb, 1975) is the capability to record data directly with an inexpensive cassette tape recorder in the field without first decoding the data. The circuit was designed with wide band modulation so as to minimise the adverse effects due to 'wow' and tape speed variations which are inherent faults of cheap cassette tape recorders. The recorded data can later be taken to the laboratory where the demodulator may be used to decode information.

Fryer, Sandler and Datnow (1969) have described a time-division multiplexing system capable of recording several channels of temperature, ECG and blood presure. Five and eight-channel devices have been successfully tested on canids and could also be adapted for larger animals. However, the discrete components of this system make it excessively bulky, though integrated circuitry could significantly miniaturise the transmitter.

While advances in multi-channel biotelemetry have been considerable, and continue, certain cautions remain. It may be difficult to record simultaneously several parameters from an animal when the signal sources are far removed from the transmitter. It is particularly difficult to maintain the continuity of the electrode leads when they are long or are attached to areas where much movement occurs. Designers have improved the mechanical properties of wires which are subjected to bending and stress; also very fine stranded stainless steel or copper wire (Fryer, Deboo and Winget, 1966; Sawby and Gessaman, 1974) has been used. Teflon insulation is preferred because of its non-irritating and physiologically inert qualities. When wiring transducers, leads should be as short as possible and should avoid areas where excessive movement occurs (that is around the neck and limbs). Obviously this is not always possible, so each case needs separate consideration. For example, if ECG and respiration were to be measured, then the best location for a transmitter would be near the heart. If EEG were also to be recorded, leads would have to run up past the neck from the heart area, and in this situation it might be preferable to have two transmitters, one at the head and the other at the chest. Systems that do not use wire leads, such as radio pills used for measuring temperature (Fryer and Sandler, 1974) are highly desirable, but of limited application.

Physiological States Determined by Telemetry

Investigations of animals with restricted mobility (for example cages) are possible using wire 'umbilical' cables tied directly to instrumentation. Thus standard laboratory equipment may be used without modification which conveniently saves time and money. Cables of this type must avoid severe restriction and entanglement as the animal moves about, which is usually accomplished by using slip rings (that is carbon brushes and armatures). Difficulty arises when the slip rings become dirty or the small gauge wires in the cable begin to break. Furthermore, experiments necessitating that animals be free ranging are impossible using this technique. A few investigations have shown that wired systems often psychologically and physiologically disturb the animal in such a way as to influence and distort the measurements (Bohus, 1974; Borbely, 1974). Also, human disturbance has been found to alter the physiological state (that is increase heart rate, raise body temperature etc.) while no external evidence of behavioural change was noted (see following examples). Consequently, researchers are turning to biotelemetry systems whenever possible, even though they are somewhat more expensive and may be limited in their flexibility of measurement. Examples follow which describe many varied situations where biotelemeters were used to measure an animal's reaction to abnormal and environmental pressures.

Temperature as an indicator of behavioural state

During a study to determine onset time of the disease leptospirosis in Pronghorn antelope *Antilocapra americana* Lonsdale, Bradach and Thorne (1971) utilised body temperature as an indicator. Direct measurements using a rectal thermometer gave almost meaningless results due to the 'stress' and 'excitement' of the animal being handled. A biotelemeter capable of transmitting temperature remotely was ideally suited to these circumstances.

Even though the animals had been raised in captivity, their body temperature still rose in the presence of their customary attendants by as much as $2.0\,^\circ$C in 10 minutes. Results from the disease study showed that 5 days after inoculation, undisturbed diseased animals exhibited a $3.0\,^\circ$C temperature rise over a 5-hour period followed by a drop of $2.0\,^\circ$C. The temperature then remained at this elevated level for 36 hours, after which the study ended.

It is known that during a defence or flight reaction in domestic fowl, the sympathetic nervous system is aroused and adrenalin is released. This action causes a redistribution of blood from the skin and splanchnic regions into the main muscle masses (Whitton, 1976). Since an insulating layer of feathers covers most body surfaces, temperature under the skin remains relatively constant both with temperature regulation in general and to fight or flight reactions in particular. Vascular changes are notably most important in controlling heat loss from the poorly insulated legs and feet. Duncan, Filshie and McGee (1975) studied blood redistribution in the legs of domestic fowl by measuring temperature shifts with a biotelemeter using a remotely located thermister on the leg. Figure 21.4 shows results of a bird's skin temperature trace during exposure to a black cloth which, when waved, was thought to simulate an aerial predator. The bird's immediate response was to become alert, alarm call for a few minutes and then resume the activity preceding disturbance with bouts of preening. In each case, the temperature dropped immediately after exposure to the stimulus and during the alarm calling. Thereafter temperature remained low, but when alarm calling ceased temperature increased to above the previous norm. Normal temperature returned about 4.5 minutes after the initial disturbance.

Certain limitations occur when telemetry techniques are applied to extremely small animals. Over-all size and weight must be kept to a minimum, especially when

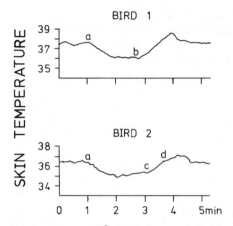

Figure 21.4 Skin temperature (°C) traces from two domestic hens during a disturbance. A black cloth was waved over the feeding birds at (a). The first bird stopped alarm calling and resumed feeding at (b); the second bird stopped calling at (c) and started preening at (d). (After Duncan *et al.*, 1975).

using telemetry on birds. During a study on body temperature of White-crowned sparrows *Zonotrichia leucophrys gambelii* Southwick (1973) was faced with this problem since these birds weigh approximately 25 g. He used a 0.86 g low power temperature telemeter that was specially designed for the study. Use of this bio-telemeter revealed (figure 21.5) that a very slight disturbance (for example such as a human silently approaching a caged bird to within 2 m and then leaving) caused a transient rise of 2–3 °C in body temperature which lasted 10 or more minutes. There was no obvious behavioural change during this disturbance. The temperature increase was such that observations alone could never have revealed this change as a result of human disturbance. The possible effect of the cage remains to be tested.

By using these examples of temperature variations, I have attempted to show how useful biotelemetry can be. These kinds of measurements and others that follow would be impossible without the use of wireless data transmission.

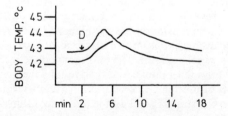

Figure 21.5 Fluctuation in telemetered intraperitoneal temperatures of two White-crowned sparrows resulting from a minor disturbance. The arrow (D) indicates the time of silent approach of a human to within 2 m of the caged birds followed by immediate departure. (After Southwick, 1973).

ECG and heart rate as indicators of behavioural state

Relationships between behavioural and physiological responses have provided a major source of information for the study of emotional behaviour. Heart rate measurement has frequently been used as an indicator of the autonomic responses accompanying behaviours. It would be extremely useful if certain types of heart rate patterns were consistent indicators of emotional states but, in practice, heart rate only gives us clues to actual emotional conditions. Bohus (1974) points out that even though large amounts of data have been gathered, contradictory observations still do not allow a uniform view to be established between 'emotionality' and heart rate changes. Some of the more obvious reasons are intra and interspecific differences, handling history of animals under study, constraints used in quantifying behaviour and methodological factors. The question of whether contradictory results could arise as a partial function of differing data-acquisition techniques was examined by Bohus (1974). A comparison was made between telemetric and direct wire lead measurements of heart rates of rats under various behavioural situations. Figure 21.6 shows results obtained by these two techniques while the rats were in their home cages. The figure indicates that heart rates were always significantly higher when recordings were made by direct wire; furthermore in animals monitored by telemetry devices, habituation to the telemetry system became evident during the first few days of the experiment. Behavioural activity did not differ between the two groups, which does not explain the cause of higher cardiac activity for wired animals. Bohus (1974) gives the more likely explanation that attachment of the wire leads caused some psychological effects, which were reflected in a sensitive autonomic measure like heart rate, but not in behavioural responses such as activity rates.

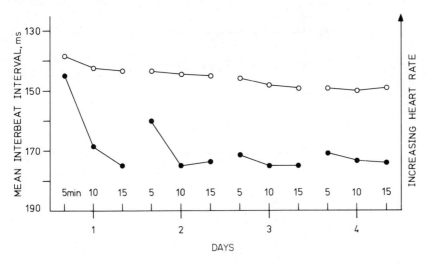

Figure 21.6 The influence of recording conditions on the heart rate of rats as measured in their home cage. ECG records were taken daily for 15-min periods with the aid of a biotelemetry transmitter (solid circles) or through wire leads (open circles). (After Bohus, 1974).

Thompson, Grant, Pearson and Corner (1968*a* and *b*) conducted a study to test the effectiveness of certain stimuli in modifying behavioural conditions of starlings *Sturnus vulgaris*. The object of their study was to determine which calls (natural or artificial) had the lowest habituation rate (that is number of times a bird would respond to call before habituation) and which caused the greatest increase in heart rate. Since handling and direct wire techniques caused abnormal heart rates, bio-telemetry was chosen as the preferred recording medium. Figure 21.7 shows average heart rate resulting from exposure to three sound stimuli used in the experiment. The distress and feeding calls were from starlings while the novel stimulus was a human voice reading a report. Habituation was found to be lowest for the distress call. There was little difference between responses to the human voice and distress call. Even though no immediate explanation for this similarity was given, certain practical applications were proposed. The probable repelling effect of sounds to free-living starlings and possibly other pest species, may be quantitatively assessed by recording heart rate under 'stressful' conditions. Heart rate then may be used as a sensitive index of fright (or stress) induced behaviour in the natural environment.

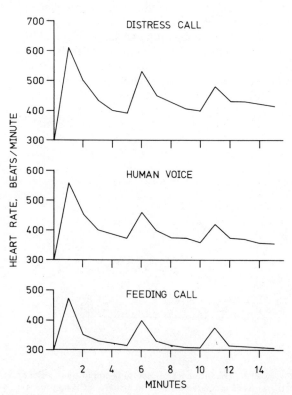

Figure 21.7 Average heart rate of starlings in response to three 10-s applications of sound stimuli. (Redrawn after Thompson *et al.*, 1968).

Speeding up (tachycardia) and slowing down (bradycardia) of heart rate has been observed in various species subjected to 'normal' and 'abnormal' behavioural pressures. Tachycardia under stress occurs in the two studies cited above. Bradycardia has been studied using biotelemetry in ducks (Butler and Woakes, 1976), ground squirrels *Citellus armatus* (Ruff, 1971) and the American alligator *Alligator mississippiensis* (Smith, Allison and Crowder, 1974).

Butler and Woakes (1976) carried out preliminary studies on the physiological responses of diving ducks in an indoor pond which showed that during enforced submersion, there was a progressive reduction in heart rate, but because of transmitter limitations they were unable to evaluate the response associated with natural submersion. An FM transmitter was then designed (Woakes and Butler, 1975) which operated effectively under water. It could transmit information about heart and respiration rates, the latter being measured by air flow over a thermister located in the trachea. Using this system they have shown that preceding a natural dive there is an increase in heart rate and respiratory frequency. As soon as the bird dives and stops breathing there is an instantaneous reduction in heart rate which is the lowest measured throughout the dive. Butler and Woakes (1976) suggest the difference between enforced and normal submersions is evidence that ducks anticipate natural dives. Furthermore, there is evidence that ducks respond to a human's approach physiologically but not necessarily behaviourally. The cardiac activity of an approached duck increased significantly and remained elevated while a human stood at the pond's edge. Immediately upon retreat of the human, cardiac activity of the duck began to decrease (Butler, personal communication).

The telemetered heart rate of ground squirrels showed a marked decline from 350 to 200 beats per minute within 1 second when trapped or 'hiding' animals were approached by a human (Ruff, 1971). This indicates a difference in response to human disturbance between squirrels (bradycardia) and ducks (tachycardia).

The measurements of Smith *et al.* (1974) for undisturbed values of alligator heart rate are 25–35 beats per minute. Those that were held in a cage out of the water always showed higher heart rate than free-ranging animals. Greater cardiac activity was also noted while animals were very active, for example swimming rapidly. Disturbing animals housed in a cage but not in water, resulted only in tachycardia. Figure 21.8 shows the heart rate measurements over a 4-hour period

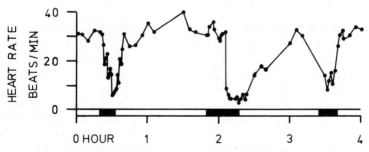

Figure 21.8 Purposely induced bradycardia in the American alligator resulting from human disturbance (solid bar) during a continuous 4-hour sample observed telemetrically. (After Smith *et al.*, 1974).

in a free-ranging alligator. During each disturbance, bradycardia was noticed imme-diately upon diving, sometimes reaching as little as two beats per minute, but this was not found to occur during natural dives. To account for this apparent anomaly it has been proposed that animals may either react to danger by 'fight or flight' or by passively 'freezing or hiding'. The latter response involves bradycardia and has been observed in reptiles and mammals while some birds have been noted to in-crease heart rates.

Effects of Telemetry Systems on Animals

Any researcher comparing telemetered with uninstrumented animals hoping to as-certain the effects of telemetry must be aware that certain techniques of telemetry may require caution in using unmarked animals as controls. An example of this consideration occurs when survival is used as a measure of impact. Researchers releasing groups of animals, and subsequently monitoring location of the telemeter-ed group, create an obvious bias because telemetered animals will always be easier to find than unmarked animals.

The effects of biotelemeters are largely a function of animal size, telemetry package size and weight attachment. Big game are not affected by telemetry pack-ages of a few hundred grams, whereas a small rodent or passerine may be severely affected by carrying a package weighing 1 or 2 g. In most experiments, radio pack-age weights (transmitter, battery and harness) are minimised and transmitters are attached in a non-restrictive manner.

Most impact studies have been conducted on birds (with the exception of Bohus, 1974). It is generally assumed that if a bird carries a telemetry device for an agreed period without any noticeable adverse effects, the telemeter then can be considered to have scarcely influenced its behaviour (Brander, 1968; Ball, 1971). Greenwood and Sargeant (1973) aptly point out that 'such an assumption could lead to erroneous interpretation of data if unrecognised subtle changes occurred in the physiology, behaviour or well-being of the bird.' Cochran (1972, p. 40) has allowed for the possibility of these kinds of effects by stating 'for a given species and study objective, a bias may be acceptable if it were known.' By using examples I shall attempt to show how effects caused by telemetric devices may be measured.

Effects on behaviour patterns

Boag (1972) studied what effects telemetry devices had on captive Red grouse *Lagopus l. scoticus*. To minimise handling effects, both telemetered and control animals were handled in similar ways. He found that activity levels for radio-equipped animals were consistently lower than among controls. Food consump-tion among experimental females was significantly less than among female controls, but not between the males and no differences in the choice of habitat were found between the two groups. The differences in activity and food intake between the instrumented and control groups were found to be greatest in the first week after the transmitters were fitted.

Research aimed at evaluating the effects of breeding behaviour on Woodcocks *Philohela minor* was carried out by Ramakka (1972). The number of courtship flights of marked males was used as a measure of courtship success. Courtship activity was reduced compared with controls and courtship flights were significantly fewer compared with unmarked males. Ramakka (1972, p. 1312) points out that poor harness, transmitter and antenna design may have each affected the behaviour. The long antennae used (30.5 cm) on a small bird may have caused instabilities in flight, being reflected by fewer flights during courtship.

Animal preoccupation with a newly installed telemetry package is commonly reported in the literature (Mackay, 1970; Dwyer, 1972; Greenwood and Sargeant, 1973; Gilmer, Ball, Cowardin and Riechmann, 1974; Lawson, Kanwisher and Williams, 1976). Abnormal behavioural activities included increased preening and smoothing of the feathers around the harness and package, and a partial aversion to swimming (Greenwood and Sargeant, 1973). Normally this preoccupation subsides after the first few hours but may last up to a week. During this time, it is advisable not to collect data to describe normal behavioural or physiological states, though such data may be valuable in determining eventual acceptance of the radio package.

Effects on animal weight

Boag's (1972) study showing that feeding behaviour was less for instrumented birds led Greenwood and Sargeant (1973) to evaluate the effects of back-mounted radio packages of three different weights on mallards and Blue-winged teal *Anas discors*. All groups with radio packages lost more weight than did control groups. No correlation was found between the weights of the transmitters and the loss in weight of the ducks. Thus birds with light transmitters lost weight at no greater rate than birds with heavier packages. There was a marked difference in weight loss within all instrumented mallard groups while in captivity during the first week compared with captive controls. Such was not the case for the teal until the fourth week of study. Marked feather wear in each group of instrumented birds within the first week was noticed. New feathers began to appear after the fourth week of study.

Effects on reproductive success

Dummy radio packages were fitted to Red grouse to compare the effects of back tabbing and telemetry techniques used for recognition (Boag, Watson and Parr, 1973). Females marked with these two techniques were found to be equally successful at hatching and raising young. The mortality rates of the groups did not significantly differ even though the transmitters were over five times the weight of the back tabs. Back tabbed and non-back tabbed controls also showed no difference in reproductive success (Watson and Miller, 1971). Therefore, Boag *et al.* (1973) concluded that transmitters did not adversely affect the reproductive success of Red grouse.

Johnson (1971) leg banded and released 785 Ring-necked pheasants *Phasianus colchicus* of which 393 were equipped with dummy radio packages. His conclusion from recoveries and bag checks was that the radio packages did not affect survival, dispersal, or growth rates of marked birds compared to uninstrumented birds.

Our own research (Amlaner, Sibly and McCleery, in preparation) supports these general conclusions when also applied to Herring gulls *Larus argentatus*. We placed dummy radio packages of various weights (10, 30 and 50 g) on gulls and found birds similarly handled but not weighted had similar success at maintaining a clutch compared with weighted birds. With each successive weight increase of dummy radio package, success at maintaining a clutch was not greatly effected.

From these examples it is clear there is a diversity of opinion as to the effects of radio packages on birds. The over-all indication points to the need to minimise weights of transmitters compared with body weight and to design non-restrictive harnesses. The general picture of telemetry devices is that when properly installed, using the above guidelines, the effects on an animal's welfare can be minimal.

Conclusions

The use of biotelemetry to record physiological parameters has several distinct advantages including unrestrained movement, ability to allow an animal to remain in his natural setting, and technical advantages (such as unambiguous signal retrieval).

Results on the effects of radio packages indicate that, with properly designed systems, animal welfare is not impaired significantly. The design process usually involves techniques that take into account skin abrasion from the harness, minimising weight of transmitter, and selection of transducer and electrode leads suitable for the particular animal in question.

The evidence reported here shows that telemetry is a preferred method by which researchers may obtain data when considering both the physiological and behavioural aspects of the animal in natural conditions. As interest continues in this field, we can look forward to further advances in weight reduction, battery design (already the solar cell is being used on some telemeters, Patton, 1973; Williams and Burke, 1973) and harnessing (harnesses which automatically release radio packages after a certain prescribed period, Mackay, 1974) that collectively minimise the impact on welfare of the individual animal.

Acknowledgements

I thank D. Macdonald, N. Ball, N. Hough and M. Thom for their very useful and enlightening comments made on earlier 'rough' drafts. Also, I thank my wife Beverly for her many hours of organising the 400 plus papers from which I made this typescript and for her painstaking efforts in typing numerous drafts.

References

Ball, I. J., Jr (1971). Movements, habitat use and behavior of wood duck (*Air sponsa*) broods in north-central Minnesota as determined by radio tracking. M.S. thesis, University of Minnesota. 56 pp.
Boag, D. A. (1972). Effect of radio packages on behavior of captive red grouse. *J. Wildl. Mgmt,* **36**, 511–518.

Boag, D. A., Watson, A. and Parr, R. (1973). Radio-marking versus back-tabbing red grouse. *J. Wildl. Mgmt,* **37** (3), 410–412.

Bohus, B. (1974). Telemetered heart rate responses of the rat during free and learned behaviour. *Biotelemetry,* **1**, 193–201.

Borbely, A. A. (1974). Monitoring neurobiological processes by cable connections or telemetry. In *Biotelemetry II,* 2nd Int. Symp. (ed. P. A. Neukomm), Karger, Basel, pp. 168–172.

Brander, R. B. (1968). A radio-package harness for game birds. *J. Wildl. Mgmt,* **32** (3), 630–632.

Butler, P. J. and Woakes, A. J. (1976). Changes in heart rate and respiratory frequency associated with spontaneous submersion of ducks. In *Biotelemetry III* (ed. T. B. Fryer, H. A. Miller, H. Sandler), Academic Press, New York, San Francisco, London, pp. 215–218.

Caceres, C. A. (1965). *Biomedical Telemetry.* Academic Press, New York.

Cochran, W. W. (1972). Long-distance tracking of birds. In *Animal Orientation and Navigation,* (ed. S. R. Galler, K. Schmidt-Koenig, G. J. Jacobs, R. E. Belleville), NASA-SP-262. US Government Printing Office, Washington, D.C. 606 pp.

Duncan, I. J. H., Filshie, J. H. and McGee, I. J. (1975). Radiotelemetry of avian shank temperature using a thin-film hybrid micro-circuit. *Med. Biol. Engng,* **13** (4), 544–550.

Dwyer, T. J. (1972). An adjustable radio-package for ducks. *Bird-Banding,* **43** (4), 282–284.

Eliassen, E. (1960). A method for measuring heart rate and stroke/pulse pressure in birds by normal flight. Arbok University Bergen. *Mat-Nat. Ser.,* **12**, 1–22.

Eliassen, E. (1963a). Preliminary results from new methods of investigating the physiology of birds during flight. *IBIS,* **105**, 234–237.

Eliassen, E. (1963b). Telemetric registering of physiological data in birds in normal flight. In *Biotelemetry* (ed. L. E. Slater), Pergamon, New York, pp. 257–265.

Fryer, T. B., Deboo, G. J. and Winget, C. M. (1966). Miniature longlife temperature telemetry system. *J. appl. Physiol.,* **21**, 295–298.

Fryer, T. B. and Sandler, H. (1974). A review of implant telemetry systems. *Biotelemetry,* **1**, 351–374.

Fryer, T. B., Sandler, H. and Datnow, B. (1969). A multichannel telemetry system. *Med. Res. Engr,* **8**, 9–15.

Gilmer, D. S., Ball, I. J., Cowardin, L. M. and Riechmann, J. H. (1974). Effects of radio packages on wild ducks. *J. Wildl. Mgmt,* **38** (2) 243–252.

Greenwood, R. H. and Sargeant, A. B. (1973). Influence of radio packs on captive mallards and blue-winged teal. *J. Wildl. Mgmt,* **37** (1), 3–9.

Johnson, R. N. (1971). Comparative survival of radio-marked and non-radio-marked pen-reared juvenile cock pheasants released into the wild. Minnesota Dept. Nat. Resource, *St. Paul. Q. Prog. Rep.,* **31** (1), 23–32.

Lawson, K., Kanwisher, J. and Williams, T. C. (1976). A UHF radio-telemetry system for wild animals. *J. Wildl. Mgmt,* **40** (2), 360–362.

Lonsdale, E. M., Bradach, B. and Thorne, E. T. (1971). A telemetry system to determine body temperature in pronghorn antelope. *J. Wildl. Mgmt,* **35**, 747–751.

Lord, R., Belrose, F. and Cochran, W. W. (1962). Radio-telemetry of the respiration of flying ducks. *Science,* **137**, 39–40.

Mackay, R. S. (1970). *Bio-medical Telemetry,* 2nd edn, Wiley, New York.

Mackay, R. S. (1974). Field studies on animals. *Biotelemetry,* **1**, 286–312.

Patton, D. R. (1973). Solar panels: an energy source for radio transmitters on wildlife. *J. Wildl. Mgmt,* **37** (2), 236–238.

Ramakka, J. M. (1972). Effect of radio-tagging on breeding behavior of male woodcock. *J. Wildl. Mgmt,* **36**, 1309–1312.

Ruff, R. L. (1971). Telemetered heart rates of free-living Uinta ground squirrels in response to social interactions. Ph.D. dissertation. Utah State University, Logan, Utah.

Sawby, S. W. and Gessaman, J. A. (1974). Telemetry of electrocardiograms from free-living birds: a method of electrode placement. *Condor,* Winter, **76** (4), 479–481.

Schladweiler, J. L. and Ball, I. J., Jr (1968). Telemetry bibliography emphasizing studies of wild animals under natural condtions. *Bell Museum Nat. Hist. Tech. Rept.,* 15. 31 pp.

Skutt, H. R., Bock, F. M., IV, Haugstad, P., Holter, J. B., Hayes, H. H. and Silver, H. (1973). Low-power implantable transmitters for telemetry of heart rate and temperature from white-tailed deer. *J. Wildl. Mgmt,* **37** (3), 413–417.

Slater, L. E. (1963). *Bio-Telemetry. The use of telemetry in animal behavior and physiology in relation to ecological problems.* Proc. of the Interdisciplinary Conf., New York, March 1962. Pergamon, New York, 372 pp.

Smith, E. N., Allison, R. D. and Crowder, W. E. (1974). Bradycardia in a free ranging American alligator. *Copeia,* **3** (October), 770–772.

Smith, E. N. and Crowder, W. E. (1974). Implantable ECG transmitter employing a magnetic switch. *J. appl. Physiol.,* **36** (5), 634–635).

Smith, E. N. and Salb, T. J., Jr. (1975). Multichannel subcarrier ECG, respiration, and temperature biotelemetry system. *J. appl. Physiol.,* **39** (2), 331–334.

Southwick, E. E. (1973). Remote sensing of body temperature in a captive 25-G bird. *Condor,* **75** (3), 464–466.

Thompson, R. D., Grant, C. V., Pearson, E. W. and Corner, G. W. (1968a). Cardiac response of starlings to sound; effects of lighting and grouping. *Am. J. Physiol.,* **214**, 41–44.

Thompson, R. D., Grant, C. V., Pearson, E. W. and Corner, G. W. (1968b). Differential heart rate response of starlings to sound stimuli of biological origin. *J. Wildl. Mgmt,* **32**, 888–893.

Varney, J. R. (1971). Radio-tracking and telemetering equipment design. Montana Cooperative Wildlife Research Unit. University of Montana, Missoula, Montana, 59801.

Watson, A. and Miller, G. R. (1971). Territory size and aggression in a fluctuating red grouse population. *J. Anim. Ecol.,* **40** (2), 367–383.

Whitton, G. C. (1976). Regulation of body temperature. In *Avian Physiology* (ed. P. D. Sturkie), Springer-Verlag, New York, pp. 146–173.

Will, G. B. and Patric, E. F. (1972). A contribution toward a bibliography on wildlife telemetry and radio tracking. *New York Fed. Aid in Fish and Wildl. Restoration Proj. W 123-R and Rhode Island Agric. Exp. Stn., Contrib. 1439.* 56 pp.

Williams, T. C. and Burke, E. H. (1973). Solar power for wildlife telemetry transmitters. *Am. Birds,* **27**, 719–720.

Woakes, A. J. and Butler, P. J. (1975). An implantable transmitter for monitoring heart rate and respiratory frequency in diving ducks. *Biotelemetry,* 2, 153-160.
Zimmermann, F., Gerard, H. and Charles-Dominique, P. (1976). Radio-tracking vertebrates: theory and practical application. *La Terre et La Vie,* 30 (3), 309-346.

Additional References

This bibliography supplements the literature cited above and Mackay's *Biomedical Telemetry* (1970) references. It includes citings from 1970 to the present. The interested reader could do no better than to obtain a copy of Mackay's book as it contains most of the essentials useful to a person just getting started in biotelemetry. I have categorised these references similarly to the chapter subheadings, with the exception that none of the references included in the chapter has been repeated here.

Biotelemetry systems

These include a diverse selection of design approaches for transmitters, receivers, demodulators, harnesses etc. I have purposely categorised 'power supplies' separately from this list because of their importance. Deserving specific note are the applications of solar cells (Patton, 1933; Williams and Burke, 1973) and nuclear cells which remain as potentially useful long-range power sources for biotelemeters.

Barr, R. E. (1972). A telemetry system for recording body temperature of large numbers of caged rodents. *Med. biol. Engng,* 10, 877-884.
Ben-Yaakov, S. (1972). Clock oscillator for telemetry systems uses CMOS chip to minimise power drain. *Electronic Design,* Information Retrieval Number 39, 20, 84.
Bray, O. E. and Corner, G. W. (1972). A tail clip for attaching transmitters to birds. *J. Wildl. Mgmt,* 36 (2), 640-642.
Collier, R. J., Diprose, M. F. and Crawley, B. E. (1976). A low-power transmitter for electrocardiograms using tunnel diodes. *Med. biol. Engng,* May, 359-360.
Decker, J. R. and Gillis, M. F. (1973). A completely implantable three channel temperature biotelemetry system. *ISI Trans.,* 12 (2), 97-102.
Djorup, A., Nielsen, J. F. and Wagner, G. (1970). Implantable FM-telemetry transmitter for long-term registration of biopotentials. *Dan. med. buttl.,* 17, 136-137.
Ellerbruch, V. G. (1973). Biotelemetry transmitter design methods. In *Research Animals in Medicine* (ed. Harmison), US Govt. Publ. DHEW No. (NIH) 72-333, pp. 1105-1117.
Fryer, T. B. (1975). A multichannel implantable telemetry system for flow, pressure and ECG measurements. *J. appl. Physiol.,* 39, 318-326.
Gier, S. (1974). A complete EEG radio telemetry equipment. *Electroenceph. clin. Neurophysiol.,* 37, 89-92.
Gill, R. W. (1976). Microtelemetry—the use of integrated circuits in biotelemetry. *Biomed. Engng,* February, 43-46, 58.

Godfrey, G. A. (1970). A transmitter harness for small birds. *Inland Bird Banding News,* **42** (1), 3-5.

Goodman, R. M. (1971). A reliable and accurate implantable temperature tele-meter. *Bioscience,*21 (8), 370-374.

Guckel, H., Scidmore, A. K., Beyer, J. B. and Chitre, S. (1976). RF telemetry system for pressure- and temperature-monitoring of free-swimming freshwater fish. In *Biotelemetry III* (ed. T. B. Fryer, H. A. Miller and H. Sandler), Academic Press, New York, San Francisco, London, pp. 203-206.

Heal, J. W. (1974). A physiological radiotelemetry system using mark/space ratio modulation of a square-wave subcarrier. *Med. biol. Engng,* **12** (6), 843-848.

Hyde, C. and Bell, D. (1972). Digital transmission of physiological data. *Biomed. sci. Instrum.,*9, 33-36.

Ijsenbrandt, H. J. B., Kimmich, H. P. and Van Den Akker, A. J. (1972). Single to seven channel lightweight biotelemetry system. In *Biotelemetry* (ed. H. P. Kimmich and J. A. Vos), Meander, Leiden, pp. 57-64.

Ivison, J. M. and Robinson, P. F. (1974). A digital phase modulator and demodu-lator for a biomedical telemetry system. *Med. biol. Engng,* January, 109-112.

Johnsen, P. E. and Horral, R. M. (1974). A temperature and pressure sensing bio-telemetry system. U.T.N.,4 (1), 13-15.

Lund, G. F. (1974). A design for receiving antennas for laboratory radio trans-mitters, witb field application. *J. Mammal.,* **55**, 237-238.

Marshall, D. A. and Celebi, G. (1970). A tunable subminiature bio-telemetry trans-mitter. *Physiol. Behav.,* **5** (6), 709-712.

McElligott, J. G. (1973). A telemetry system for the transmission of single and multiple channel data from individual neurons in the brain. In *Brain Unit Activity during Behavior* (ed. M. I. Phillips), C. C. Thomas Press, Springfield, pp. 53-66.

McEwen, G. N., Jr, Miranda, R., Fryer, T. B., Satinoff, E. and Williams, B. A. (1976). A system for continuous measurement of metabolism, body tempera-ture, feeding, drinking and activity in unrestrained rats. In *Biotelemetry III* (eds., T. B. Fryer, H. A. Miller and H. Sandler), Academic Press, New York, San Francisco, London, pp. 195-198.

Meijer, A. A. (1974). A simple, wide-band FM transmitter for telemetering bio-potentials. *Med. biol. Engng,* **12**, 875-876.

Morrow, J. L. (1976). A telemetry system for recording heart rates of unrestrained game birds. *J. Wildl. Mgmt ,* **40**, 359-360.

Pauley, J. D. and Reite, M. (1977). Automatic antenna selector for use in biotele-metry applications. *Physiol. Behav.,* **18** (1), 169-170.

Pauley, J. D., Reite, M. and Walker, S. (1974). An implantable multichannel bio-telemetry system. *Electroenceph. clin. Neurophysiol.,*37, 153-160.

Radar, R. D., Meehan, J. P. and Henriksen, J. K. C. (1973). An implantable tele-metry system and its application in the study of renal hemodynamics. In *Chronically Implanted Cardiovascular Instrumentation* (ed. E. P. McCutcheon), Academic Press, New York, pp. 377-399.

Riley, J. L. (1972). Transmitter for recording respiration rate information by radio-telemetry. *J. appl. Physiol.,* **32** (2), 259-260.

Sandler, H., Fryer, T. B. and Stone, H. L. (1973). Implantable telemetry systems for use in animal monitoring. *Biomaterials, Medical Devices, and Artificial Organs,* **1** (2), 405–417.

Sharp, R. W., Breeyear, J. J. and Simmons, K. R. (1974). Improved temperature telemetry system. *J. appl. Physiol.,* **37** (4), 617–619.

Smith, E. N. (1974). Multichannel temperature and heart rate radio-telemetry transmitter. *J. appl. Physiol.,* **36** (2), 252–255.

Standora, E. A. (1972). A multichannecl transmitter for monitoring shark behavior at sea. *U.T.N.,* **2** (1), 1, 8–13.

Topham, W. S. (1973). Review of animal instrumentation: transducer capability. In *Research Animals in Medicine* (ed. Harmison), US Govt. Publ. DHEW No. (NIH) 72-333, pp. 1229–1241.

Voegeli, F. and Kraft, W. (1972). Multichannel telemetry of physiological parameters (body temperature, ECG, EEG) in the rat. In *Biotelemetry* (ed. H. P. Kimmich and J. A. Vos) Meander, Leiden, pp. 371–380.

Vreeland, R. W. and Yeager, C. L. (1974). Low level COS/MOS multi-plexing for simplified EEG telemetry. In *Biotelemetry II* 2nd Int. Symp. (ed. P. A. Neukomn), Karger, Basel, pp. 55–57.

Weller, C. (1973). An inexpensive diversity receiving system for medical telemetry. *Biomed. Engng,* April, 157–159.

Power Supplies

Fryer, T. B. (1974). Power sources for implanted telemetry systems. *Biotelemetry J.,* **1** (1), 31–40.

Greatbatch, W. and Bustard, T. S. (1973). A Pu^{238} O_2 nuclear power source for implantable cardiac pacemakers. *IEEE Trans. Biomed. Engng, BME,* **20** (5), 336–345.

Harding, P. J. R., Chute, F. S. and Doell, A. C. (1976). Increasing battery reliability for radio transmitters. *J. Wildl. Mgmt,* **40** (2), 357–358.

Ko, W. H. and Hymecek, J. (1974). Implant evaluation of a nuclear power source. Betacel battery. *IEEE Trans. Biomed. Engng.,BME,***21**, 238–241.

Roy, O. Z. (1971). Biological energy sources. A review. *Biomed. Engng,* **6**, 250–256.

Tseung, A. C. C. (1971). An encapsulated implantable metal-oxygen cell as a long-term power source for medical and biological application. *Med. biol. Engng,* **9**, 175–184.

Wan, B. Y. C. and Tseung, A. C. C. (1974). Some studies related to electricity generation from biological fuel cells and galvanic cells *in vitro* and *in vivo. Med. biol. Engng,* **12**, 14–27.

Physiological measurements

The 'Physiological Measurements' section includes a wide list of parameters not dealt with in the chapter, for example EMG, pressure and flow. Most of the following papers stress actual results obtained through the use of biotelemetry systems rather than describing the systems themselves.

Berger, M., Hart, J. S. and Roy, O. Z. (1970*a*). The co-ordination between respiration and wing beats in birds. *Z. vergl. Physiol.,* **66**, 190–200.

Berger, M., Hart, J. S. and Roy, O. Z. (1970*b*). Respiration, oxygen consumption and heart rate in some birds during rest and flight. *Z. vergl. Physiol.*, **66**, 201-214.

Boyd, J. C. and Sladen, W. J. L. (1971). Telemetry studies of the internal body temperatures of Adelie and emperor penguins at Cape Crozier, Rose Island, Antarctica. *Auk*, **88**, 366-380.

Burns, J., Horlington, M., Shaffer, M. and White, E. H. (1971). Miniature transmitters for heart rate measurements in groups of unrestrained rats. *Arch. int. Pharmacodyn. Ther.*, **193**, 213-225.

Cleworth, P. B. and Verberne, G. (1976). Telemetered EEG activity from the isolated olfactory bulb of rabbits. In *Biotelemetry III* (ed. T. B. Fryer, H. A. Miller and H. Sandler), Academic Press, New York, San Francisco, London, pp. 223-226.

Cogger, E. A., Otis, R. E. and Ringer, R. K. (1974). Heart rates in restrained and freely moving Japanese quail via radiotelemetry. *Poultry Sci.*, **53**, 430.

Conway, M. J., Parker, D. and Soutter, L. P. (1973). Radio telemetry of blood pO_2 *in vivo*. *Biomed. Engng*, October, 428-430.

Cupal, J. J., Weeks, R. W. and Kaltenbach, C. (1976). A heart rate activity biotelemetry system for use on wild big game animals. In *Biotelemetry III* (ed. T. B. Fryer, H. A. Miller and H. Sandler), Academic Press, New York, San Francisco, London, pp. 219-222.

Davis, S. D. (1970). Telemetering in thermobiology: A study of mammalian hair. *Proc. Vi A. Meeting Int. Telemetering Conf.*, pp. 103-109.

Devaney, M. J., Deavers, D. R., Coria, A. M., Tempel, G. E. and Musacchia, X. J. (1976). Telemetry of body temperature and heart rate of hibernating and normothermic ground squirrels. In *Biotelemetry III* (ed. T. B. Fryer, H. A. Miller and H. Sandler), Academic Press, New York, San Francisco, London, pp. 207-210.

Downhower, J. F. and Pauley, J. D. (1970). Automated recordings of body temperature form free-ranging yellow-bellied marmots. *J. Wildl. Mgmt*, **34** (3), 639-641.

Evans, B. T. (1972). A remotely operated ECG telemetry for chronic implantation in rats. In *Biotelemetry* (ed. H. P. Kimmich and J. A. Vos), Meander, Leiden, pp. 353-359.

Grant, C. V., Thompson, R. D. and Corner, G. W. (1971). Determining avian ECG and respiration with a single-channel radio transmitter. *J. appl. Physiol.*, **30** (2), 302-303.

Hartley, J., Murphy, V. G., Devaney, M., Barr, R. E. and Hahn, A. W. (1976). Short-range telemetry of tissue oxygen tensions. In *Biotelemetry III* (ed. T. B. Fryer, H. A. Miller, H. Sandler), Academic Press, New York, San Francisco, London, pp. 259-262.

Holter, J. B., Urban, W. E., Jr, Hayes, H. H. and Silver, H. (1976). Predicting metabolic rate from telemetered heart rate in white-tailed deer. *J. Wildl. Mgmt*, **40** (4), 626-629.

Kroll, J. C., Clark, D. R., Jr and Albert, J. W. (1973). Radio telemetry for studying thermoregulation in free-ranging snakes. *Ecology*, **54**, 454-456.

Manson, G. (1974). EEG radio telemetry. *Electroenceph. clin. Neurophysiol.*, **37**, 411-413.

McGinnis, S. M., Finch, V. A. and Harthoorn, A. M. (1970). A radio-telemetry technique for monitoring temperatures from unrestrained ungulates. *J. Wildl. Mgmt,* **34** (4), 921-925.

Millard, R. W., Johnansen, K. and Milson, W. K. (1973). Radio-telemetry of cardiovascular responses to exercise and diving in penguins. *Comp. Biochem. Physiol.,* **46A**, 227-240.

Morhardt, J. E. (1972). Temperature transmission from biopotential radio-telemetry transmitters. *J. appl. Physiol.,* **33**, 397-399.

Osgood, D. W. (1970). Thermoregulation in water snakes studied by telemetry. *Copeia,* **3**, 568-571.

Prochazka, V. J., Tat, K., Westerman, R. A. and Ziccone, S. P. (1974). Remote monitoring of muscle length and EMG in unrestrained cats. *Electroenceph. clin. Neurophysiol.,* **37** (6), 649-653.

Radar, R. D. and Stevens, C. M. (1974). Renal parameter estimates in unrestrained dogs. *Med. biol. Engng,* **12** (4), 465-477.

Rochelle, J. M. and Coutant, C. C. (1974). Ultrasonic tag for extended temperature monitoring from small fish. *U.T.N.,* **4** (1), 1, 4-7.

Scidmore, A. K., Weiss, D., Beyer, J. B. and Guckel, H. (1976). EEG monitor for free-swimming fish. In *Biotelemetry III* (ed. T. B. Fryer, H. A. Miller and H. Sandler), Academic Press, New York, San Francisco, London, pp. 227-230.

Shore, J. R. and Burbage, A. M. R. (1972). A telemetry system for the remote measurement of breathing pressures. *Med. biol. Engng,* **10**, 105-108.

Smith, E. N. (1975a). Thermoregulation of the American alligator, *Alligator mississippiensis. Physiol. Zool.,* **47** (2), 177-194.

Smith, E. N. (1975b). Oxygen consumption, ventilation, and oxygen pulse of the American alligator during heating and cooling. *Physiol. Zool.,* **48** (4), 326-337.

Smith, E. N., Peterson, C. and Thigpen, K. (1976). Body temperature, heart rate and respiration rate on an unrestrained domestic mallard duck, *Anas platyrhynchos domesticus. Comp. Biochem. Physiol.,*54A, 19-20.

Stuart, J. L. and Zervanos, S. M. (1976). Heart flux and temperature data telemetering system for mammalian energy flow studies. In *Biotelemetry III* (ed. T. B. Fryer, H. A. Miller and H. Sandler), Academic Press, New York, San Francisco, London, pp. 199-202.

Varney, J. R. and Ellis, D. H. (1974). Telemetering egg for use in incubation and nesting studies. *J. Wildl. Mgmt,* **38** (1), 142-148.

Venables, B. and Smith, E. N. (1972). A simple method for recording opercular rate and heart rate of unrestrained fish. *Progressive Fish-Culturist,*34, 233-234.

Zigmond, M. J., Holmquest, D. L. and Wurtman, R. J. (1970). Telemetric measurements of effects of light and drugs on diurnal body temperaure rhythms. In *Proc. IV Int. Congr. Pharmacol. 1969.* (ed. R. Eigenmann), Schwabe, Basel, pp. 279-287.

Measured effects

'Measured effects' by telemetry not only include system impact but also include survival studies, which are becoming increasingly popular among wildlife organisations in assessing various impact parameters on wild animals.

Beale, D. M. and Smith, A. D. (1973). Mortality of pronghorn antelope fawns in western Utah. *J. Wildl. Mgmt,* **37** (3), 343–352.

Brand, C. J., Vowles, R. H. and Keith, L. B. (1975). Snowshoe hare mortality monitored by telemetry. *J. Wildl. Mgmt,* **39** (4), 741–747.

Dumke, R. T. and Pils, C. M. (1973). Mortality of radio-tagged pheasants on the Waterloo wildlife area. *Wisconsin Dept. Nat. Resour. Tech. Bull.,* 72, 52 pp.

Hessler, E., Tester, J. R., Siniff, D. B. and Nelson, M. M. (1970). Biotelemetry study of survival of pen reared pheasant released in selected habitats. *J. Wildl. Mgmt,* **34**, 267–274.

Knight, A. E. (1974). Fish mortality studies during passage through Northfield pumped storage hydroelectric facility. Fishery Field Studies in Holyoke and Turners Pools 1945: A tuned-antenna radio telemetric tag for fish. *U.T.N.,***5** (1), 13–16.

Radar, R. D., Stevens, C. M., Meehan, J. P. and Henry, J. P. (1972*a*). Implant telemetry and social strain. *Biomed. sci. Instrum.,* **9**, 144–150.

Reite, M., Pauley, J. D., Kaufman, I. C., Stynes, A. J. and Marker, V. (1974). Normal physiological patterns and physiological-behavioral correlations in unrestrained monkey infants. *Physiol. Behav.,* **12**, 1021–1033.

Schladweiler, J. L. and Tester, J. R. (1972). Survival and behavior of hand-reared mallards released in the wild. *J. Wildl. Mgmt,* **36** (4), 1118–1127.

Shepherd, B. G. (1973). Transmitter attachment and fish behaviour. *U.T.N.,***3** (1), 8–11.

Stoddart, L. C. (1970). A telemetric method for detecting Jack rabbit mortality. *J. Wildl. Mgmt,* **34** (3), 501–507.

Sweeney, J. R., Marchinton, R. L. and Sweeney, J. M. (1971). Responses of radio-monitored white-tailed deer chased by hunting dogs. *J. Wildl. Mgmt,* **35** (4), 707–716.

Tester, J. R. (1971). Interpretation of ecological and behavioral data on wild animals obtained by telemetry with special reference to errors and uncertainties. In *Proc. Symp. Biotelemetry S 57,* CSIR, Pretoria, South Africa, pp. 385–408.

Miscellaneous

Obviously, there were a few papers that did not fit into the above categories and I have put them under 'miscellaneous'. I would like to draw particular attention to the approach by Bojsen (1976). His application of semiconductor memory systems is truly innovative and with microminiturisation techniques (Gill, 1976), future applications of this type to biotelemetry should be possible.

Adey, W. R. (1972). Biotelemetry and computer analysis of sleep processes on earth and in space. *Astronautica Acta,* **17** (1 and 2), 185–202.

Bojsen, J. (1976). A semiconductor memory system for data storage in biotelemetry of radionuclide tracers. In *Biotelemetry III* (ed. T. B. Fryer, H. A. Miller and H. Sandler), Academic Press, New York, San Francisco, London, pp. 283–286.

Cook, G. R. and Sandler, H. (1970). An implantable ultrasonic telemeter for the measurement of blood flow in animals. *Proc. 23rd Ann. Conf. Engr. Med. Biol.,* Washington, D.C., Nov. 15–19, p. 281.

Donohoe, R. W. and Beal, R. O. (1972). Squirrel behavior determined by biotelemetry. *Ohio Fish Wildl. Rep.,* No. 2.

GPO (1968). *Performance specification for radio equipment for medical and biological telemetry devices.* HMSO SO Code No. 88-5438.

Howard, W. H. and Young, D. R. (1976). *In vivo* bone strain telemetry systems. In *Biotelemetry III* (ed. T. B. Fryer, H. A. Miller and H. Sandler), Academic Press, New York, San Francisco, London, pp. 251-254.

Konigsberg, E., Cothran, L. and Hawthrone, E. W. (1976). Implantable accelerometer for telemetry. In *Biotelemetry III* (ed. T. B. Fryer, H. A. Miller and H. Sandler), Academic Press, New York, San Francisco, London, pp. 271-274.

Lawson, K. and Kanwisher, J. (1973). Acoustic telemetry in studies of fish behaviour and physiology. *U.T.N.,* 3 (2), 5-7.

Perachio, A. A., Lide, E., Rice, D. H. and Sikes, J. (1976). A remotely controlled device for controlling electrical stimulations of the central nervous system. In *Biotelemetry III* (ed. T. B. Fryer, H. A. Miller and H. Sandler), Academic Press, New York, San Francisco, London, pp. 231-234.

Salmons, S. (1972). A telemetric technique for measuring muscle tension in conscious, unrestrained animals. In *Biotelemetry* (ed. H. P. Kimmich and J. A. Vos), Meander, Leiden, pp. 337-343.

Snyder, F., Bak, A. F., Bryan, J. S. and Carr, P. J. (1972). A method for telemetric study of sleep in small animals. *Psychophysiology,* (Abstracts of papers presented to the 11th Annual Meeting of the Association for the Psychophysiological Study of Sleep), 9 (1), 122.

Verberne, G. and Hofman, M. (1976). Telemetered neurophysiological activity in the olfactory system in rabbits and pheromones. In *Biotelemetry III* (ed. T. B. Fryer, H. A. Miller and H. Sandler), Academic Press, New York, San Francisco, London, pp. 235-238.

Wagner, G. (1975). Electrical activity of grafted myometrium and its recording by radiotelemetry in unrestrained rabbits. *J. Physiol.,* 244 (2), 353-364.

Manufacturers

A short list of manufacturers is included who supply ready built biotelemetry systems, power supplies and various types of electrodes and transducers for physiological measurements. Each will supply a catalogue or data sheet on request.

AVM Instrument Company 810 Dennison Drive Champaign, Illinois 61820, U.S.A.	Radio-tracking transmitters, battery packs, harnesses and receivers
BIOCom Incorporated 9522 West Jefferson Boulevard Culver City, California 90230, U.S.A	Single and multi-channel telemetry system (receiver and transmitter for ECG, EEG, EMG, vector-ECG, temperature, respiration, goniometry, activity, vibration, acceleration, force blood pressure, GSR

Devices Instruments Limited
26–28 Hyde Way
Welwyn Garden City, Herfordshire, UK

Lightweight miniature telemeter for
ECG, EEG, EMG

Biotelemetry Systems Inc.
P.O. Box 10
Rush, New York 14543, U.S.A.

Single-channel FM transmitter for ECG,
FM/AM subcarrier ECG, respiration, and
temperature telemetry system, single-
channel, two-channel, three-channel
transmitters, and demodulators.

Dynamic Electronics Limited
Roslyn Road,
London N15 5JB

Biotelemetry system comprising receiver
and miniature FM transmitter.

The Mini-Mitter Company, Inc.
P.O. Box 88210-G
Indianapolis, Indiana 46208, U.S.A.

Miniature temperature-sensitive radio
transmitters, short and long range.

Narco Bio-systems, Inc.
P.O. Box 12511/7651 Airport Boulevard
Houston, Texas 77017, U.S.A

Telemetry transmitters for ECG, EMG,
EEG, GSR and respiration, and telemetry receivers

Telemetry Systems, Inc.
5830 North Shore Drive
Milwaukee, Wisconsin, 53217, U.S.A.

Receivers, one and two-stage transmitters,
mercury and lithium solar battery packs,
temperature transmitters, dart transmitters, fish and snake transmitters, ECG
transmitters

Postscript: towards humane methods of identification

Richard D. Ryder*

From the point of view of the R.S.P.C.A. there can be only one criterion for judging the success or otherwise of this symposium: will it lead to a lessening of animal suffering?

I would like to begin by referring to matters arising from introductory chapters by Professor Delany and Dr Eltringham. I was interested by these and amazed by, for example, the description of elephants painted with huge white numbers, tottering off across the savannah, like travelling motorway signs.

In the case of all wild animals, and with some laboratory species, the subjects must usually be caught and restrained before any marking can take place. This immediately raises problems for the humanitarian, since anyone who has seen a wild animal caught in a cage or, worse still, being handled by his 'natural' enemy, man, must have been struck by the obvious terror that this often causes. The concerned layman can sometimes be pacified by soothing reassurances about cages with rubber coated bars or the use of tranquillisers, but the use of some immobilising drugs may itself occasion considerable psychological distress. This was particularly true of the earlier paralysing drugs, and any drug which causes only loss of motor control or paralysis cannot be said to be humane. An animal apprehending danger and then finding itself without its basic responses of fight and flight must be alarmed. The reaction to the actual physical collapse must also be considered.

It is a common component of nightmares to find oneself unable to escape from threat. Loss of control over one's body, even in the absence of believed danger, is one of man's deepest dreads, probably arising out of our basic predator/prey programming. Why should it be less true of other species, whose previous experiences of threat and avoidance are almost certainly more intense than those of most scientists? Extreme situations of drug-induced paralysis are, so we are informed, being used as some of the most effective forms of modern torture for political purposes. One must conclude that the use of paralysing drugs alone, for animal study, can never be condoned.

The fight against the effects of other immobilising drugs can also be very disturbing. I have seen animals resisting the effects of chloroform and barbiturates, and it is a pathetic sight. Fortunately we now have in use more sophisticated tran-

*Richard D. Ryder qualified in Experimental Psychology from Cambridge University and is currently a Clinical Psychologist at Oxford. He is Chairman of the Council of the Royal Society for the Prevention of Cruelty to Animals, and is author of *Victims of Science*, *Speciesism* and various other publications on animal welfare topics.

quilisers and analgesics. But even with these there are question-marks. There are, for example, major differences in reaction between the species, and what may be humane for a primate may not be humane for a cat.

Subdued behaviour does not necessarily indicate an absence of psychological or even physical distress. Terrified animals can become quite motionless in a state believed to correspond to catatonia in the human—a state subsequently recalled as being one of acute distress by some patients I have talked to. Another example is the classic tranquiliser chlorpromazine, which can cause highly unpleasant hypotensive effects. I once took an experimental dose and was prostrated; a zoologist observing me lying down on my bed might assume that I was tranquil and content— I can assure you that I was not! I was miserable.

We must always strive to reduce fear and pain—but we can never assume with certainty that we have eliminated these conditions. I don't believe we should waste too much time arguing about whether other animals—especially mammals— do or do not experience pain and fear. There are few scientists today who would take other than a common-sense view on this. The philosophers tend now to take the view that the evidence that a member of *another* species suffers is no less adequate than the evidence that another member of our *own* species experiences distress. The Brambell Committee took very much the line that we can assume suffering in animals by 'comparing the symptoms exhibited by animals with those which are known to accompany mental suffering in human beings' (Report of the Technical Committee to Enquire into the Welfare of Animals kept under Intensive Livestock Husbandry Systems. H.M.S.O. Cmnd. 2836. 1965: Chairman: Professor F. W. Rogers Brambell, F.R.S., p. 83). The Scott-Henderson Committee was satisfied that animals suffer physical pain 'in much the same way as human beings' (Report of the Committee on Cruelty to Wild Animals. H.M.S.O. Cmd. 8266. 1951: Chairman: Mr. John Scott-Henderson, K. C., p. 12) and that they can suffer 'acute fear and terror.' They based these conclusions on three sorts of evidence: (1) that all mammals may be 'presumed to have the nervous apparatus which in human beings is known to mediate the sensation of pain', (2) that 'animals squeal, struggle and give other "behavioural" evidence which is generally regarded as the accompaniment of painful feelings'; and (3) that 'pain is of the utmost biological value to animals' and essential for survival.

One might add that drugs known to be analgesic in man usually have similar effects in other animals also. More recently the concept of mental suffering in animals has been taken a stage further and is now recognised as a legal reality in this country. Psychologists have long assumed states of pain and fear in mammals and other animals and although *absolute* evidence of suffering in any individual other than oneself is impossible, the hypothesis of common sense—*that animals can suffer*—is surely the wisest working hypothesis until refuted.

To return to the case of the captured animal; it should not be forgotten that the common denominator in nearly all situations creating experimental neurosis, is *unescapability*. When an animal finds itself in a threatening situation from which it cannot escape, then it is likely to be under the greatest stress. I would suggest that for most animals, the approach of man, confinement within a small cage, and the perceived loss of motor control arising from drug intoxication, will all be perceived as threats in themselves. It is known that such disturbances, especially in phylogenetically higher animals can cause pathological changes, increased susceptibility to disease and deterioration in general bodily condition. Furthermore, there may sometimes be gross behavioural effects such as the killing of young, the cessation of breeding or migration from the area.

How then can a humane scientist make his first moves towards marking his subjects? What methods are we left with?

I would say we need, ideally, methods of marking which are so gentle that the subject animal remains unaware of having been marked. These would not only satisfy the principles of humanity but would create less disturbance to the behaviour under observation, since an animal exposed to a traumatic marking procedure may show distortions of behaviour for days afterwards, or even for ever. One-trial learning can and does occur. So, for scientific as well as for humane reasons, the marking process must be non-traumatic. In this respect, *humane and scientific objectives coincide.*

Marking from a distance would seem to be one solution, and could, perhaps, be achieved by the use of 'marker guns' firing dyes or chemically or physically detectable tags. Here I am speculating about techniques which are not yet developed or are in their infancy. But one day it may be possible to use marking procedures, borrowed perhaps from the police or military, which mark a subject without his being aware that he is under observation. An alternative method would be to use immobilising drugs that cause no alarm. These would have to be administered without the subject being aware of any untoward procedure, perhaps by being administered at a distance, by being automatically triggered by the animal itself, or by being given while the animal is asleep. In order to avoid a panic reaction to symptoms, one would require a perfect tranquiliser (which does not yet exist) or a very rapidly acting general anaesthetic, where unconsciousness supervenes before alarm is experienced. I doubt whether such techniques have yet been invented, but I am certain that totally non-traumatic marking is an ideal to be aimed for. I am looking into the future.

The five main sections of the symposium have treated the following subjects:

(1) the marking of *captive* animals
(2) *tagging* a variety of animals
(3) marking by tissue removal or modification
(4) radio and radioactive tracking
(5) recognition by naturally occurring features.

Now I shall consider these sections in turn. First, the *Identification of captive animals*, so comprehensively dealt with by Mr Jordan, Mr Ashton and Dr Lane-Petter. There are quite a range of techniques available, some humane and some not (such as the 'Nottingham Lace Syndrome' in rodents' ears). In the first category I would put some non-toxic painting, fur-clipping, ringing and collaring. Obviously paint, clipping or collaring which interferes with the animal's natural behaviour, inasmuch as this causes frustration or other stress, cannot be entirely humane. However, I have had some experience of using dyes on fur and tails and I am fairly confident that it is effective and need cause the animal no distress or handicap.

Other methods, including clipping of flesh or vibrissae, or punching ears or webs are not acceptable. The captive animal (unlike the wild one) is continuously controlled, should not be afraid of people, and is under daily observation, so when dye marks become faint they can easily and humanely be renewed. Cages are themselves labelled and may entirely obviate the need for marking their inhabitants at all. I feel there is absolutely no excuse for causing distress or mutilation in the marking of captive animals, whether in zoo, farm or laboratory.

Mr Ashton mentions hot branding but in no way advocates it: surely the branding of sensitive tissue is a barbarity that should have been outlawed along with bear-baiting? Thankfully this is now almost completely discontinued in this country.

Perhaps the test of good zoo-keepers, good farmers or good animal technicians is whether they can identify each individual animal by its natural characteristics. They should be sufficiently interested in the animals to be able to recognise them individually; then marking would be superfluous or merely an additional aid or stand-by.

Tagging was the next section to be ably considered under Lord Medway's Chairmanship. Dr Patterson has described in detail a number of techniques for use with birds, including collars, streamers, imped feathers, dyes and patagial tags. Here the object is to produce a marker which can be identified at some distance and which causes no impediment for the wearer of it. Dr Laird dealt with the marking of fish and Drs Summers and Witthames with seals.

Mr Spencer mentioned methods which remove the necessity for recapture. Included in this category are metal and plastic leg rings carrying large figures, small plastic rings in coded colour combinations, bill disks and neck collars.

I do not feel happy about some of these, and it is certainly true that tagging must be species-specific; for example, what is humane for a waterbird may be inhumane for other birds. However, I am sure that Mr Spencer has touched on an important principle: where a marker can be worn permanently without deleterious effect to the wearer (or if it decays away after the period for which it is needed for observation—and one wonders if there is not more scope for the use of 'biodegradable' materials as markers) then recapture can and should be avoided. Mr Spencer also emphasised the importance of experience and skill in choosing and fitting rings correctly, and offered the assistance of the British Trust for Ornithology.

Animals in the wild should be harassed and interfered with as little as possible. Scientists marking them should use techniques that do not necessitate repeated recapture of the subject.

Dr Stebbings has given some warnings as to how damaging the marking process itself can be; any such procedure which kills or injures the subject is morally unacceptable as well as scientifically useless. Indeed in the United States a moratorium on bat-banding has recently been declared, because of the unacceptably high injury and mortality rates.

We now come to the marking by *tissue removal or modification*: this is the section that worries me most. Dr Twigg has excellently surveyed the field and lists the clipping of ears, toes and fur, the docking of tails, heat branding and freeze branding and tattooing. Freeze branding has also been described by Mr Newton and other methods were mentioned by Dr Spellerberg and Mr Prestt. Of these, I think only fur clipping (and possibly some forms of tattooing) can be recommended as entirely humane. I would not consider the clipping of vibrissae as humane in any species. Dr Swingland has quite rightly raised the question, in the case of reptiles, as to which techniques are known not to affect adversely the individual or its ecology.

Fourthly, I comment on *radioactive and radio-tracking* techniques: Mr Linn discussed these for the case of small mammals and brought out the real dangers of radiation damage to the animals under observation. Mr Amlaner has reviewed bio-telemetry in free-ranging animals and considered possible applications for the animals' welfare. Personally, I am opposed to the use of techniques involving the implantation of electrodes into sensitive tissues. Where physiological measures can be recorded from the surface this is less objectionable.

Dr Macdonald's meticulous survey makes one aware of the range of techniques and their limitations. Attaching transmitters by collar or harness sounds harmless, but one wonders a little at the reactions of a wild animal to finding itself unable to shake off or get away from a strange clinging 'parasite' that smells of man and is associated with the experience of capture. For example, how long does it take for a fox to grow sufficiently accustomed to its harness or radio-collar to be able to sleep naturally? Such questions need to be asked for humanitarian as well as scientific reasons. In the case of carnivores, the evidence is reassuring but not conclusive—with birds there have been disturbing reports of increased mortality, as Mr Amlaner pointed out.

I am worried by the tendency to recapture—or worse, kill—an animal in order to recover a piece of radio-equipment. Surely this is unnecessary. Is it past the wit of man to devise a radio-collar that can itself be remotely released by radio?

Finally, *Recognition by naturally occurring body surface features*: although this may sometimes be a less certain approach, it should be the method of choice from the humane viewpoint and Dr Kear emphasised this aspect. Dr Pennycuick has provided helpful guides as to how to assess the reliability of using natural markings in particular cases, and Miss Scott has pointed to some definite advantages for the short-term study of Bewick's swans. Dr Ingram confirmed the usefulness of such techniques in the case of larger primates. These were encouraging contributions to the symposium.

It is only after one has taken the trouble fully to acquaint oneself with the animals under observation that their individuality gradually becomes apparent. A herd of cows may all look much the same to the motorist driving past, but to the careful stockman they are each clearly distinguishable one from another. The behavioural scientist who flashes past his subject matter, glancing at it en route between lecture hall and computer room, is not worthy of his name. The field-worker who really gets to know his animals will find progressively less difficulty in identifying individuals by their natural characteristics.

Conclusion

Men have been marked with numbers in prisons and concentration camps—evidence that the usual natural external cues we use to differentiate man from man were insufficient for the prison guards. This analogy raises the wider moral issues, for marking is too often a sign of oppression—of man by man, or of man's exploitation of the other species. It was once considered essential to brand slaves with their owner's mark. But do we own the animals we study? Can one creature own another? In law certainly—but morally?

I happen to believe in the rights of animals to live and pursue contentment through the satisfaction of their natural drives. If we study animals, let us do so in a spirit of friendliness approaching them as our evolutionary kin.

Marking them may cause physical or psychological suffering in three ways: (i) in the act of marking, (ii) in the wearing of the mark, (iii) in the observing of it. If marking does cause suffering, then I can see no justification in it (save only if we honestly believe that marking is necessary in a particular case, for the wellbeing of the individual animal which is marked.)

The whole question of the *Rights of Animals* (Singer, 1976) has now become an issue for serious debate: the RSPCA has recently held a two-day Symposium on the subject at Trinity College, Cambridge, (August 18th—19th 1977), of which proceedings will ultimately be published. It has always seemed to me to be a matter of simple logic to extend the concept of rights across the thin dividing lines between the species. I can see no rational defence of *speciesism* (Ryder, 1975) anymore than racism. If we accept the basic Darwinian premise of biological kinship, then surely there should be moral kinship also. The conservation and welfare ethics, although not identical, *are* closely allied.

As part of the broadening scope of its animal welfare operations, the R.S.P.C.A. holds symposia such as this one on the marking of research animals, in the hope that by bringing together leading experts in various fields who do look upon animals with sympathy and not just as objects for exploitation, it will facilitate the work of scientists who wish to treat with respect the animals that they are studying, and prevent suffering by the use of better techniques.

Let us then endeavour to use only those entirely humane methods of identification which I hope this Symposium has helped to define.

References

Ryder, Richard D. 1975. *Victims of Science.* Davis-Poynter, London.
Singer, Peter. 1976. *Animal Liberation: A new Ethic for our Treatment of Animals.* Jonathan Cape, London.

Author index

235

238   *Author Index*

Subject index